W9-DFT-435

ATHEIST DELUSIONS

DAVID BENTLEY HART

Atheist Delusions

THE CHRISTIAN REVOLUTION AND ITS FASHIONABLE ENEMIES

YALE UNIVERSITY PRESS   NEW HAVEN & LONDON

Published with assistance from the Mary Cady Tew Memorial Fund.

Copyright © 2009 by David Bentley Hart.
All rights reserved.
This book may not be reproduced, in whole or in part, including illustrations, in any form
(beyond that copying permitted by Sections 107 and 108 of the U.S. Copyright Law and
except by reviewers for the public press), without written permission from the publishers.

Set in FontShop Scala and Scala Sans by Duke & Company, Devon, Pennsylvania.
Printed in the United States of America by Sheridan Books, Ann Arbor, Michigan.

The Library of Congress has cataloged the hardcover edition as follows:
Hart, David Bentley.
Atheist delusions : the Christian revolution and its fashionable enemies / David Bentley
Hart.
p.   cm.
Includes bibliographical references and index.
ISBN 978-0-300-11190-3 (cloth : alk. paper) 1. Church history—Primitive and early church,
ca. 30–600. 2. Civilization, Western. 3. Christianity—Influence. I. Title.
BR162.3.H37 2009
909'.09821—dc22   2008040641

ISBN 978-0-300-16429-9 (pbk.)

A catalogue record for this book is available from the British Library.

10 9 8 7 6 5 4

For Solwyn

CONTENTS

INTRODUCTION

THIS BOOK IS IN NO SENSE an impartial work of history. Perfect detachment is impossible for even the soberest of historians, since the writing of history necessarily demands some sort of narrative of causes and effects, and is thus necessarily an act of interpretation, which by its nature can never be wholly free of prejudice. But I am not really a historian, in any event, and I do not even aspire to detachment. In what follows, my prejudices are transparent and unreserved, and my argument is in some respects willfully extreme (or so it might seem). I think it prudent to admit this from the outset, if only to avoid being accused later of having made some pretense of perfect objectivity or neutrality so as to lull the reader into a state of pliant credulity. What I have written is at most a "historical essay," at no point free of bias, and intended principally as an apologia for a particular understanding of the effect of Christianity upon the development of Western civilization.

This is not to say, I hasten to add, that I am in any way forswearing claims of objective truth: to acknowledge that one's historical judgments can never be absolutely pure of preconceptions or personal convictions is scarcely to surrender to a thoroughgoing relativism. It may be impossible to provide perfectly irrefutable evidence for one's conclusions, but it is certainly possible to amass evidence sufficient to confirm them beyond plausible doubt, just as it is possible to discern when a particular line of interpretation has exceeded or contradicted the evidence altogether and become little better than a vehicle for the writer's own predilections, interests, or allegiances. I can, moreover, vouch for the honesty of my argument: I have not consciously distorted any aspect of the history I discuss or striven to conceal any of its more disheartening elements. Such honesty costs me little, as it happens. Since the case I wish to make is *not* that the Christian gospel can magically transform whole societies in an instant, or summon the charity it enjoins out of the depths of every soul, or entirely extirpate cruelty and violence from human nature, or miraculously lift men and women out of their historical contexts, I feel no need to evade or excuse the innumerable failures of many Christians through the ages to live lives of charity or peace. Where I come to the defense of historical Christianity, it is only in order to raise objections to certain popular calumnies of the church, or to demur from what I take to be disingenuous or inane arraignments of Christian belief or history, or to call attention to achievements and virtues that writers of a devoutly anti-Christian bent tend to ignore, dissemble, or dismiss.

Beyond that, my ambitions are small; I make no attempt here to convert anyone to anything. Indeed, the issue of my personal belief or disbelief is quite irrelevant to—and would be surprisingly unilluminating of—my argument. Some of the early parts of this book, for instance, concern the Roman Catholic Church; but whatever I say in its defense ought not to be construed as advocacy for the institution itself (to which I do not belong), but only for historical accuracy. To be honest, my affection for institutional Christianity as a whole is rarely more than tepid; and there are numerous forms of Christian belief and practice for which I would be hard pressed to muster a kind word from the depths of my heart, and the rejection of which by the atheist or skeptic strikes me as perfectly laudable. In a larger sense, moreover, nothing I argue below—even if all of it is granted—implies that the Christian vision of reality is true. And yet, even so, the case I wish to make is intended to be provocative, and its more apologetic moments are meant to clear the way for a number of much stronger, and even perhaps somewhat immoderate, assertions.

This book chiefly—or at least centrally—concerns the history of the early church, of roughly the first four or five centuries, and the story of how Christendom was born out of the culture of late antiquity. My chief ambition in writing it is to call attention to the peculiar and radical nature of the new faith in that setting: how enormous a transformation of thought, sensibility, culture, morality, and spiritual imagination Christianity constituted in the age of pagan Rome; the liberation it offered from fatalism, cosmic despair, and the terror of occult agencies; the immense dignity it conferred upon the human person; its subversion of the cruelest aspects of pagan society; its (alas, only partial) demystification of political power; its ability to create moral community where none had existed before; and its elevation of active charity above all other virtues. Stated in its most elementary and most buoyantly positive form, my argument is, first of all, that among all the many great transitions that have marked the evolution of Western civilization, whether convulsive or gradual, political or philosophical, social or scientific, material or spiritual, there has been only one—the triumph of Christianity—that can be called in the fullest sense a "revolution": a truly massive and epochal revision of humanity's prevailing vision of reality, so pervasive in its influence and so vast in its consequences as actually to have created a new conception of the world, of history, of human nature, of time, and of the moral good. To my mind, I should add, it was an event immeasurably more impressive in its cultural creativity and more ennobling in its moral power than any other movement of spirit, will, imagination, aspiration, or accomplishment in the history of the West. And I am convinced that, given how radically at variance Christianity was with the culture it slowly and relentlessly displaced, its eventual victory was an event of such improbability as to strain the very limits of our understanding of historical causality.

There is also, however, a negative side to my argument. It is what I suppose I should call my rejection of modernity—or, rather, my rejection of the ideology of "the modern" and my rejection, especially, of the myth of "the Enlightenment." By modernity, I should explain, I certainly do not mean modern medicine or air travel or space exploration or any of the genuinely useful or estimable aspects of life today; I do not even mean modern philosophical method or social ideology or political thought. Rather, I mean the modern age's grand narrative of itself: its story of the triumph of critical reason over "irrational" faith, of the progress of social morality toward greater justice and freedom, of the "tolerance" of the secular state, and of the unquestioned ethical primacy of either individualism or collectivism (as the case may be). Indeed, I want in part to argue that what many of us are still in the habit of calling the "Age of Reason" was in many significant ways the beginning of the eclipse of reason's authority as a cultural value; that the modern age is notable in large measure for the triumph of inflexible and unthinking dogmatism in every sphere of human endeavor (including the sciences) and for a flight from rationality to any number of soothing fundamentalisms, religious and secular; that the Enlightenment ideology of modernity *as such* does not even deserve any particular credit for the advance of modern science; that the modern secular state's capacity for barbarism exceeds any of the evils for which Christendom might justly be indicted, not solely by virtue of the superior technology at its disposal, but by its very nature; that among the chief accomplishments of modern culture have been a massive retreat to superstition and the gestation of especially pitiless forms of nihilism; and that, by comparison to the Christian revolution it succeeded, modernity is little more than an aftereffect, or even a counterrevolution—a reactionary flight back toward a comfortable, but dehumanizing, mental and moral servitude to elemental nature. In fact, this is where my story both begins and ends. The central concern of what follows is the early centuries of the church, but I approach those centuries very much from the perspective of the present, and I return from them only to consider what the true nature of a post-Christian culture must be. Needless to say, perhaps, my prognostications tend toward the bleak.

Summary is always perilous. I know that—reduced thus to its barest elements—the argument I propose lacks a certain refinement. I must leave it to the reader to judge whether, in filling in the details below, I in fact achieve any greater degree of subtlety. What, however, animates this project is a powerful sense of how great a distance of historical forgetfulness and cultural alienation separates us from the early centuries of the Christian era, and how often our familiarity with the Christianity we know today can render us insensible to the novelty and uncanniness of the gospel as it was first proclaimed—or even as it was received by succeeding generations of ancient and mediaeval Christians. And this is more than merely unfortunate. Our normal sense of the continuity of history, though it can accommodate ruptures and upheavals of a certain magnitude, still makes it difficult for us to comprehend the sheer immensity of what I want to call the Western tradition's "Christian interruption." But it is something we must comprehend if we are properly to understand who we have been and what we have become, or to understand both the happy fortuity and poignant fragility of many of those moral "truths" upon which our sense of our humanity rests, or even to understand what defenses we possess against the eventual cultural demise of those truths. And, after all, given how enormous the force of this Christian interruption was in shaping the reality all of us inhabit, it is nothing less than our obligation to our own past to attempt to grasp its true nature.

I have called this book an essay, and that description should be kept in mind as one reads it. What follows is not a history at all, really, if by that one means a minutely exhaustive, sequential chronicle of social, political, and economic events. In large part, this is because I simply lack many of the special skills required of genuinely proficient historians and am acutely conscious of how much my efforts in that direction would suffer by comparison to their work. What I have written is an extended meditation upon certain facts of history, and no more. Its arrangement is largely thematic rather than chronological, and it does not pretend to address most of the more contentious debates in modern historical scholarship regarding the early church (except where necessary). So my narrative will move at the pace my argument dictates. As this is an essay, I would have preferred to do without scholarly apparatus altogether, in order to make it as concise and fluid as possible; but I found I could not entirely dispense with notes, and so I had to satisfy myself by making them as few and as chastely minimal as common sense and my conscience would allow. The arrangement of my argument is simple and comprises four "movements": I begin, in part 1, from the current state of popular antireligious and anti-Christian polemic, and attempt to identify certain of the common assumptions informing it; in part 2, I consider, in a somewhat desultory fashion, the view of the Christian past that the ideology of modernity has taught us to embrace; in part 3, the heart of the book, I attempt to illuminate (thematically, as I say) what happened during the early centuries of the church and the slow conversion of the Roman Empire to the new faith; and in part 4 I return to the present to consider the consequences of the decline of Christendom.

What I have tried to describe in this book, I should finally note, is very much a personal vision of Christian history, and I acknowledge that it is perhaps slightly eccentric in certain of its emphases, in its shape, even occasionally in its tone. This is not to say that it is merely a collection of subjective impressions; I am keen to score as many telling blows as I can against what I take to be false histories and against dishonest or incompetent historians, and that requires some quantity of substantive evidence. I think one must grant, though, that to communicate a personal vision one must do more than prove or refute certain claims regarding facts; one must invite others to see what one sees, and must attempt to draw others into the world that vision descries. At a particular moment in history, I believe, something happened to Western humanity that changed it at the deepest levels of consciousness and at the highest levels of culture. It was something of such strange and radiant vastness that it is almost inexplicable that the memory of it should have so largely faded from our minds, to be reduced to a few old habits of thought and desire whose origins we no longer know, or to be displaced altogether by a few recent habits of thought and desire that render us oblivious to what we have forsaken. But perhaps the veil that time draws between us and the distant past in some sense protects us from the burden of too much memory. It often proves debilitating to dwell too entirely in the shadows of vanished epochs, and our capacity to forget is (as Friedrich Nietzsche noted) very much a part of our capacity to live in the present. That said, every natural strength can become also an innate weakness; to live entirely in the present, without any of the wisdom that a broad perspective upon the past provides, is to live a life of idiocy and vapid distraction and ingratitude. Over time, our capacity to forget can make everything come to seem unexceptional and predictable, even things that are actually quite remarkable and implausible. The most important function of historical reflection is to wake us from too complacent a forgetfulness and to recall us to a knowledge of things that should never be lost to memory. And the most important function of Christian history is to remind us not only of how we came to be modern men and women, or of how Western civilization was shaped, but also of something of incalculable wonder and inexpressible beauty, the knowledge of which can still haunt, delight, torment, and transfigure us.

PART ONE FAITH, REASON, AND FREEDOM: A VIEW FROM THE PRESENT

CHAPTER ONE

The Gospel of Unbelief

ONE WOULD THINK these would be giddy days for religion's most passionate antagonists; rarely can they have known a moment so intoxicatingly full of promise. A mere glance in the direction of current trends in mass-market publishing should be enough to make the ardent secularist's heart thrill with the daring and delicious hope that we just might be entering a golden age for bold assaults on humanity's ancient slavery to "irrational dogma" and "creedal tribalism." Conditions in the world of print have never before been so propitious for sanctimonious tirades against religion, or (more narrowly) monotheism, or (more specifically) Christianity, or (more precisely) Roman Catholicism. Never before have the presses or the press been so hospitable to journalists, biologists, minor philosophers, amateur moralists proudly brandishing their baccalaureates, novelists, and (most indispensable of all) film actors eager to denounce the savagery of faith, to sound frantic alarms against the imminence of a new "theocracy," and to commend the virtues of spiritual disenchantment to all who have the wisdom to take heed. As I write, Daniel Dennett's latest attempt to wean a credulous humanity from its reliance on the preposterous fantasies of religion, *Breaking the Spell,* has arrived amid a clamor of indignant groans from the faithful and exultant bellowing from the godless. *The God Delusion,* an energetic attack on all religious belief, has just been released by Richard Dawkins, the zoologist and tireless tractarian, who—despite

3

his embarrassing incapacity for philosophical reasoning—never fails to entrance his eager readers with his rhetorical recklessness. The journalist Christopher Hitchens, whose talent for intellectual caricature somewhat exceeds his mastery of consecutive logic, has just issued *God Is Not Great*, a book that raises the wild non sequitur almost to the level of a dialectical method. Over the past few years, Sam Harris's extravagantly callow attack on all religious belief, *The End of Faith*, has enjoyed robust sales and the earnest praise of sympathetic reviewers.[1] Over a slightly greater span, Philip Pullman's evangelically atheist (and rather overrated) fantasy trilogy for children, *His Dark Materials*, has sold millions of copies, has been lavishly praised by numerous critics, has been adapted for the stage, and has received partial cinematic translation; its third volume, easily the weakest of the series, has even won the (formerly) respectable Whitbread Prize. And one hardly need mention the extraordinary sales achieved by Dan Brown's *Da Vinci Code*, already a major film and surely the most lucrative novel ever written by a borderline illiterate. I could go on.

A note of asperity, though, has probably already become audible in my tone, and I probably should strive to suppress it. It is not inspired, however, by any prejudice against unbelief as such; I can honestly say that there are many forms of atheism that I find far more admirable than many forms of Christianity or of religion in general. But atheism that consists entirely in vacuous arguments afloat on oceans of historical ignorance, made turbulent by storms of strident self-righteousness, is as contemptible as any other form of dreary fundamentalism. And it is sometimes difficult, frankly, to be perfectly generous in one's response to the sort of invective currently fashionable among the devoutly undevout, or to the sort of historical misrepresentations it typically involves. Take for instance Peter Watson, author of a diverting little bagatelle of a book on the history of invention, who, when asked not long ago by the *New York Times* to name humanity's worst invention, blandly replied, "Without question, ethical monotheism. . . . This has been responsible for most of the wars and bigotry in history."[2] Now, as a specimen of the sort of antireligious chatter that is currently chic, this is actually rather mild; but it is also utter nonsense. Not that there is much point in defending "monotheism" in the abstract (it is a terribly imprecise term); and devotees of the "one true God" have certainly had their share of blood on their hands. But the vast majority of history's wars have been conducted in the service of many gods; or have been fought under the aegis, or with the blessing, or at the command of one god among many; or have been driven by the pursuit of profits or conquest or power; or have been waged for territory, national or racial destiny, tribal supremacy, the empire, or the "greater good"; or, indeed, have been prosecuted in obedience to ideologies that have no use for any gods whatsoever (these, as it happens, have been the most murderous wars of all). The pagan rhetorician Libanius justly bragged that the gods of the Roman Empire had directed the waging of innumerable wars.[3] By contrast, the number of wars that one could plausibly say have actually been fought on behalf of anything one might call "ethical monotheism" is so vanishingly small that such wars certainly qualify as exceptions to the historical rule. Bigotry and religious persecution, moreover, are any-thing but peculiar to monotheistic cultures, as anyone with a respectable grasp of human culture and history should know. And yet, absurd as it is, Watson's is the sort of remark that sets many heads sagely nodding in recognition of what seems an undeniable truth. Such sentiments have become so much a part of the conventional grammar of "enlightened" skepticism that they are scarcely ever subjected to serious scrutiny.

My own impatience with such remarks, I should confess, would probably be far smaller if I did not suffer from a melancholy sense that, among Christianity's most fervent detractors, there has been a consider-able decline in standards in recent years. In its early centuries, the church earned the enmity of genuinely imaginative and civilized critics, such as Celsus and Porphyry, who held the amiable belief that they should make some effort to acquaint themselves with the object of their critique. And, at the end of Europe's Christian centuries, the church could still boast antagonists of real stature. In the eighteenth century, David Hume was unrivaled in his power to sow doubt where certainty once had flourished. And while the diatribes of Voltaire, Denis Diderot, and the other Enlight-enment philosophes were, on the whole, insubstantial, they were at least marked by a certain fierce elegance and occasional moral acuity. Edward Gibbon, for all the temporal parochialism and frequent inaccuracy of his account of Christianity's rise, was nevertheless a scholar and writer of positively titanic gifts, whose sonorously enunciated opinions were the fruit of immense labors of study and reflection. And the extraordinary scientific, philosophical, and political ferment of the nineteenth century provided Christianity with enemies of unparalleled passion and visionary intensity. The greatest of them all, Friedrich Nietzsche, may have had a somewhat limited understanding of the history of Christian thought, but he was nevertheless a man of immense culture who could appreciate the magnitude of the thing against which he had turned his spirit, and who had enough of a sense of the past to understand the cultural crisis that the fading of Christian faith would bring about. Moreover, he had the good manners to despise Christianity, in large part, for what it actually was— above all, for its devotion to an ethics of compassion—rather than allow himself the soothing, self-righteous fantasy that Christianity's history had been nothing but an interminable pageant of violence, tyranny, and sexual neurosis. He may have hated many Christians for their hypocrisy, but he hated Christianity itself principally on account of its enfeebling solicitude for the weak, the outcast, the infirm, and the diseased; and, because he was conscious of the historical contingency of all cultural values, he never deluded himself that humanity could do away with Christian faith while simply retaining Christian morality in some diluted form, such as liberal social conscience or innate human sympathy. He knew that the disappearance of the cultural values of Christianity would gradually but inevitably lead to a new set of values, the nature of which was yet to be decided. By comparison to these men, today's gadflies seem far lazier, less insightful, less subtle, less refined, more emotional, more ethically complacent, and far more interested in facile simplifications of history than in sober and demanding investigations of what Christianity has been or is.

Two of the books I have mentioned above—*Breaking the Spell* and *The End of Faith*—provide perhaps the best examples of what I mean, albeit in two radically different registers. In the former, Daniel Dennett—a professor of philosophy at Tufts University and codirector of that university's Center for Cognitive Studies—advances what he takes to be the provocative thesis that religion is an entirely natural phenomenon, and claims that this thesis can be investigated by methods proper to the empirical sciences. Indeed, about midway through the book, after having laid out his conjectures regarding the evolution of religion, Dennett confidently asserts that he has just successfully led his readers on a "nonmiraculous and matter-of-fact stroll" from the blind machinery of nature up to humanity's passionate fidelity to its most exalted ideas. As it happens, the case he has actually made at this point is a matter not of fact but of pure intuition, held together by tenuous strands of presupposition, utterly inadequate as an explanation of religious culture, and almost absurdly dependent upon Richard Dawkins's inane concept of "memes" (for a definition of which one may consult the most current editions of the *Oxford English Dictionary*). And, as a whole, Dennett's argument consists in little more than the persistent misapplication of quantitative and empirical terms to unquantifiable and intrinsically nonempirical realities, sustained by classifications that are entirely arbitrary and fortified by arguments that any attentive reader should notice are wholly circular. The "science of religion" Dennett describes would inevitably prove to be no more than a series of indistinct inferences drawn from behaviors that could be interpreted in an almost limitless variety of ways; and it could never produce anything more significant than a collection of biological metaphors for supporting (or, really, simply illustrating) an essentially unverifiable philosophical materialism.

All of this, however, is slightly beside the point. Judged solely as a scientific proposal, Dennett's book is utterly inconsequential—in fact, it is something of an embarrassment—but its methodological deficiencies are not my real concern here (although I have written about them elsewhere).[4] And, in fact, even if there were far more substance to Dennett's project than there is, and even if by sheer chance his story of religion's evolution were correct in every detail, it would still be a trivial project at the end of the day. For, whether one finds Dennett's story convincing or not—whether, that is, one thinks he has quite succeeded in perfectly bridging the gulf between the amoeba and the *St. Matthew Passion*—not only does that story pose no challenge to faith, it is in fact perfectly compatible with what most developed faiths already teach regarding religion. Of course religion is a natural phenomenon. Who would be so foolish as to deny that? It is ubiquitous in human culture, obviously forms an essential element in the evolution of society, and has itself clearly evolved. Perhaps Dennett believes there are millions of sincere souls out there deeply committed to the proposition that religion, in the abstract, is a supernatural reality, but there are not. After all, it does not logically follow that simply because religion is natural it cannot become the vehicle of divine truth, or that it is not in some sense oriented toward ultimate reality (as, according to Christian tradition, all natural things are).

Moreover—and one would have thought Dennett might have noticed this—religion in the abstract does not actually exist, and almost no one (apart from politicians) would profess any allegiance to it. Rather, there are a very great number of systems of belief and practice that, for the sake of convenience, we call "religions," though they could scarcely differ more from one another, and very few of them depend upon some fanciful notion that religion itself is a miraculous exception to the rule of nature. Christians, for instance, are not, properly speaking, believers in religion; rather, they believe that Jesus of Nazareth, crucified under Pontius Pilate, rose from the dead and is now, by the power of the Holy Spirit, present to his church as its Lord. This is a claim that is at once historical and spiritual, and it has given rise to an incalculable diversity of natural expressions: moral, artistic, philosophical, social, legal, and religious. As for "religion" as such, however, Christian thought has generally acknowledged that it is an impulse common to all societies, and that many of its manifestations are violent, superstitious, amoral, degrading, and false. The most one can say from a Christian perspective concerning human religion is that it gives ambiguous expression to what Christian tradition calls the "natural desire for God," and as such represents a kind of natural openness to spiritual truth, revelation, or grace, as well as an occasion for any number of delusions, cruelties, and tyrannies. When, therefore, Dennett solemnly asks (as he does) whether religion is worthy of our loyalty, he poses a meaningless question. For Christians the pertinent question is whether Christ is worthy of loyalty, which is an entirely different matter. As for Dennett's amazing discovery that the "natural desire for God" is in fact a desire for God that is natural, it amounts to a revolution not of thought, only of syntax.

The real significance of Breaking the Spell (at least for me) becomes visible when it is set alongside Sam Harris's The End of Faith. This latter is also a book that, in itself, should not detain anyone for very long. It is little more than a concatenation of shrill, petulant assertions, a few of which are true, but none of which betrays any great degree of philosophical or historical sophistication. In his remarks on Christian belief, Harris displays an abysmal ignorance of almost every topic he addresses—Christianity's view of the soul, its moral doctrines, its mystical traditions, its understandings of scripture, and so on. Sometimes it seems his principal complaint must be against twentieth-century fundamentalists, but he does not even get them right (at one point, for example, he nonsensically and scurrilously charges that they believe Christ's second coming will

usher in a final destruction of the Jews). He declares all dogma pernicious, except his own thoroughly dogmatic attachment to nondualistic
contemplative mysticism, of a sort which he mistakenly imagines he has
discovered in one school of Tibetan Buddhism, and which (naturally) he
characterizes as purely rational and scientific. He provides a long passage
ascribed to the (largely mythical) Tantric sage Padmasambhava and then
breathlessly informs his readers that nothing remotely as profound is
to be found anywhere in the religious texts of the West—though, really,
the passage is little more than a formulaic series of mystic platitudes, of
the sort to be found in every religion's contemplative repertoire, describing the kind of oceanic ecstasy that Christian mystical tradition tends to
treat as one of the infantile stages of the contemplative life. He makes
his inevitable pilgrimage to the dungeons of the Spanish Inquisition,
though without pausing to acquaint himself with the Inquisition's actual
history or any of the recent scholarship on it. He more or less explicitly
states that every episode of violence or injustice in Christian history is
a natural consequence of Christianity's basic tenets (which is obviously
false), and that Christianity's twenty centuries of unprecedented and still
unmatched moral triumphs—its care of widows and orphans, its almshouses, hospitals, foundling homes, schools, shelters, relief organiza-
tions, soup kitchens, medical missions, charitable aid societies, and so
on—are simply expressions of normal human kindness, with no necessary connection to Christian conviction (which is even more obviously
false). Needless to say, he essentially reverses the equation when talking
about Buddhism and, with all the fervor of the true believer, defends the
purity of his elected creed against its historical distortions. Admittedly,
he does not actually discuss Tibet's unsavory history of religious warfare,
monastic feudalism, theocratic despotism, and social neglect; but he does
helpfully explain that most Buddhists do not really understand Buddhism
(at least, not as well as he does). And in a disastrous chapter, reminiscent
of nothing so much as a recklessly ambitious undergraduate essay, he
attempts to describe a "science of good and evil" that would discover the
rational basis of moral self-sacrifice, apart from religious adherences: an
argument composed almost entirely of logical lacunae. In short, *The End
of Faith* is not a serious—merely a self-important—book, and merits only
cursory comment.

If Harris's argument holds any real interest here, it is as an epitome—

verging on unintentional parody—of contemporary antireligious rhetoric at its most impassioned and sanctimonious. As such, it gives especially vivid and unalloyed expression to two popular prejudices that one finds also in the work of Dennett (and of Dawkins and many others), but nowhere in so bracingly simplistic a form. These prejudices are, first, that all religious belief is in essence baseless; and, second, that religion is principally a cause of violence, division, and oppression, and hence should be abandoned for the sake of peace and tolerance. The former premise—the sheer passive idiocy of belief—is assumed with such imperturbable confidence by those who hold it that scarcely any of them bothers to argue the point with any systematic care. That there might be such a thing as religious experience (other, of course, than states of delusion, suffered by the stupid or emotionally disturbed) is naturally never considered, since it goes without saying that there is nothing to experience. Dawkins, for instance, frequently asserts, without pausing actually to think about the matter, that religious believers have no reasons for their faith. The most embarrassingly ill-conceived chapter in *Breaking the Spell* consists largely in Dennett attempting to convince believers, in tones of excruciating condescension, that they do not really believe what they think they believe, or even understand it, and attempting to scandalize them with the revelation that academic theology sometimes lapses into a technical jargon full of obscure Greek terms like "apophatic" and "ontic." And Harris is never more theatrically indignant than when angrily reminding his readers that Christians believe in Christ's resurrection (for example) only because someone has told them it is true.

It is always perilous to attempt to tell others what or why they believe; and it is especially unwise to assume (as Dennett is peculiarly prone to do) that believers, as a species, do not constantly evaluate or reevaluate their beliefs. Anyone who actually lives among persons of faith knows that this is simply untrue. Obviously, though, there is no point in demanding of believers that they produce criteria for their beliefs unless one is willing to conform one's expectations to the kind of claims being made. For, while it is unquestionably true that perfectly neutral proofs in support of faith cannot generally be adduced, it is not a neutral form of knowledge that is at issue. Dennett's belief that no one need take seriously any claim that cannot be tested by scientific method is merely fatuous. By that standard, I need not believe that the battle of Salamis ever took place, that the widower next door loves the children for whom he tirelessly provides, or that I might be wise to trust my oldest friend even if he tells me something I do not care to hear. Harris is quite correct to say, for instance, that Christ's resurrection—like any other historical event—is known only by way of the testimony of others. Indeed, Christianity is the only major faith built entirely around a single historical claim. It is, however, a claim quite unlike any other ever made, as any perceptive and scrupulous historian must recognize. Certainly it bears no resemblance to the vague fantasies of witless enthusiasts or to the cunning machinations of opportunistic charlatans. It is the report of men and women who had suffered the devastating defeat of their beloved master's death, but who in a very short time were proclaiming an immediate experience of his living presence beyond the tomb, and who were, it seems, willing to suffer privation, imprisonment, torture, and death rather than deny that experience. And it is the report of a man who had never known Jesus before the crucifixion, and who had once persecuted Jesus's followers, but who also believed that he had experienced the risen Christ, with such shattering power that he too preferred death to apostasy. And it is the report of countless others who have believed that they also—in a quite irreducibly personal way—have known the risen Christ.

It cannot be gainsaid that Christians have faith in Easter largely because they belong to communities of believers, or that their faith is a complex amalgam of shared confession, personal experience, spiritual and ethical practice, and reliance on others, or that they are inevitably obliged to make judgments about the trustworthiness of those whose word they must take. Some also choose to venture out upon the vast seas of Christianity's philosophical or mystical traditions; and many are inspired by miracles, or dreams, or the apparent working of grace in their lives, or moments of aesthetic transport, or strange raptures, or intuitions of the Holy Spirit's presence, and so on. None of this might impress the committed skeptic, or seem like adequate grounds for faith, but that does not mean that faith is essentially willful and irrational. More to the point, it is bizarre for anyone to think he or she can judge the nature or credibility of another's experiences from the outside. If Dennett really wishes to undertake a "scientific" investigation of faith, he should promptly abandon his efforts to describe religion (which, again, does not really exist), and attempt instead to enter into the actual world of belief in order to weigh its phenomena from within. As a first step, he should certainly—purely in the interest of sound scientific method and empirical rigor—begin praying, and then continue doing so with some perseverance. This is a drastic and implausible prescription, no doubt; but it is the only means by which he could possibly begin to acquire any knowledge of what belief is or of what it is not.

Rather than court absurdity, however, let us graciously grant that there is indeed such a thing as unthinking religious conviction, just as there is a great deal of unthinking irreligious materialism. Let us also, more magnanimously, grant the truth of the second conviction I attributed to these writers above: that religion is violent, that religion in fact kills. At least, let us grant that it is exactly as true, and as intellectually significant, as the propositions "politics kills" and "color reddens." For many things are true in a general sense, even when, in the majority of specific cases, they are false. Violent religion or politics kills, and red reddens; but peaceful religion or politics does not kill, even if it is adopted as a pretext for killing, just as green does not redden, even if a certain kind of color blindness creates the impression that it does. For, purely in the abstract, "religious" longing is neither this nor that, neither admirable nor terrible, but is at once creative and destructive, consoling and murderous, tender and brutal.

I take it that this is because "religion" is something "natural" to human beings (as Dennett so acutely notes) and, as such, reflects human nature. For the broader, even more general, and yet more pertinent truth is that men kill (women kill too, but historically have had fewer opportunities to do so). Some kill because their faiths explicitly command them to do so, some kill though their faiths explicitly forbid them to do so, and some kill because they have no faith and hence believe all things are permitted to them. Polytheists, monotheists, and atheists kill—indeed, this last class is especially prolifically homicidal, if the evidence of the twentieth century is to be consulted. Men kill for their gods, or for their God, or because there is no God and the destiny of humanity must be shaped by gigantic exertions of human will. They kill in pursuit of universal truths and out of fidelity to tribal allegiances; for faith, blood and soil, empire, national greatness, the "socialist utopia," capitalism, and "democratization." Men will always seek gods in whose name they may perform great deeds or commit unspeakable atrocities, even when those gods are not gods but "tribal honor" or "genetic imperatives" or "social ideals" or "human destiny" or "liberal democracy." Then again, men also kill on account of money, land, love, pride, hatred, envy, or ambition. They kill out of conviction or out of lack of conviction. Harris at one point approvingly cites a platitude from Will Durant to the effect that violence follows from religious certitude—which again, like most empty generalities, is vacuously true. It is just as often the case, however, that men are violent solely from expedience, because they believe in no higher law than the demands of the moment, while only certain kinds of religious certitude have the power to temper their murderous pragmatism with a compassionate idealism, or to freeze their wills with a dread of divine justice, or to free them from the terrors of present uncertainty and so from the temptation to act unjustly. Caiaphas and Pilate, if scripture is to be believed, were perfect examples of the officious and practical statesman with grave responsibilities to consider; Christ, on the other hand, was certain of a Kingdom not of this world and commanded his disciples to love their enemies. Does religious conviction provide a powerful reason for killing? Undeniably it often does. It also often provides the sole compelling reason for refusing to kill, or for being merciful, or for seeking peace; only the profoundest ignorance of history could prevent one from recognizing this. For the truth is that religion and irreligion are cultural variables, but killing is a human constant.

I do not, I must note, doubt the sincerity of any of these writers. I maintain only that to speak of the evil of religion or to desire its abolition is, again, as simpleminded as condemning and wanting to abolish politics. Dennett, for example, on several occasions in *Breaking the Spell* proclaims his devotion to democracy, a devotion that one can assume remains largely undiminished by the knowledge that democratic governments—often in the name of protecting or promoting democracy—have waged unjust wars, incinerated villages or cities full of noncombatants, abridged civil liberties, tolerated corruption and racial inequality, lied to their citizens, aided despotic foreign regimes, or given power to evil men (Hitler seems a not insignificant example of this last). By the same token, one may remain wholly unswayed from one's devotion to Christianity by the knowledge that men and women have done many wicked things in Christ's name. If the analogy fails in any respect, it is only that Christianity expressly forbids the various evils that have been done by Christians, whereas democracy, in principle, forbids nothing (except, of course, the defeat of the majority's will). Moreover, I am fairly certain that Dennett would not be so feeble of intellect as to abandon his faith in democratic institutions simply because someone of no political philosophy whatsoever had emerged from the forest and told him in tones of stirring pomposity that politics is divisive and violent and therefore should be forsaken in the interests of human harmony. Similarly, the vapid truism that "religion is violent" is less than morally compelling. As no one has any vested interest in "religion" as such, it is perfectly reasonable for someone simultaneously to recite the Nicene Creed and to deplore Aztec human sacrifice (or even the Spanish Inquisition) without suffering any of the equivocator's pangs of conscience, or indeed sensing the least tension between the two positions.

What I find most mystifying in the arguments of the authors I have mentioned, and of others like them, is the strange presupposition that a truly secular society would of its nature be more tolerant and less prone to violence than any society shaped by any form of faith. Given that the modern age of secular governance has been the most savagely and sublimely violent period in human history, by a factor (or body count) of incalculable magnitude, it is hard to identify the grounds for their confidence. (Certainly the ridiculous claim that these forms of secular government were often little more than "political religions," and so only provide further proof of the evil of religion, should simply be laughed off as the shabby evasion it obviously is.) It is not even especially clear why these authors imagine that a world entirely purged of faith would choose to be guided by moral prejudices remotely similar to their own; and the obscurity becomes especially impenetrable to me in the case of those who seem to believe that a thoroughgoing materialism informed by Darwinian biology might actually aid us in forsaking our "tribalism" and "irrationality" and in choosing instead to live in tolerant concord with one another. After all, the only ideological or political factions that have made any attempt at an ethics consistent with Darwinian science, to this point at least, have been the socialist eugenics movement of the early twentieth century and the Nazi movement that sprang from it. Obviously, stupid or evil social and political movements should not dictate our opinions of scientific discoveries. But it scarcely impugns the epochal genius of Charles Darwin or Alfred Russel Wallace to note that—understood purely as a bare, brute, material event—nature admits of no moral principles at all, and so can provide none; all it can provide is its own "moral" example, which is anything but gentle. Dennett, who often shows a propensity for moral pronouncements of almost pontifical peremptoriness, and for social prescriptions of the most authoritarian variety, does not delude himself that evolutionary theory is a source of positive moral prescriptions. But there is something delusional nonetheless in his optimistic certainty that human beings will wish to choose altruistic values without invoking transcendent principles. They may do so; but they may also wish to build death camps, and may very well choose to do that instead. For every ethical theory developed apart from some account of transcendent truth—of, that is, the spiritual or metaphysical foundation of reality—is a fragile fiction, credible only to those sufficiently obstinate in their willing suspension of disbelief. If one does not wish to be convinced, however, a simple "I disagree" or "I refuse" is enough to exhaust the persuasive resources of any purely worldly ethics.

Not that one needs an ethical theory to be an upright person. Dennett likes to point out that there is no evidence that believers are more law-abiding or principled than unbelievers, which is presumably true. Most persons are generally compliant with the laws and moral customs of their societies, no matter what their ultimate convictions about the nature of reality; and often it is the worst reprobates of all who—fearing for their souls or unable to correct their own natures—turn to faith. I might add, though (drawing, I admit, mostly on personal observation) that outside the realm of mere civil obedience to dominant social values—in that world of consummate hopelessness where the most indigent, disabled, forsaken, and forgotten among us depend upon the continuous, concrete, heroic charity of selfless souls—the ranks of the godless tend to thin out markedly. And it is probably also worth noting that the quantity of charitable aid in the world today supplied and sustained by Christian churches continues to be almost unimaginably vast. A world from which the gospel had been banished would surely be one in which millions more of our fellows would go unfed, unnursed, unsheltered, and uneducated. (But I suppose we could always hope for the governments of the world to unite and take up the slack.) Still, it seems obvious that both the religious and the irreligious are capable of varying degrees of tolerance or intolerance, benevolence or malice, depending on how they understand the moral implications of their beliefs.

What, however, we should never forget is where those larger notions of the moral good, to which even atheists can feel a devotion, come from; and this is no small matter. Compassion, pity, and charity, as we understand and cherish them, are not objects found in nature, like trees or butterflies or academic philosophers, but are historically contingent conventions of belief and practice, formed by cultural convictions that need never have arisen at all. Many societies have endured and indeed flourished quite well without them. It is laudable that Dennett is disposed (as I assume he is) to hate economic, civil, or judicial injustice, and that he believes we should not abandon our fellow human beings to poverty, tyranny, exploitation, or despair. Good manners, however, should oblige him and others like him to acknowledge that they are inheritors of a social conscience whose ethical grammar would have been very different had it not been shaped by Christianity's moral premises: the ideals of justice for the oppressed the church took from Judaism, Christianity's own special language of charity, its doctrine of God's universal love, its exaltation of forgiveness over condemnation, and so on. And good sense should prompt them to acknowledge that absolutely nothing ensures that, once Christian beliefs have been finally and fully renounced, those values will not slowly dissolve, to be replaced by others that are coarser, colder, more pragmatic, and more "inhuman." On this score, it would be foolish to feel especially sanguine; and there are good causes, as I shall discuss in the final part of this book, for apprehension. This is one reason why the historical insight and intellectual honesty of Nietzsche were such precious things, and why their absence from so much contemporary antireligious polemic renders it so depressingly vapid.

It is pointless, however, to debate what it would truly mean for Western culture to renounce Christianity unless one first understands what it meant for Western culture to adopt Christianity; and this one cannot do if one is content to remain fixated upon fruitless abstractions concerning "religion" rather than turning to the actual particularities of Christian history and belief. Nor, surely, does that turn constitute some sort of safe retreat for the Christian: the realm of the particular is, by its nature, one of ambiguity, where wisdom and mercy are indissolubly wedded to ignorance and brutality, often within the same institution, or indeed the same person. It is hardly novel to observe that Christianity's greatest historical triumph was also its most calamitous defeat: with the conversion of the

Roman Empire, the faith that was born proclaiming the overthrow of the powers of "this age" all at once found itself in alliance with, subordinate to, and too often emulous of those powers. It would be foolish to deny or regret the magnificent achievements of Christendom, moral no less than cultural. Even so, the gospel has at best flickered through the history of the West, working upon hard and intractable natures—the frank brutality of barbarians, the refined cruelty of the civilized—producing prodigies of sanctity and charity in every age, institutional and personal, and suffering countless betrayals and perversions in every generation.

It should be uncontroversial (though, given the mood of the times, it probably is not) to say that if the teachings of Christianity were genuinely to take root in human hearts—if indeed we all believed that God is love and that we ought to love our neighbors as ourselves—we should have no desire for war, should hate injustice worse than death, and should find indifference to the sufferings of others impossible. But, in fact, human beings will continue to make war, and to slay the innocent and the defenseless with cheerful abandon; they will continue to distract themselves from themselves, and from their mortality, and from morbid boredom by killing and dying on a magnificent scale, and by exulting in their power to destroy one another. And human society will continue, in various times and places, to degenerate into a murderous horde, even if it remains so civilized as to depute the legal, political, and military machineries of the state to do its murdering for it. In such a world, Christians have no choice but to continue to believe in the power of the gospel to transform the human will from an engine of cruelty, sentimentality, and selfishness into a vessel of divine grace, capable of union with God and love of one's neighbor. Many of today's most obstreperous critics of Christianity know nothing more of Christendom's two millennia than a few childish images of bloodthirsty crusaders and sadistic inquisitors, a few damning facts, and a great number of even more damning legends; to such critics, obviously, Christians ought not to surrender the past but should instead deepen their own collective memory of what the gospel has been in human history. Perhaps more crucially, they ought not to surrender the future to those who know so little of human nature as to imagine that a society "liberated" from Christ would love justice, or truth, or beauty, or compassion, or even life. The Christian view of human nature is wise precisely because it is so very extreme: it sees humanity, at once, as an image of the divine, fashioned for infinite love and imperishable glory, and as an almost inexhaustible wellspring of vindictiveness, cupidity, and brutality. Christians, indeed, have a special obligation not to forget how great and how inextinguishable the human proclivity for violence is, or how many victims it has claimed, for they worship a God who does not merely take the part of those victims, but who was himself one of them, murdered by the combined authority and moral prudence of the political, religious, and legal powers of human society.

Which is, incidentally, the most subversive claim ever made in the history of the human race.

CHAPTER TWO

The Age of Freedom

AT THE END OF THE DAY, it is probably the case that arguments of
the sort rehearsed in the previous chapter are somewhat futile, since they
are more or less confined to the surface of an antagonism that runs far
deeper than reasonable dispute can possibly reach. The sorts of "scientific," "moral," or "rational" objections to faith I have described above are
not really scientific, moral, or rational in any but a purely rhetorical sense.
There is no serious science in Dennett's "science of religion"; and there is
no genuine moral cogitation or rigorous reflection in any of the moral in-
dictments of religion advanced by him or his fellow "New Atheists." These
are attitudes masquerading as ideas, emotional commitments disguised as
intellectual honesty. However sincere the current evangelists of unbelief
may be, they are doing nothing more than producing rationales—bal-
lasted by a formidable collection of conceptual and historical errors—for
convictions that are rooted not in reason but in a greater cultural will, of
which their arguments are only reflexes. This is only to be expected: we
all inhabit cultural and linguistic worlds that determine to a great extent
what we think important, how we see reality, what fundamental premises
we assume, and even what we most deeply desire. We are not entirely
confined to these worlds—we are living souls, not merely machines—but
it requires considerable effort to see beyond their horizons.

The reason that today's cultured despisers of religion tend to employ such extraordinarily bad arguments for their prejudices, without realizing how bad those arguments are, is that they are driven by the precritical and irrational impulses of the purest kind of fideism. At the deepest level of their thoughts and desires, they are obedient to principles and promptings that rest upon no foundation but themselves. Dennett believes that all of reality consists of matter in motion not because he can reason his way to such a conclusion, and not because that is his experience of reality; rather, both his reasoning and his experiences are fixed within a world picture of absolutely primordial authority for him. It would make no sense, really, to suggest that he, say, run off to Mt. Athos to explore (by practicing) the Eastern Christian hesychastic tradition, or that he reconsider whether the testimony of so many disciplined minds over the centuries regarding encounters with supernatural reality are prima facie worthless simply because they cannot be examined in the way one might examine an animal zygote, or that he immerse himself with somewhat more than a superficial resolve in the classical philosophical arguments of religious traditions (concerning which *Breaking the Spell* demonstrates that he possesses practically no knowledge whatsoever, despite his philosophical training). In all likelihood, these would be impossibilities for someone of his temperament and basic vision of things; he could not do them with a good will or unclouded mind, and so they would have little power to unsettle him. And, in a far wider sense, all the manifestations of the currently fashionable forms of principled unbelief are understandable only within the context of a larger "project": the largely preconscious (or, at any rate, prerational) will of Western humanity toward the values of modernity and toward—more specifically—the modern understanding of human freedom. To understand what it is that drives certain of us not only to unbelief but to a passionate and often articulate hatred of belief in God, and to an evangelical dedication to its eradication, one must understand what it is they—and perhaps, in a larger sense, all of us—believe *in*, and why it demands of us the overthrow of the faith it seeks to displace.

These are all very presumptuous claims, perhaps, and my only excuse for making them is that I happen to think them true. Given this, I shall venture an even more presumptuous, and intentionally provocative, assertion: To be entirely modern (which very few of us are) is to believe in nothing. This is not to say it is to have no beliefs: the truly modern person may believe in almost anything, or even perhaps in everything, so long as all these beliefs rest securely upon a more fundamental and radical faith in *the* nothing—or, better, in nothingness as such. Modernity's highest ideal—its special understanding of personal autonomy—requires us to place our trust in an original absence underlying all of reality, a fertile void in which all things are possible, from which arises no impediment to our wills, and before which we may consequently choose to make of ourselves what we choose. We trust, that is to say, that there is no substantial criterion by which to judge our choices that stands higher than the unquestioned good of free choice itself, and that therefore all judgment, divine no less than human, is in some sense an infringement upon our freedom. This is our primal ideology. In the most unadorned terms possible, the ethos of modernity is—to be perfectly precise—nihilism.

This word is not, I want immediately to urge, a term of abuse, and I do not employ it dismissively or contemptuously. There are today a number of quite morally earnest philosophers (especially in continental Europe) who are perfectly content to identify themselves as nihilists, because they understand nihilism to be no more than the rejection of any idea of an ultimate source of truth transcendent of the self or the world—a rejection, that is, not of the various objective *truths* that can be identified within the world but of the notion that there is some total or eternal *Truth* beyond the world, governing reality and defining the good, the true, or the beautiful for all of us here below. As such, some would argue, nihilism is potentially the most peaceful and pluralistic of intellectual conditions, precisely because it presumes no system of beliefs that ought to be imposed upon others and no single correct path to truth that others ought to be made to tread. To be truly nihilist, in this sense of the word, is simply to have been set free from subservience to creeds, or to religious fantasy, or to any form of moral or cultural absolutism, and so ideally to have relinquished every desire to control one's fellows.

Again, however, almost no one is entirely modern in this way, and very few of us are conscious or consistent nihilists, even of the extremely benign variety I have just described. The majority of us, if polls are to be trusted, even believe in God. And even the majority of unbelievers are aware that human nature and human society place not merely necessary but desirable limits upon the will's free exercise. Nevertheless, we live in an age whose chief value has been determined, by overwhelming consensus, to be the inviolable liberty of personal volition, the right to decide for ourselves what we shall believe, want, need, own, or serve. The will, we habitually assume, is sovereign to the degree that it is obedient to nothing else and is free to the degree that it is truly spontaneous and constrained by nothing greater than itself. This, for many of us, is the highest good imaginable. And a society guided by such beliefs must, at least implicitly, embrace and subtly advocate a very particular "moral metaphysics": that is, the nonexistence of any transcendent standard of the good that has the power (or the *right*) to order our desires toward a higher end. We are, first and foremost, heroic and insatiable consumers, and we must not allow the specters of transcendent law or personal guilt to render us indecisive. For us, it is choice itself, and not what we choose, that is the first good, and this applies not only to such matters as what we shall purchase or how we shall we live. In even our gravest political and ethical debates—regarding economic policy, abortion, euthanasia, assisted suicide, censorship, ge- netic engineering, and so on—"choice" is a principle not only frequently invoked, by one side or by both, but often seeming to exercise an almost mystical supremacy over all other concerns.

All of this, undoubtedly, follows from an extremely potent and persua- sive model of freedom, one that would not have risen to such dominance in our culture if it did not give us a sense of liberty from arbitrary author- ity, and of limitless inner possibilities, and of profound personal dignity. There is nothing contemptible in this, and there is no simple, obvious moral reproach to be brought against it. Nevertheless, as I have said, it is a model of freedom whose ultimate horizon is, quite literally, nothing. More- over, if the will determines itself principally in and through the choices it makes, then it too, at some very deep level, must also be nothing: simply a pure movement of spontaneity, motive without motive, absolute poten- tiality, giving birth to itself. A God beyond us or a stable human nature within us would confine our decisions within certain inescapable chan- nels; and so at some, usually unconscious level—whatever else we may believe—we stake ourselves entirely upon the absence of either. Those of us who now, in the latter days of modernity, are truest to the wisdom and ethos of our age place ourselves not at the disposal of God, or the gods, or the Good, but before an abyss, over which presides the empty power of our isolated wills, whose decisions are their own moral index. This is what it means to have become perfect consumers: the original nothingness of the will gives itself shape by the use it makes of the nothingness of the world—and thus we are free.

Now this is, as I have said, a willfully extreme formulation of the matter, and life is rarely lived at the extremes. For most of us, the forces of conformity that surround and seduce us—political, religious, patriotic, and popular—are necessary shelters against the storm of infinite possibility. A perfectly consistent ethics of choice would ultimately erase any meaningful distinction between good and evil, compassion and cruelty, love and hatred, reverence and transgression, and few of us could bear to inhabit the world on those terms. We may more or less unreflectively believe that the will becomes progressively freer the more it is liberated from whatever constraints it suffers. This may mean that, over the course of time, even cherished moral traditions can come to seem like onerous nuisances to us, impinging upon our rights; but few of us are so demented, demonic, or incorrigibly adolescent as to choose to live without visible boundaries. Even when we have shed the moral and religious precepts of our ancestors, most of us try to be ethical and even, in many cases, "spiritual." It is rare, however, that we are able to impose anything like a coherent pattern upon the somewhat haphazard collection of principles and practices by which we do this. Our ethics, especially, tends to be something of a continuous improvisation or bricolage: we assemble fragments of traditions we half remember, gather ethical maxims almost at random from the surrounding culture, attempt to find an inner equilibrium between tolerance and conviction, and so on, until we have knit together something like a code, suited to our needs, temperaments, capacities, and imaginations. We select the standards or values we find appealing from a larger market of moral options and then try to arrange them into some sort of tasteful harmony. As for our religion, much the same may be said: few of us really feel that the creeds we espouse are more important in giving shape to our ethical predispositions than are our own judgments. We certainly, at any rate, do not draw near to the "mystery of God" with anything like the fear and trembling of our ancestors, and when we tire of our devotions and drift away we do not expect to be pursued, either by the furies or by the hounds of conscience.

This is especially obvious at modern Western religion's pastel-tinged margins, in those realms of the New Age where the gods of the boutique hold uncontested sway. Here one may cultivate a private atmosphere of "spirituality" as undemanding and therapeutically comforting as one likes simply by purchasing a dream catcher, a few pretty crystals, some books on the goddess, a Tibetan prayer wheel, a volume of Joseph Campbell or Carl Jung or Robert Graves, a Nataraja figurine, a purse of tiles engraved with runes, a scattering of Pre-Raphaelite prints drenched in Celtic twilight, an Andean flute, and so forth, until this mounting congeries of string, worthless quartz, cheap joss sticks, baked clay, kitsch, borrowed iconography, and fraudulent scholarship reaches that mysterious point of saturation at which religion has become indistinguishable from interior decorating. Then one may either abandon one's gods for something new or bide with them for a time, but in either case without any real reverence, love, or dread. There could scarcely be a more thoroughly *modern* form of religion than this. It certainly bears no resemblance to the genuine and honorable idolatries of old, or to the sort of ravenous religious eclecticism that characterized the late Roman Empire. The peoples of early and late antiquity actually believed in, adored, and feared their gods. No one really believes in the gods of the New Age; they are deities not of the celestial hierarchy above but of the ornamental *étagère* in the corner, and their only "divine" office is to give symbolic expression to the dreamier sides of their votaries' personalities. They are purchased gods, gods as accessories, and hence are merely masks by means of which the one true god—the will—at once conceals and reveals itself.

It should not be forgotten that the concept of freedom that most of us take for granted, and that is arguably modernity's central "idea," has a history. In the more classical understanding of the matter, whether pagan or Christian, true freedom was understood as something inseparable from one's nature: to be truly free, that is to say, was to be at liberty to realize one's proper "essence" and so flourish as the kind of being one was. For Plato or Aristotle, or for Christian thinkers like Gregory of Nyssa, Augustine, Maximus the Confessor, John of Damascus, or Thomas Aquinas, true human freedom is emancipation from whatever constrains us from living the life of rational virtue, or from experiencing the full fruition of our nature; and among the things that constrain us are our own untutored passions, our willful surrender to momentary impulses, our own foolish or wicked *choices*. In this view of things, we are free when we achieve that end toward which our inmost nature is oriented from the first moment of existence, and whatever separates us from that end—even if it comes from our own wills—is a form of bondage. We become free, that is, in something of the same way that (in Michelangelo's image) the form is "liberated" from the marble by the sculptor. This means we are free not merely because we can choose, but only when we have chosen well. For to choose poorly, through folly or malice, in a way that thwarts our nature and distorts our proper form, is to enslave ourselves to the transitory, the irrational, the purposeless, the (to be precise) subhuman. To choose well we must ever more clearly see the "sun of the Good" (to use the lovely Platonic metaphor), and to see more clearly we must continue to choose well; and the more we are emancipated from illusion and caprice, the more perfect our vision becomes, and the less there is really to choose. We see and we act in one unified movement of our nature toward God or the Good, and as we progress we find that to turn away from that light is ever more manifestly a defect of the mind and will, and ever more difficult to do. Hence Augustine defined the highest state of human freedom not as "being able not to sin" (*posse non peccare*) but as "being unable to sin" (*non posse peccare*): a condition that reflects the infinite goodness of God, who, because nothing can hinder him in the perfect realization of his own nature, is "incapable" of evil and so is infinitely *free*.

That, though, was a very long time ago, and we have journeyed far from there. Even many theologians, as the Middle Ages gave way to the early modern period (and ever thereafter), ceased to think of God quite in this way. The story the modern world tells of itself now is the story of how we Westerners finally learned to be free, for the first time ever; and so it is also necessarily a story about the bondage from which we have escaped. After all, the freedom we now possess in the aftermath of Christendom has vouchsafed us (has it not?) so many and such prodigious marvels: free inquiry, which has given rise to all the marvelous achievements of modern science, technology, and medicine, and which (we are told) the church once violently discouraged; all those political liberties that only a secular polity can guarantee and that (as we all know) the church always feared and strove to suppress; the freedom from sectarian violence and "wars of religion" that only a rigorously secular regime can preserve and that (obviously) Christian society was unable to provide; and the immense wealth produced by modern market economies, which are nourished by the incalculable diversity of consumer wants and needs, and which (everyone agrees) should never be limited by the imposition of "private" religious concerns upon society as a whole. Modernity is an exhilarating and intoxicating promise, not only of a kind of personal autonomy inconceivable in earlier ages, but also of peace, progress, and prosperity. As a result, the older model of freedom must now be remembered, if at all, only as a form of servitude.

But, then, that is the question: Do we remember this older model *at all*? Do we really know what the Christian centuries were? And are freedom and rationality distinctively modern values, or have we merely been indoctrinated to believe that it is modernity alone that is free and rational? And how free are we? And from what have we been freed? After all, modernity was a cultural revolution: it was not merely the result of a natural evolution from one phase of economic and social development to another but a positive ideological project, the active creation of an entire "secular" sphere that had never before existed and that (because it had not yet been invented) had never before sought to be "liberated" from the bondage of faith. And every revolution must justify itself by telling again and again how it came to pass and why it was necessary, until it gets the story just right; which is to say that every revolution depends, in the long run, upon the scope, audacity, and persuasiveness of its propaganda.

PART TWO THE MYTHOLOGY OF THE SECULAR
AGE: MODERNITY'S REWRITING
OF THE CHRISTIAN PAST

CHAPTER THREE

Faith and Reason

AT ONE POINT in his magisterial *Medieval Civilization,* Jacques Le Goff, one of the more brilliant medievalists of the latter half of the twentieth century, makes this observation: "[Christendom's] attitude towards the excluded remained ambiguous. The Church seemed to detest and admire them simultaneously; it was afraid of them, but the fear was mixed with a sense of fascination. It kept them at a distance, but fixed the distance so that it would be close enough for the outcasts to be within reach. What it called its charity towards them was like the attitude of a cat playing with a mouse. Thus leper hospitals had to be sited 'a stone's throw from the town' so that 'fraternal charity' could be exercised towards the lepers. Mediaeval society needed these pariahs, who were exiled because they were danger-ous, and who yet had to be visible, because it eased its conscience by the cares which it expended on them. Even better, it could project on to and fix in them, magically, all the evils which it was banishing away from itself."[1] Indeed. I must say, it is difficult not to envy Le Goff's ability to gaze with such unwavering acuity back through the centuries, to peer into the hearts of persons long dead, to glimpse motives hidden even from them, and to lay those motives bare with such penetrating psychological insight. At least, I would envy such an ability if in fact it existed; but it does not.

Admittedly, the condition of lepers in medieval Western society— social and legal, to say nothing of medical—was anything but happy. But scholars less confident of their perspicacity than Le Goff would probably have paused, at least for a moment, to marvel at the very existence of lepers' hospitals in an age when the fear of contamination was so great, and might have leadenly ascribed the location of these hospitals at the edges of towns to nothing more sinister than the exigencies of quarantine. They might even have noted the amazing willingness of Christian towns to tolerate the proximity (a mere "stone's throw" away) of persons whom other societies would have banished far from all human habitation, and the willingness of monks, nuns, and even laity to minister to those persons' needs. There was, after all, a long tradition of Christian monastic hospitals for the destitute and dying, going back to the days of Constantine and stretching from the Syrian and Byzantine East to the Western fringes of Christendom, a tradition that had no real precedent in pagan society (unless one counts, say, the *valetudinaria* used by the military to restore soldiers to fighting form). St. Ephraim the Syrian (A.D. c. 306–373), when the city of Edessa was ravaged by plague, established hospitals open to all who were afflicted. St. Basil the Great (A.D. 329–379) founded a hospital in Cappadocia with a ward set aside for the care of lepers, whom he did not disdain to nurse with his own hands. St. Benedict of Nursia (A.D. c. 480–c. 547) opened a free infirmary at Monte Cassino and made care of the sick a paramount duty of his monks. In Rome, the Christian noblewoman and scholar St. Fabiola (d. A.D. c. 399) established the first public hospital in Western Europe and—despite her wealth and position—often ventured out into the streets personally to seek out those who needed care. St. John Chrysostom (A.D. 347–407), while patriarch of Constantinople, used his influence to fund several such institutions in the city; and in the *diakoniai* of Constantinople, for centuries, many rich members of the laity labored to care for the poor and ill, bathing the sick, ministering to their needs, assisting them with alms. During the Middle Ages, the Benedictines alone were responsible for more than two thousand hospitals in Western Europe. The twelfth century was particularly remarkable in this regard, especially wherever the Knights of St. John—the Hospitallers—were active. At Montpellier in 1145, for example, the great Hospital of the Holy Spirit was founded, soon becoming a center of medical training and, in 1221, of Montpellier's faculty of medicine. And, in addition to medical care, these hospitals provided food for the hungry, cared for widows and orphans, and distributed alms to all who came in need. I could go on; but my point is that, surely, this history must be, at the very least, germane to our understanding of the lepers' hospitals Le Goff describes.[2]

Admittedly, it is probably far more diverting, and a far better way to make a show of the historian's subtlety, to ignore the declared and explicit purpose of such hospitals, and to attribute the entire phenomenon of Christian care of lepers to the ambiguous allure of "exclusion" and "curse," or to "expose" an apparently sincere social labor of charity as nothing more than a thin salve for scabrous consciences, concealing a particularly unwholesome and voyeuristic kind of malice. Even granting all the quite legitimate observations one might make regarding the injustices of late medieval society, however, Le Goff's remarks here are less than worthless. They tell us nothing about medieval society, but merely record a personal impression without any basis in the historical evidence. Other historians, looking at the same period, have found it possible—without becoming cheerful apologists for medieval culture—to take the medieval world somewhat at its word, at least provisionally, and so to descry a society that, for all its brutalities, mixed motives, and inconstancies, was in some genuine way constructed around a central ideal of Christian love.[3] Certainly Le Goff wins no marks for superior perceptiveness on this matter; his desire to reduce an extraordinary example of imperfect compassion to a completely ordinary example of perfect spite is, if not a mere reflex of prejudice, at the very least fantastic and cynical ("a cat playing with a mouse," for goodness' sake). And yet, outrageous as his remarks are, they are likely to strike us as sober and plausible, because we are so predisposed to believe not only that social morality is something that naturally evolves over time toward higher and higher expressions but also that we today are vastly more enlightened than those poor, uncouth, benighted brutes who slouched through the swamps of medieval fanaticism, superstition, and hypocrisy. Not that Le Goff would himself ever be so unsophisticated as to embrace the narrower bigotries of his age explicitly or uncritically; but here, certainly, his inability to enter imaginatively into another epoch leads him to prefer a set of empty abstractions to a serious engagement with the complexities of a society historically remote from him. And these are the remarks of a scholar who is, as I have already said, quite brilliant.

This, perhaps, is no more than one should expect. Every age necessarily reinterprets—and rewrites—the past in accord with its own interests, ideals, and illusions. Most purely ideological reconstructions of the past are too crude to be especially convincing—for instance, the Marxist reduction of history to material dialectic and class warfare. But modernity is itself an ideology, pervasive and enormously powerful, which most of us have absorbed at a far profounder level of thought and conviction than the boringly simplistic myths of Marxism could ever reach. For centuries now the story of humanity's emergence from what Gibbon called "the darkness and confusion of the middle ages"[4] into a new and revolutionary age of enlightenment and reason has been the reigning historical narrative that most of us imbibe from school, the press, popular entertainment, even frequently our churches—in short, the entire fabric of our society. And along with this narrative, as an indispensable concomitant, comes an elaborate mythology of what it was that was overcome when modernity was born out of the turmoils of the waning centuries of the "age of faith."

What, after all, does it mean for a whole society to be truly "modern"? Completely modern, that is, as opposed to merely possessing modern technologies or obeying the axioms of modern economics. I have already offered a partial answer to this: it has a great deal to do with a society's understanding of freedom. But, in a more purely historical sense, if we take the word "modernity" to mean not simply whatever happens to be contemporary with us but rather the culture of the Western world as it has evolved over the last four or five centuries, then it seems obvious that a society is truly modern to the extent that it is post-Christian. This is not to say, obviously, that modern society is predominantly inhabited by non-Christians or atheists; it is only to say that modernity is what comes "after Christendom," when Christianity has been displaced from the center of a culture and deprived of any power explicitly to shape laws and customs, and has ceased to be regarded as the source of a society's highest values or of a government's legitimacy, and has ceased even to hold preeminent sway over a people's collective imagination. And the term "post-Christian" must be given its full weight here: modernity is not simply a "postreligious" condition; it is the state of a society that has been specifically a Christian society but has "lost the faith." The ethical presuppositions intrinsic to modernity, for instance, are palliated fragments and haunting echoes of Christian moral theology. Even the most ardent secularists among us generally cling to notions of human rights, economic and social justice, providence for the indigent, legal equality, or basic human dignity that pre-Christian Western culture would have found not so much foolish as unintelligible. It is simply the case that we distant children of the pagans would not be able to believe in any of these things—they would never have occurred to us—had our ancestors not once believed that God is love, that charity is the foundation of all virtues, that all of us are equal before the eyes of God, that to fail to feed the hungry or care for the suffering is to sin against Christ, and that Christ laid down his life for the least of his brethren. That said, it is undeniable that—however much certain Christian moral presuppositions may continue to exercise their vestigial influence over us—the history of modernity is the history of secularization, of the retreat of Christian belief to the private sphere; and this, for many of us, is nothing less than the history of human freedom itself, the grand adventure of the adulthood of the race (so long delayed by priestcraft and superstition and intolerance), the great revolution that liberated society and the individual alike from the crushing weight of tradition and doctrine.

Hence modernity's first great attempt to define itself: an "age of reason" emerging from and overthrowing an "age of faith." Behind this definition lay a simple but thoroughly enchanting tale. Once upon a time, it went, Western humanity was the cosseted and incurious ward of Mother Church; during this, the age of faith, culture stagnated, science languished, wars of religion were routinely waged, witches were burned by inquisitors, and Western humanity labored in brutish subjugation to dogma, superstition, and the unholy alliance of church and state. Withering blasts of fanaticism and fideism had long since scorched away the last remnants of classical learning; inquiry was stifled; the literary remains of classical antiquity had long ago been consigned to the fires of faith, and even the great achievements of "Greek science" were forgotten till Islamic civilization restored them to the West. All was darkness. Then, in the wake of the "wars of religion" that had torn Christendom apart, came the full flowering of the Enlightenment and with it the reign of reason and progress, the riches of scientific achievement and political liberty, and a new and revolutionary sense of human dignity. The secular nation-state arose, reduced religion to an establishment of the state or, in the course of time, to something altogether separate from the state, and thereby rescued Western humanity from the blood-steeped intolerance of religion. Now, at last, Western humanity has left its nonage and attained to its majority, in science, politics, and ethics. The story of the travails of

Galileo almost invariably occupies an honored place in this narrative, as exemplary of the natural relation between "faith" and "reason" and as an exquisite epitome of scientific reason's mighty struggle during the early modern period to free itself from the tyranny of religion. This is, as I say, a simple and enchanting tale, easily followed and utterly captivating in its explanatory tidiness; its sole defect is that it happens to be false in every identifiable detail.

To be fair, serious historians do not for the most part speak in such terms. This tale of the birth of the modern world has largely disappeared from respectable academic literature and survives now principally at the level of folklore, "intellectual journalism," and vulgar legend. One continues, of course, to see the entire medieval period now and then vaguely described as the "Dark Ages" in popular histories; but scholars are generally loath to use that term even of the era to which it "properly" refers: the period between the final fall of the Western Roman Empire in A.D. 476 and the rise of the Holy Roman Empire in A.D. 800 (or, more broadly, between the fifth and eleventh centuries); and they have abandoned the term not only because it sounds derogatory. The very idea of an unnaturally protracted period of general darkness after the fall of the Western Roman Empire began its life among the humanists of the Italian Renaissance, who liked to characterize the "new learning" they advocated as a reawakening of ancient wisdom from a millennium of inglorious slumber. But most good historians know that the intellectual and cultural revolution of the Renaissance was the flowering of innumerable high medieval developments, fecundated by a late infusion into Italy of scholarship and classical Greek texts from the dying Byzantine Empire of the Christian East.

Admittedly, the early Middle Ages were a surpassingly harsh period in Western European history. As the Western Roman world gradually dissolved—as a result of mercantile, military, cultural, and demographic decline, and as successive immigrations and occasional invasions of "barbarians" continued to alter the shape of Western European society, and as agrarian economies gradually replaced urban, and as successions of plagues and famines exacted their toll—there was a prolonged period when many of the achievements of classical antiquity were largely lost in the Christian West (though not in the Christian East), and the monasteries became the sole repositories of what remained of ancient learning. But the Middle Ages as a whole, especially from the time of the Carolingian

Renaissance of the late seventh and early eighth centuries, were marked by considerable dynamism, in the arts, scholarship, engineering, agronomy, architecture, law, philosophy, and natural science, despite economic and material adversity of a sort now hard even to imagine. Perhaps most importantly, few historians of science now endorse a "catastrophist" account of nascent modern science—even those who believe in a great scientific paradigm shift at the dawn of modernity—and instead tend to acknowledge the continuity of scientific inquiry from the High Middle Ages through the modern period, the technological advances made by medieval society, both early and late, and the first stirrings of a genuinely empirical scientific method in late medieval scholastic thought (but more of this below).

Sadly, however, it is not serious historians who, for the most part, form the historical consciousness of their times; it is bad popular historians, generally speaking, and the historical hearsay they repeat or invent, and the myths they perpetuate and simplifications they promote, that tend to determine how most of us view the past. However assiduously the diligent, painstakingly precise academical drudge may labor at his or her meticulously researched and exhaustively documented tomes, nothing he or she produces will enjoy a fraction of the currency of any of the casually composed (though sometimes lavishly illustrated) squibs heaped on the front tables of chain bookstores or clinging to the middle rungs of best-seller lists. For everyone whose picture of the Middle Ages is shaped by the dry, exact, quietly illuminating books produced by those pale dutiful pedants who squander the golden meridians of their lives prowling in the shadows of library stacks or weakening their eyes by poring over pages of barely legible Carolingian minuscule, a few hundred will be convinced by what they read in, say, William Manchester's dreadful, vulgar, and almost systematically erroneous *A World Lit Only by Fire*.[5] After all, few have the time or the need to sift through academic journals and monographs and tedious disquisitions on abstruse topics trying to separate the gold from the dross. And so, naturally, among the broadly educated and the broadly uneducated alike, it is the simple picture that tends to prevail, though in varying shades and intensities of color, as with any image often and cheaply reproduced; and the simple picture, in this case, is the story that Western society has been telling about itself for centuries now.

CHAPTER FOUR

The Night of Reason

PART OF THIS "story of the modern world," in one of its more venerable variants, is that the "faith" that modern "reason" superseded was *uniquely* irrational, and unprecedentedly hostile to the appeals of rationality; that, in fact, this faith had barbarously purged Western culture of the high attainments of the classical world—had burned its books, abandoned its science, forsaken its "pluralism"—and had plunged the Western world into a millennium of mental squalor. Christianity, so the tale goes, induced the so-called Dark Ages by actively destroying the achievements of Roman culture. Here the ghastly light of a thousand inane legends burns with an almost inextinguishable incandescence.

Take, for example, this from a recent book by Jonathan Kirsch entitled *God against the Gods:* "In 390 . . . a mob of Christian zealots attacked the ancient library of Alexandria, a place where works of the greatest rarity and antiquity had been collected. Here were preserved the oldest manuscripts of the Bible and other writings of Jewish and Christian origin, far older than the Dead Sea Scrolls, and the pagan texts were even more ancient and even more abundant, some 700,000 volumes and scrolls in all. The whole collection of parchment and papyri was torched, the library itself was pulled down, and the loss to Western civilization is beyond calculation or even imagination. . . . The next year, Theodosius I ordered the destruction of the Serapeum, a magnificent temple that served as the principal shrine

of Isis and Serapis."[1] Not everyone, admittedly, is at leisure to drink deep
from the Pierian Spring. Kirsch is not a historian and so can perhaps be
forgiven for relying on popular rather than original sources; and obviously
he is repeating in good faith a tale he has heard so often that he cannot
distinguish it from fact. But it is quite absurd for all that.

There is, as it happens, a story to be told about (at least) the ruin of the
Serapeum, and it is not particularly creditable for either the Christian or
the pagan citizens of late fourth-century Alexandria; but Kirsch's rendition
of that story is hopelessly confused. For one thing, unless some long-lost
catalogue of the Library of Alexandria has recently turned up in a pawn
shop in Cairo, the list of works that Kirsch claims the library possessed is
sheer fantasy. The only copy of the Jewish Bible we can be reasonably sure
belonged to the collection was the Greek translation called the Septuagint;
and while it was certainly part of the purpose of the Great Library that
it should be a repository of other Greek translations of foreign texts, we
do not know how many it succeeded in procuring. Far more egregiously,
though, Kirsch has both divided one tale into two and collapsed two libraries into one. The great Royal Library of Alexandria that some ancient historians claimed, rather incredibly, had contained seven hundred thousand
scrolls (or five hundred thousand, or four hundred thousand, or indeed as
few as forty thousand) was established by King Ptolemy II Philadelphus
(304–246 B.C.) as part of the grand Museum his father Ptolemy I Soter
(c. 367–c. 282 B.C.) had established in the Brucheium, the royal quarter
at the northeast of the city. Some ancient sources claim that this library
was indeed destroyed by fire, but certainly not by Christians. Julius Caesar
was generally reckoned to be the culprit; it was said, at least, that in 48 or
47 B.C., when his war with Pompey had taken him to Alexandria, Caesar
inadvertently started a fire in the royal quarter—whether by burning his
enemy's ships in the harbor or by other means—that destroyed the library,
either whole or in part, or that at least destroyed tens of thousands of scrolls
stored in granaries near the docks. How credible this tale is remains an
object of scholarly debate. If the library survived, however, or was restored,
as some think, many believe it to have perished along with the rest of the
Museum in A.D. 272, during the wars waged by the emperor Aurelian (A.D.
c. 215–275) to reunite the empire. In all likelihood, though, the original
Great Library was very much a part of the distant (and somewhat legend-
ary) past by that time. It was certainly no longer in existence in A.D. 390.[2]

There was, however, a "daughter" library, which may have been located in the grounds of the Serapeum, perhaps placed there by Ptolemy III Euergetes (fl. 246–221 B.C.) when he built the original temple, or perhaps established there only when the temple was rebuilt, far more resplendently, in the late second century A.D. There were at least stacks, it seems, among the colonnades, perhaps at the periphery of the temple complex; but how many, and how plenteously stocked, we cannot say.[3] The twelfth-century Byzantine historian John Tzetzes claimed that Callimachus of Cyrene (c. 305–c. 240 B.C.) catalogued forty-two thousand scrolls in the library built by Euergetes outside the Brucheium, but whether this is to be trusted, and whether that library was in fact at the Serapeum, cannot be determined. In any event, it is this library that *could* have been destroyed when Roman soldiers and Christian civilians tore down the Serapeum (as indeed did happen in 391). Of this, however, there is no evidence whatsoever. None of the ancient accounts of the destruction of the temple says anything about the destruction of a library, not even that of the devoutly pagan rhetorician and historian Eunapius of Sardis (A.D. c. 345–c. 420), who despised Christians and certainly was not anxious to exculpate them of any perfidy that could be laid at their feet, and who as a man of enormous learning would have been enraged by the mass destruction of precious texts. Moreover, the demolition was a military operation, it seems, not simply a spontaneous orgy of wanton destruction, even if a Christian mob joined in. It is not even certain that anything other than the actual sanctuary of the god—the inner temple building—was demolished.

Edward Gibbon, however, in his account of the event, speaks with strange confidence of the library being "pillaged or destroyed," and adds that "the appearance of empty shelves excited the regret and indignation of every spectator whose mind was not totally darkened by religious prejudice." But the only source he cites in corroboration of his claim is a cursory remark made by the Christian historian Paul Orosius (fl. A.D. 414–417), who, while recounting the tale of Caesar's fire, observes in passing that he himself has seen "caskets for books" in certain temples that were "emptied out" by "our own men" when those temples were plundered: an admission at which, Gibbon correctly notes, "Orosius seems to blush." But by "our own men" Orosius may mean simply "men of our time," because he then goes on to praise, in contrast, the men of previous generations who, "more honorably," had collected those books in the first place, in emulation of the Alexandrian scholars of old. Whatever the case, and though it may seem shameful that temples were despoiled of their riches, including their books, either by Christians or others of the time, the lurid, tragic, scandalous story that one sees repeated again and again—that Christian hordes took seven hundred thousand scrolls from the Great Library of Alexandria and, intoxicated by their fanatical and brutish detestation of profane learning and heathen science, burned them in open fires in the streets, setting back the advance of Western civilization by centuries in the process —is pure fiction. Indeed, before the modern genesis of this legend, it was the Arab invaders of A.D. 642 under General Amr ibn al'As who tended to receive the blame for the "final" destruction of the Alexandrian library, on the orders of the caliph Umar himself. Gibbon discounts this tale, as do most historians today (perhaps too hastily), on account of how late the story appears in Arab and Christian literature. In the course of doing so, however, he inadvertently provides a powerful argument against his own suppositions regarding a Christian spoliation of the Serapeum library: he notes—as evidence that the library was no longer in existence at the time of the Arab conquest—that the pagan historian Ammianus Marcellinus (A.D. c. 330–395), describing the Serapeum a few years before its destruction, speaks of its library in the "*past* tense," in words "remarkably strong." The full significance of that fact seems, however, to have eluded Gibbon's notice.[4]

In a sense, this is all of very limited importance. Even if the sordid fable of the destruction of the Great Library by a Christian mob were true (and it definitely is not), or even if there had been a substantial collection of books at the Serapeum that was stolen or destroyed by the soldiers and their Christian accomplices in 391 (and the silence of Eunapius, to say nothing of Ammianus's tenses, is sufficient evidence that there was not), this would tell us nothing about the Christian view of pagan learning or classical culture. Local riots rarely tell us much, in any event, apart from certain things we already know about the more unseemly characteristics of human mass behavior. Colorful myths aside, the early church did not systematically destroy the literature of pagan antiquity, and there was no universal Christian prejudice against profane learning (as is obvious from Orosius's remarks). Alexandria was the most violent city in the most violent imperial territory in an exceedingly violent age, and it was often not so much disturbed as governed by rioting mobs of pagans, Jews, or

Christians. It was also a seat of immense learning and home to many of the greatest scholars and philosophers—pagan, Jewish, and Christian—of its time. It was here, for instance, that the School of Alexandria, the first Christian institution of higher learning in the empire, was established midway through the second century by the philosopher Pantaenus (d. before A.D. 200), a convert from Stoicism, and then led successively by Clement of Alexandria (A.D. c. 150–c. 213) and Origen (A.D. c. 185–c. 254), two men of vast erudition, who made free use of Greek methods of textual interpretation and of pagan philosophy. Origen even attended lectures by Ammonius Saccas, the "Socrates of Neoplatonism," and required his students to regard no path of wisdom as forbidden to them, and to apply themselves to the study of geometry, astronomy, and all the religious and philosophical texts of pagan culture. It is no anomaly that, in the middle of the third century, one of the city's more accomplished scholars of Aristotle was the Christian rhetorician and mathematician Anatolius. In the fourth century, perhaps the finest private collection of texts in Alexandria, both Christian and pagan—theology, philosophy, history, rhetoric—belonged to the Christian (Arian) patriarch George of Cappadocia. Indeed, that collection was impressive enough that, when George was murdered in 361 by an Alexandrian mob, the emperor Julian "the Apostate" (A.D. 331–363), a convert to paganism from Christianity, commanded that it be sent to him (expressing his regret as he did so that he could not mandate the burning of the Christian books in the collection, lest the soldiers charged with the task prove incapable of correctly separating the wheat from the chaff).

In truth, if one really wishes to make Alexandria of the first four centuries one's index for understanding the interaction of Christian and pagan culture, and proceeds without excessive prejudice, what one will find is that pagans and Christians alike had their scholars and philosophers, who frequently studied at one another's feet regardless of religious adherence, that both also had their cruel, superstitious, violent rabble, and that the priests of both traditions were as likely to occupy one class as the other. One will find too that, at the most elevated levels of philosophical discourse, both traditions admitted of debates concerning the degree to which the power of natural reason was sufficient to attain to divine truth, and the degree to which one must rely on divine revelation; and that a tendency toward a "pure" and contemplative monotheism, and a consequent disdain for or indifference toward popular cults, was pronounced among many pagans of a more philosophical cast of mind. And one will find also that, at the lower levels of society, the Christians and the pagans were distinct tribes that sometimes lived in harmonious—even exogamous—concord and that sometimes went to war with one another. It would have been wonderful, obviously, and a splendid testament to the power of high ideals, if Greek prudence or Christian charity had governed every person of the time and pervaded every stratum of society. It would have been wonderful especially if all the baptized Christians of the age, whose ideals were by far the higher and nobler, had never yielded to their hatred for the cults of their erstwhile persecutors as fervidly as they sometimes did. But human beings frequently disappoint.

As for the actual destruction of the Serapeum, it came late in a period of particularly intense religious persecution and violence that had begun a century and a half earlier under the pagan emperor Decius (A.D. c. 201–251). In the years leading up to his short reign (A.D. 249–251), persecution of Christians had tended to be limited and intermittent; but in January of 250 he issued an edict requiring every citizen to make a token oblation at a pagan altar before an official witness. Many Christians who refused were arrested, certain prominent bishops were executed, and for a year the persecution persisted. But the project proved something of a failure, systematic persecution ceased even before Decius's death in June 251, and his successor Gallus (d. A.D. 253) was apparently content that it not resume. Gallus's successor Valerian (d. A.D. 260), however, renewed the persecution in 257, with greater vigor. Among those who lost their lives were the great bishop of Carthage, Cyprian (A.D. 200–258), and bishop Sixtus II of Rome (d. A.D. 258). The last and most terrible persecution of Christians across the empire began in 303, under the emperor Diocletian (A.D. 245–316), a particularly credulous champion of the old gods, who seems to have blamed the new religion for the inability of his augurs to divine the future with any accuracy. Diocletian's ferocious lieutenant, General Galerius (d. A.D. 311), whose hatred of the Christians was absolute, urged the persecution with a special enthusiasm. Believers were imprisoned, tortured, mutilated, disfigured, and killed; martyrs' tombs were desecrated, churches were destroyed, and Christian books were seized and burned. When Diocletian abdicated for reasons of health in 305, Galerius became the Augustus of the Eastern half of the empire and appointed his equally brutal nephew Maximinus (d. A.D. 313) as Caesar (that is, a subordinate emperor), and together they sustained the persecution for another half dozen years; but when Galerius was himself stricken by a particularly painful (and ultimately fatal) illness in 311, he suspected the affliction had been visited upon him by the Christian God and so issued an edict absolving Christians of the obligation to make offerings to the gods of Rome, and in the winter of 312 the persecution largely ceased.

The next year, Constantine (A.D. c. 280–337), the new Augustus of the Western Empire and a new convert (of a sort) to Christianity, along with Licinius (d. A.D. 325), the Eastern Augustus, promulgated the Edict of Milan, which granted Christians complete toleration of their faith and full legal rights. After 324, Constantine was emperor of both East and West, and during his reign he demonstrated his loyalty to his new faith principally by shifting state patronage away from the old cults to the church and, later, by making somewhat sporadic attempts to discourage and suppress pagan devotions and the consecration of idols; and his son Constantius II (317–361), while remaining a Christian (in name if not in character), largely turned a blind eye on the devotions of the pagan aristocracy of Rome. Constantine's nephew Julian, however, in a hopeless attempt to restore the ancient religion and overthrow the new, spent much of his exceedingly brief reign (A.D. November 361–June 363) taking measures against the "Galilaeans" that quickly gravitated from the merely prejudicial to the positively cruel. Julian was an intelligent, courageous, and formidable man, with a host of amiable virtues and an enthusiasm for philosophy as great as his capacity was small. He was also mildly hysterical, vindictive, and deeply superstitious, blessed with boundless energy and possessed of an insatiable appetite for magic, mystery, and animal sacrifice. He is the one Roman emperor of this period, pagan or Christian, whom one could unreservedly call a religious fanatic, and while he officially proscribed the use of violence against the Christians, he was willing on occasion unofficially (but openly) to tolerate it. Among his policies was a law forbidding Christians to teach classical rhetoric, literature, and philosophy, a measure that even his generally sympathetic biographer Ammianus Marcellinus considered infamous (and a law, obviously, that would have been unnecessary had the Christians of the time been universally hostile to classical culture and learning).

When the temple of Serapis was razed, however, Theodosius I (A.D. 347–395) was emperor, and with him the pendulum of religious oppression had swung almost entirely to the opposite extreme. He was not simply a brutal despot like Galerius or an excitable monomaniac like Julian; but he ultimately took it upon himself—for political and religious reasons—to extinguish the fires of the old devotions and to purge the empire of foreign creeds and "deviant" forms of Christianity. For most of his reign, he tolerated pagans and did not exclude them from high office (as Julian had excluded Christians), but in 381 and 382 he issued or reinstituted laws forbidding sacrifices and making it illegal even to enter pagan temples for purposes of worship. Thereafter, in the East (and especially, predictably enough, in Egypt), bands of "monks"—little more, actually, than black-robed brigands who used the new laws as license for their outrages—began demolishing rural temples, stealing their treasures, abusing and robbing the peasants who lived on the estates where the temples were found, gorging themselves on the cattle and grain they stole, and apparently even killing some who resisted.[5] A more direct result of Theodosius's proscriptions, however, was that the abandoned urban temples—many of which had been effectively reduced to historical curiosities even before Theodosius came to power—were often converted into churches. In Alexandria, where nothing was ever done by half measures and no difference was ever peacefully resolved, the implacable patriarch Theophilus was apparently all too eager to turn the vacant sanctuaries to holier uses; and this eagerness seems to have begun the chain of events that ended in the Serapeum's destruction. Accounts of what happened vary, as is always the case, and the most that one can ascertain is that there were episodes of mass violence instigated now by one side, now by the other.

The earliest surviving Christian version of the story is that of Rufinus (A.D. c. 345–c. 411), who may have been a witness. According to him, the trouble began when the bishop of Alexandria secured permission to renovate an old temple (perhaps of Mithras) long fallen into disuse and considerable disrepair, one that may have been used by Arian Christians before him. When, in the course of the work, hidden caverns were exposed and human skulls exhumed, local pagans began to riot. Christian crowds engaged them, and the "two peoples" were soon fighting in open battles in the streets, which continued until certain pagans, as the tide of battle began to turn against them, retreated to the fortified enclosure of the Serapeum, taking a number of Christians with them as hostages. Once inside the temple precincts, the pagans forced their Christian prisoners to make sacrifice at the altars of the god, or tortured them at length and then murdered them, or crippled them with shattering blows to the shins and flung them into the caverns where the blood and offal of sacrificial animals used to be thrown. When word of this reached Theodosius, he issued orders that the pagan rioters not be punished, lest the glory of the Christians martyred during the unrest be impugned, but that the cause of the unrest be destroyed; and so the temple was demolished. The account offered by the later Christian historian Socrates (A.D. c. 380–c. 450) is vaguer. It says nothing very clear about what led up to the destruction of the temple, but merely reports that when Theophilus made a public display of "superstitions" and "sanguinary mysteries" and grotesque images attached to the worship of Serapis, Mithras, and Priapus, pagan throngs, at a preordained signal, fell upon the Christians and murdered as many as they could; ultimately, though, the attackers were repelled, and many fled the city. Socrates even mentions that two of the pagan rioters were grammarians under whom he had been a student in Constantinople, one of whom boasted in later years that he had killed nine Christians during the commotions of 391. After the riots, says Socrates, heathen temples were razed and, at the emperor's command, their idols melted down and refashioned into vessels and utensils to be distributed for the relief of the poor. There are other accounts of the unrest as well, none of them very pleasant.

I doubt we would much like any of these people. Not to be glib, but it was a very different age, one in which blood flowed fairly copiously in the streets and almost everyone believed that supernatural forces were constantly at work in nature and beyond it. As for the failure of many of the Christians of the time to transcend their circumstances, it is enough to observe that it is easier to baptize a culture than to change it, and the general culture of the time and the specific culture of Egypt were habitually brutal to a degree sometimes difficult to comprehend. Still, for all the persecutions each side visited upon the other, the two peoples—for the better part of four centuries, throughout the empire—generally lived together, conducted business with one another, studied together, even attended one another's festivals, and left one another's shrines, fanes, and basilicas unmolested. The shocking and horrifying stories are plentiful, of course, and tend to fix themselves in memory. In the days of Julian, for instance, certain Christian virgins of Heliopolis, for refusing to surrender themselves to a night of sacred prostitution before their nuptials, were publicly stripped, mocked, and abused; then they were eviscerated and—swine fodder having been mixed among their entrails—left to be finished off by pigs. Bishop Mark of Arethusa, also during Julian's reign, was brutally beaten by a pagan mob—his beard torn out, his ears severed, his flesh pierced again and again by the styluses of schoolboys—and then smeared with a mixture made from honey and suspended in a basket in the sun to be devoured by flies and wasps.[6] Hypatia (A.D. c. 355–415), the female pagan lecturer in mathematics and philosophy, was savagely assassinated and dismembered by the *parabalani* of Alexandria (originally a Christian *charitable* fraternity devoted to the impoverished ill) because she was suspected of having prevented a rapprochement between the patriarch Cyril (A.D. c. 375–444) and the Christian imperial prefect Orestes.[7] But, over the most prolonged periods of change, the slow transformation of the empire from pagan to Christian was effected without much violence, and even without great disruption to the rhythm of life. And, while it is correct to deplore Christians whose behavior betrayed the morality of the faith they professed, it is also worth noting that one cannot do the same where the pagans devoted to the temple cults are concerned, since their religions had practically no morality to betray.

It is also probably wise to recall that the Christians of the early centuries won renown principally for their sobriety, peacefulness, generosity, loyalty to their spouses, care for the poor and the sick, and ability, no matter what their social station, to exhibit virtues—self-restraint, chastity, forbearance, courage—that pagan philosophers frequently extolled but rarely practiced with comparable fidelity. And these Christians brought something new into the ancient world: a vision of the good without precedent in pagan society, a creed that prescribed charitable service to others as a *religious* obligation, a story about a God of self-outpouring love. In long retrospect, the wonder of this new nation within the empire is not that so many of its citizens could not really live by the ideals of their faith, nor even simply that so many could, but that anyone could even have imagined such ideals in the first place. Even the emperor Julian, who was all too conscious of the hypocrisies of which Christians were often capable, was forced to lament, in a letter to a pagan priest, "It is a disgrace that these impious Galilaeans care not only for their own poor but for ours as well."[8]

What was certainly not the case was that paganism and Christianity confronted one another as, on the one hand, a tradition of "pluralism" and rational inquiry and, on the other, a movement of "irrational" fideism. It is an almost infallible rule that, whenever any popular history relates the story of the murder of Hypatia—to which I have just referred—it repeats the fashionable myth that she was murdered by Christian zealots on account of her paganism and of her sex (which, supposedly, Christians would have thought disqualified her for a public career). Admittedly, more twaddle tends to be written about Hypatia than about any other figure from early or late antiquity, and this particular image of her—the martyr to misogyny and religious intolerance—is merely the most current of the many silly romances that have sprung up around her over the years. Even the most recent editions of the *Encyclopaedia Britannica,* somewhat behind the fashion in this instance, solemnly suggest that she died because she "symbolized learning and science, which at that time in Western history were largely identified with paganism." This is nonsense. To begin with, there was no particularly pronounced prejudice against woman scholars at the time, especially not in the Eastern Empire, among either Christians or pagans; such women were to be found in both communities, in Alexandria particularly. And "learning and science" were associated simply with the educated class, which comprised Christians and pagans alike; in fact, the greatest theoretical scientist and natural philosopher in Alexandria before the Muslim conquest was the sixth-century Christian John Philoponus. It seems clear, moreover, that Hypatia was on perfectly good terms with the Christian intellectuals of Alexandria, being as far as we can tell neither a particularly doctrinaire pagan nor an habituée of local cults (nor even, perhaps, much more sympathetic to pagan polytheism than the Christians), and she could number many Christians among her students and associates. One of her most devoted friends, in fact, was Synesius of Cyrene (d. A.D. c. 414), a Neoplatonist and convert (or semiconvert) to Christianity who was made bishop of Ptolemais in 409; and one of the warmest portraits of her that we possess, as well as the frankest account of her murder, can be found in the work of a Christian, the church historian Socrates. Hypatia died, as far as we can tell, because she became inadvertently involved in one of the conflicts that were constantly erupting at the demotic level of Alexandrian society between those warring tribes that made life in the city so constant an adventure.[9] But, in the social and intellectual world to which she belonged, all the attainments of classical culture were the common property of all philosophies that made use of them, including the Christian "philosophy." And even in society at large, calm coexistence was necessarily the normal state of affairs. As Ramsay MacMullen correctly says, "The elite went to university all together, regardless of religion: that is, together they attended law classes in Beirut and elsewhere, or the lectures of Hypatia on philosophy in Alexandria or of Libanius on rhetoric in Antioch. Pagans occasionally sought out the masters of eloquence in the very churches, for the brilliance of the performances to be heard there. And high or low, rich or poor, together the two populations somehow met, married, and raised their children in whatever beliefs seemed most natural and profitable."[10]

When, however, either side inveighed against the other's religious observances, each was likely to indict its rival of gross superstition. The emperor Julian, for example, accused the "Galilaeans" of demanding faith without philosophical rationale, yet his own "philosophy" emerged from one very large stream of the higher paganism of his time: initiation into mystery cults that claimed special access to divine secrets, magical invocations of gods into statuary or into human mediums, blood sacrifice, divination, and childlike faith in the "divine revelations" contained in the *Chaldean Oracles* (a fascinating but farraginous morass of Hellenistic and Asiatic religion, mysticism, hermeticism, and philosophy). Perhaps the most devastating blow delivered when the Serapeum fell was delivered by the axe of a particularly—as Gibbon says—"intrepid" soldier who approached the massive idol (the arms of which reached the temple walls on either side), climbed a ladder, and "aimed a vigorous stroke against the cheek of Serapis": for it was believed that "if any impious hand should dare to violate the majesty of the god, the heavens and earth would instantly return to their original chaos." But "the cheek fell to the ground; the thunder was still silent, and both the heavens and the earth continued to preserve the accustomed order and tranquillity."[11] And when the statue was destroyed and thousands of rats began to pour out of the nests they had gnawed in its rotten interior, even many of the pagan witnesses were apparently persuaded to change sides.[12] To many of the Christians of the age, it was the pagan subservience to magic and idols and demons that was the coarse superstition that their immeasurably more reasonable faith in a transcendent God, creator of a rationally ordered universe, had come to displace. Some Christians, it is true, could be viciously caustic regarding the achievements of classical culture; two figures from the second century, Tatian (A.D. 120–173) and Tertullian (A.D. c. 155–after 220), are especially notable in this regard (though, one should mention, both were of such an "enthusiast" religious temper that they ultimately abandoned the Catholic fold). Certainly, moreover, during the first two centuries of the church, Christians were often suspicious of pagan culture, high and low. And it was not strange for persons of a more contemplative cast of mind, pagan or Christian, to speak dismissively of natural philosophy and of too great a fascination with the material world. The Stoic sage Epictetus (A.D. 55–c. 135), for instance, thought natural science a waste of mental effort and a distraction from a proper knowledge of good and evil. But this was simply part of the established "spiritual" rhetoric of the age and did not much affect the degree to which such men employed the resources of higher culture (as, for example, Tertullian's free use of Stoic metaphysics and classical rhetoric in his theology demonstrates).

CHAPTER FIVE

The Destruction of the Past

A LITTLE FURTHER ALONG from his remarks on the Serapeum, Kirsch goes on to assert: "[The] Islamic civilization that came to power after the death of Mohammed was willing to spare the pagan writings that the Christian civilization of medieval Europe was so quick to burn. For example, the scientific writings of Aristotle were preserved in Arabic long after the original Greek texts had been destroyed. . . . [The] Crusaders were exposed to the remnants of classical Greece and Rome that had been preserved under Islam, and they returned to Europe as the bearers of a lost civilization. From the very moment that the West reconnected with the traditions of classical paganism, the so-called Dark Ages—an era of obscurantism, stagnation, and terror in the service of true belief—slowly began to recede."[1] Once again, there is the garbled anecdote: in this case, the claim that Aristotle's scientific works were preserved only in Arabic, the Greek originals having perished at the hands of Christian censors. In fact, we possess largely intact Greek texts of all of Aristotle's extant works, thanks largely to the Christian scholars of the Byzantine East; many of his writings, including all of his dialogues, we no longer possess, but they were lost well before the Christian period of the empire.

It is true that, during the days of the late empire, few translations of even the most vital Greek texts were made into Latin. Thus, with the decay of Western imperial order, the rise of the barbarian kingdoms, and the evaporation of almost all knowledge of Greek in the West (with the exception of some parts of Italy), the Western European world was progressively sealed off from the high civilization of the Eastern Christian world, and scholars were forced to rely upon a few isolated or fragmentary translations and a few scholarly digests of the great works of Greek antiquity, pagan or Christian. As early as the sixth century, the Christian philosopher Boethius (A.D. c. 475–524) undertook to shore up such fragments as he could against the ruin of the West by producing translations of all of Plato and Aristotle, writing commentaries upon them, and preparing manuals of music, mathematics, geometry, and astronomy. He succeeded in translating part of Aristotle's logical corpus, a classic introduction to these works by the Neoplatonist Porphyry (A.D. c. 234–c. 305), and perhaps a few other major works; and he wrote at least two handbooks and a few commentaries. But his grand project was rather abruptly (and rather rudely) curtailed when the Ostrogoth king Theodoric (d. A.D. 526) had him executed on suspicion of disloyalty. In Italy, from the fifth to the seventh century, translations were made of the medical works of Hippocrates (c. 460–c. 377 B.C.), Galen (A.D. 129–c. 216), and others.[2] The Irish scholar John Scotus Eriugena (A.D. 810–c. 877), in the days of the Carolingian Renaissance, produced translations of some of the greatest Greek Christian thinkers of the patristic period—Gregory of Nyssa (A.D. c. 335–c. 394), Pseudo-Dionysius (fl. A.D. c. 500), Maximus the Confessor (A.D. c. 580–662). But, for the most part, the literary treasures of Greek antiquity were the property only of the Christians of the East and, in time, their Muslim conquerors.

There was, it is true, a late introduction into the West of Greek classics not hitherto translated, especially from the twelfth century through the fifteenth, and Arab scholarship, Islamic and Christian, did indeed have a large part to play in that. Before the rise of Islam, Syrian Christians had carried Greek philosophical, medical, and scientific wisdom far eastward and had already begun to translate Greek texts into a Semitic tongue. The Christian academies of Edessa and then Nisibis and Jundishapur became some of the principal vehicles of Greek thought's eastern migrations after the fifth century; the latter two institutions may also have been centers of the medical training for which Nestorian Christianity in Persia was justly renowned. After the Islamic conquests of the Persian Empire and the Middle Eastern reaches of the East Roman, it was Syriac-speaking

Christians who provided an invaluable caste of scholars and physicians, and through them the achievements of Greek and Roman antiquity passed into Islamic culture. After the caliphate was moved to Baghdad in 762, a grand library and academy called the House of Wisdom was established and administered principally by Syrian Christians; and what followed was a golden age for the translation of Greek classical texts into Arabic, either directly from the Greek or from Syriac versions. Perhaps the greatest translator of all was the chief physician to the caliph, the Nestorian Christian Hunayn ibn Ishaq (A.D. 808–873), who in addition to his own treatises produced an enormous number of scrupulous Syriac and Arabic versions of Greek philosophical and medical texts. From Baghdad, then, a vast body of translations went forth into the greater Islamic world, including those parts of Spain occupied by the Muslims. In the tenth century, Cordoba and Toledo became centers of learning from which a great deal of the intellectual patrimony of ancient Greece would at last enter—by way of this gradual circuitous passage through Syrian Christian and Islamic scholarship—into Latin translations, produced by Mozarabic Christians (that is, the Arabic-speaking Christians of Spain), Western European scholars, and Spanish Jews.

Italy, though, was perhaps a more important port of entry for Greek texts into Western Europe. The Norman court of Palermo in the south, in the late eleventh century, welcomed scholars who spoke Greek, Latin, and Arabic; and Venice and Pisa were in constant contact—diplomatic, commercial, theological, and scholarly—with the Christian court of Constantinople. Thus, from the eleventh century onward, Italy was the chief conduit through which texts could pass from Greek directly into Latin. And with the Crusades, especially the disastrous Fourth Crusade, which left Constantinople in the possession of Latin conquerors from 1204 to 1261, the intellectual riches of the Christian East became even more readily available to Western Europe. During the thirteenth and fourteenth centuries, the rate at which Latin versions were made of Greek texts was quite astonishing. Among the most momentous accomplishments of the period were the admirably faithful and lucid renderings by William of Moerbeke (A.D. c. 1215–c. 1286) of many of Aristotle's major works, as well as of ancient commentaries on Aristotle, the *Elements of Theology* by Proclus (A.D. c. 410–485), the last major pagan Neoplatonist, the works of Ptolemy (A.D. c. 100–c. 170), and so on. And, of course, as the Byzantine Empire entered its death throes, culminating in the fall of Constantinople in 1453 to the Ottoman Turks, scholars and texts flowed westward: the Byzantine polymath Bessarion (1403–1472), for instance, donated his immense personal library to the Venetian Senate, was united to the Roman Church, and was even created cardinal by Pope Eugenius IV. In the eleventh century, Byzantine civilization had enjoyed its last golden age before entering into its long, agonizing final period of constant siege and contraction. The brilliant Michael Psellus (A.D. 1018–c. 1078), among his many accomplishments, had reformed the university curriculum of Constantinople and inspired a Platonic revival; and as the Byzantine Empire was passing away, four centuries later, the intellectual movement to which he had helped give birth in the Christian East (and which enjoyed a last glorious crescendo in the fourteenth century) flowered anew in the Italian Renaissance.

Much more ought to be said, really, if one is adequately to describe the extraordinarily complex history of the late medieval movement of the texts of Greek antiquity into the Christian West. What is important to stress here, however, is what a crude burlesque of medieval history it is to speak of a miraculous retreat of a Christian Dark Ages of "obscurantism, stagnation, and terror" before the cleansing gales of Islamic civilization. Latin Christendom was for centuries deprived of the classical inheritance that Eastern Christendom had preserved and Islam had captured, but not because it had rejected that inheritance. Nor was the Baghdad caliphate the rescuer of a "lost civilization" that the Christian world had sought to extinguish; Islam was the beneficiary of Eastern Christendom, and Western Christendom in its turn was the beneficiary of both. Talk of medieval Christian civilization being "quick to burn" the writings of ancient pagans, moreover, is tantamount to a confession of an almost total ignorance of that civilization. In fact, not only did medieval Christians not burn pagan texts, the literary remains of ancient Rome were hoarded and jealously guarded in monastic libraries even as the Western Roman world was disintegrating. At the Vivarium monastery of Cassiodorus (A.D. 490–c. 585), near modern Squillace in Italy, monks were set to work copying and preserving works of Roman antiquity and Greek Christian thought; and, for centuries, there were monasteries throughout Western Europe, from the Mediterranean to Britain, that housed collections containing the writings of Virgil, Ovid, Cicero, Pliny, Horace, Statius, Persius, Lucan, Suetonius, Seneca, Martial, Apuleius, Juvenal, Terence, and so forth, as well as such portions of Plato, Aristotle, and the Greek church fathers as were available in Latin. And it was a consequence of historical misfortune, not of willful rejection, that more had not survived.[3]

The true story, however, is ever so much more mundane than the legend. Here is Kirsch one last time: "Rome under the Christian emperors set out to destroy its own rich patrimony. . . . Scribes were forbidden to copy out the old pagan texts on pain of death or . . . the amputation of the scribe's writing hand."[4] This is false—though it can perhaps be defended by pointing out that it is no more than a paraphrase of a vaguely worded remark made by the generally anti-Christian classicist Ramsay MacMullen (who, admittedly, makes no great effort to be understood on this point).[5] It was, it is true, possible to lose one's hand under various emperors at various times in the history of the Christian empire; in fact, perhaps the single subtlest, most brilliant, and most philosophically innovative theologian in the entire history of the Eastern Church, Maximus the Confessor, lost both his hand and his tongue (and ultimately, as a result, his life) to an emperor who disapproved of his Christology. But there was certainly never a systematic imperial purge of the literature of pagan antiquity. The emperor Justinian I (A.D. 483–565) used various forms of legal coercion, such as confiscation of property, to discourage the reproduction of certain proscribed texts; those, however, were not works of classical literature or philosophy but "heretical" Christian writings, anti-Christian polemic, and the religious texts of illegal sects. And one anecdote related by the historian John Malalas (A.D. c. 491–c. 578), regarding pagans who were arrested for their devotions under Justinian, tells of how their books (their religious books, obviously) were burned along with their idols.

Even after Justinian had expelled pagan professors from what remained of the ancient Academy of Athens in 529, however, neither pagan nor Christian scholars were forbidden to study and write commentaries upon the philosophers. Christianity had for centuries drawn trained philosophers into its ranks—Justin Martyr (A.D. c. 100–c. 165), Pantaenus, Marius Victorinus (A.D. c. 300–after 362), Synesius of Cyrene—and as time passed the inheritors of ancient philosophy who made the most creative use of its principles and methods were Christians such as Origen, Gregory of Nyssa, Augustine, Pseudo-Dionysius, and Maximus. That is as much as one should expect. Pagan and Christian emperors both occasionally destroyed books, it cannot be denied—books of divination, magic, and forbidden religions, primarily—and no one was quite as sentimental about the preservation of knowledge as we are today. But even MacMullen, desperate to provide some evidence of a special Christian malice toward ancient literature, can do no better than to point to the decision of the Christian imperial regent Flavius Stilicho (A.D. 365–408) to destroy the Sibylline books, an act for which, MacMullen rather oddly claims, "Constantine had set the precedent, prescribing the burning of Arian tracts in 333."[6] The precedent, in point of fact, was set by Augustus Caesar, who according to Suetonius destroyed thousands of rival prophetic books before sealing the Sibylline books themselves away from public scrutiny in the Palatine temple of Apollo. A suspicion of oracular literature was quite pronounced in Roman society well before the Christian period. And certainly no Roman emperor can credibly be said to have demonstrated greater delight in the combustion of books he found obnoxious than did Diocletian.

None of this, however, in any way warrants fabulous claims regarding a Christian purge of pagan antiquity's literary remains. Throughout the Christian period, obviously, as was true during the pagan period as well, innumerable and often precious texts disappeared through inattention, indifference, mishap, political upheaval, riot, warfare, invasion, plunder, or mere forgetfulness. Moreover, the limitations of the technology of the written word—the friability of papyrus, the delibility of vellum, the evanescence of ink, the porosity of every available defense against fire, flood, contamination, mold, or insects—conspired to consign much of the literature of the past to utter oblivion without the premeditated connivance of anyone in particular. And naturally Christians were often at greatest pains to make copies of their own antiquities, a circumstance that occasionally left the posterity of some pagan writers without any passionate champions. But all of that must be considered the result of (to employ a serviceable cliché) the "ravages of time."

In any event, I have lingered over these matters long enough. Slovenly scholarship is a sin, perhaps, but bad scholars might almost be forgiven for believing what they have always been told: that Christianity rejected classical civilization, even sought to destroy it root and branch, and thus inaugurated the Dark Ages. In truth, there is no intelligible sense in which the rise of Christianity can be held responsible for the decline of late Roman culture, some supposed triumph of dogma over reason, or the retardation of science. In fact, the last flowering of classical literary culture, in the fourth and early fifth centuries, was for the most part the work of the church fathers: they provided the period with its greatest rhetoricians, its most sophisticated metaphysicians, and its most innovative stylists. Few pagan writers of the period could match the ravishing power of John Chrysostom's Greek, or the serenely flowing classical grandeur of Gregory Nazianzen's, or the unprecedented fluidity, suppleness, and immediacy of Augustine's Latin, or the elegance and precision of Jerome's or Ambrose's. No pagan writer graced posterity with anything as new, rich, humane, or psychologically subtle as the intense lyric interiority of Augustine's *Confessions,* or as searchingly honest and movingly human as Nazianzen's autobiographical poetry.[7] Moreover, with the collapse of the empire of the West—which was induced by centuries of internal wasting and external pressure: of plague, warfare, and demographic decline—it was the church's monasteries alone that saved classical civilization from the total eclipse it would otherwise have suffered. And, in the East, it was a Christian civilization that united the intellectual cultures of the Greek, Egyptian, and Syrian worlds, and that preserved Hellenic wisdom in academies and libraries in Greece, Syria, and Asia Minor. And, to be perfectly honest, despite the calamities that ravaged Roman civilization, many of the greatest intellectual, aesthetic, and spiritual achievements of the Hellenistic world were taken up into Christian metaphysics, theology, ethics, and art, and were occasionally even somewhat improved in the process.

CHAPTER SIX

The Death and Rebirth of Science

OF ALL THE INERADICABLE MYTHS concerning a Christian Dark Ages, none enjoys greater currency than the wildly romantic fable of a golden age of Hellenistic science brought to an abrupt halt by the church's "war against reason." In the latter part of the nineteenth century, two now notorious books appeared that, for an unpleasantly prolonged period, exercised an influence entirely disproportionate to their merits: John William Draper's *History of the Conflict between Religion and Science* (1874) and Andrew Dickson White's *History of the Warfare of Science with Theology in Christendom* (1896). The second volume was still occasionally consulted as an authoritative study as late as the middle of the twentieth century. Each, in its own way, was a masterpiece of temerity; neither Draper nor White even bothered to distort the evidence to support his case; both discovered that, where evidence was lacking, literary invention proved a happy expedient. Fortunately, respectable historians of science today have no use for either of these books and are well aware that the supposed war between Christian theology and Western science is mythology of the purest water. Unhappily, a myth can be discredited and still be devoutly believed.

In 2003, for example, the amateur historian Charles Freeman published a volume called *The Closing of the Western Mind* that is an almost perfect compendium of every trite caricature of early Christianity devised since Gibbon departed to his long home. Once upon a time, Freeman's tale unfolds, there was a late Roman Hellenistic culture that cherished the power of reason and pursued science and high philosophy. Then came Christianity, which valued only blind obedience to irrational dogma, and which maliciously extinguished the light of pagan wisdom. Then, thanks to Islam, thirteenth-century Christendom suddenly rediscovered reason and began to chafe against the bondage of witless fideism. And then, as if by magic, Copernicus discovered heliocentrism, and reason began its inexorable charge toward victory through the massed and hostile legions of faith. Or, in even more simplified form, Freeman's is the old familiar story that Christianity is somehow to be blamed for a sudden retrogression in Western civilization that set back the cause of human progress by, say, a thousand years. Along the way, Freeman provides a few damning passages from the church fathers (always out of context and without any mention of the plentiful counterexamples found in the same authors), attempts long discourses on theological disputes he simply does not understand, continually falls prey to vulgar misconstruals of the materials he is attempting to interpret, makes large claims about early Christian belief that are simply false, offers vague assertions about philosophers he clearly has not studied, and delivers himself of opinions regarding Christian teaching that are worse than simply inaccurate. And natural science is his special concern. He bewails the "death" of something he whimsically calls "the Greek empirical tradition": in the first millennium after the conversion of Constantine, he asserts, only the Islamic world made any creative use of Greek science and medicine; for more than a thousand years after the "last recorded astronomical observation in the ancient Greek world" in 475 by Proclus (c. 410–485), he says, such studies lay dormant, until Copernicus (1473–1543) published his *De revolutionibus orbium coelestium* and they began again to move forward.[1]

In regard to this last claim, a few things should immediately be said. First, the suggestion that astronomy suddenly ceased in the Western world in the fifth century, or that it was not pursued by Christians, is simply absurd. Second, there could scarcely be an odder candidate for the role of hero of Hellenistic science than Proclus, a doctrinaire Platonist who mocked the Pythagoreans of old for imagining the earth could move, contrary to the infallible doctrine of "the Philosopher." And third, and most important, scientific thought does not lurch from one mind to another across gulfs of time, nor do great scientists suddenly and miraculously emerge from the darkness, like Athena springing from the head of Zeus. To suggest that Copernicus merely took up a thread that had been severed by the church in antiquity and arrived at his hypothesis by his own unaided lights defies not only the historical record but all historical logic. Copernicus, having matriculated at a number of Christian universities, was heir to a long tradition of Christian scholastic mathematical and theoretical work in astronomy and the science of motion, stretching back at least to the early thirteenth century; but for this tradition, his thought would have had no theoretical basis.

Islamic and Christian cosmology alike had remained largely wedded through the late antique and early medieval periods to the Aristotelian image of the universe, according to which the stationary earth was surrounded by a series of hollow homocentric crystalline planetary spheres turning on a terrestrial axis, urged on by an outermost sphere called the "prime mover." No one questioned the Aristotelian principles that motion is always caused by an immediate and continuous external force and that there can be no vacuum in the order of nature (principles that, among late antique natural philosophers, only John Philoponus rejected). Almost equally authoritative was the astronomy of Ptolemy, which was a remarkably elaborate mathematical model whose sole purpose was to reconcile the observable celestial phenomena with Aristotelian cosmology. To accomplish this, however, it had been necessary for Ptolemy—in order to explain such things as the apparent retrograde motion of planets or variations in planetary brightness—to invent an exquisitely involved and brilliantly imagined system of secondary and even tertiary motions and axes. He was obliged, for instance, to displace the terrestrial axis of certain planetary spheres to an extraterrestrial "eccentric." Then he had to calculate an "equant" for each of the planetary cycles, located at neither the terrestrial nor the eccentric axes, around which the motion of the cycle could be measured as both uniform in speed and perfectly circular, even though from earth the speed would have to be reckoned as irregular. And then, for most planets, he had to posit yet another axis called a "deferent," located *within* the substance of the planetary sphere itself, around which the planet itself turned in a smaller local orbit called an "epicycle." Moreover, it was still impossible to calculate a stable eccentric in every instance; in the case of Mercury, for instance, the eccentric had to be calculated as shifting in the course of the planet's orbit, rendering the planetary path appropriately mercurial perhaps, but circular only according to a geometrical fiction.

The Ptolemaic model was never perfectly congruent with the actual Aristotelian physical model of the cosmos: epicycles were especially difficult to reconcile with the idea of solid homocentric planetary spheres, and both they and equants seemed inconsistent with the principle that motion must have an immediate exterior cause. Attempts were occasionally made to resolve these problems. The Muslim astronomer Ibn al'Haytham (c. 965–c. 1040), for example, suggested that each planet traveled in a channel within the "crystal" of its sphere, a channel aligned not with the contours of the sphere itself, but centered rather upon the appropriate "eccentric." But, when the Ptolemaic system was subjected to critique by Muslim scientists, it was not principally because of its failure accurately to predict planetary movements; rather, it was because it did not conform properly to Aristotelian physics. In twelfth century Spain, especially, several Muslim astronomers were disturbed by the absence of any efficient cause to account for the planetary movements described by Ptolemy. Ibn Rushid (1126–1198)—called Averroës in Latin—argued for the superiority of Aristotle's cosmic machinery over the impossible abstractions of Ptolemy's calculations. And thirteenth century theorists such as al'Qaswini and al'Jagmini reimagined each planetary epicycle as a smaller crystalline sphere lodged between, and so rolled along by, the surfaces of the greater spheres.

Neither Muslim nor Christian scientists are to be faulted, obviously, for clinging so long to late antique cosmology; it accounted fully for the phenomena of celestial rotation, and the geocentric picture of the universe accorded with common sense. And, after all, the Aristotelian model of the universe was an object of rare beauty, with its immense ethereal machineries, its imperishable splendors, its innumerable wellsprings of harmony and synchrony; and the Ptolemaic system, with its intricate coils and spirals and elaborately exact actions, was as exquisitely glittering a cage as any reasoning mind could hope to inhabit. Practically every educated intellect was in thrall to that model and confined in that cage; a few perceptive souls were aware that the two systems did not perfectly coincide, but were still more or less condemned to circle back and forth between them. By the time of Copernicus, though, other models had become conceivable. In the early thirteenth century, the mathematician

Gerard of Brussels had begun to consider the motion of bodies in abstraction from any causal theory; and this approach was taken up and elaborated upon with ever increasing sophistication in the fourteenth century by scholars at Oxford—William of Ockham (c. 1285–c. 1348), Walter Burleigh (1275–after 1343), Thomas Bradwardine (c. 1290–1349), William Heytesbury (fl. 1335), Richard Swineshead (fl. 1348), and John of Dumbleton (d. c. 1349)—and then by scholars at the University of Paris —Jean Buridan (1300–1358), Nicholas Oresme (c. 1320–1382), and Albert of Saxony (c. 1316–1390). Buridan, for instance, ventured (without embracing) the hypothesis that the earth could revolve upon its own axis, rejected the ancient Aristotelian claim that an object in flight is continuously propelled by displaced air closing behind it again, and suggested that an object, once moved, might persist in motion without continuous cause on account of an impressed "impetus," measurable by material volume and velocity. Oresme (the most brilliant of the Parisians) devised geometric models of, among other things, uniform constant motions and uniformly accelerating motions, and offered more ingenious arguments for the possibility (though not actuality) of terrestrial rotation. Albert applied himself to, among other things, the velocity of falling bodies and objects' centers of gravity.[2]

All of these men worked with a concept of impetus that, admittedly, was not yet a concept of momentum or inertia; but it allowed for a more "kinematic" understanding of motion, as opposed to the strictly "dynamic" concept proper to Aristotelian theory: which is to say, it allowed one to consider the laws of motion in themselves, rather than seek the external force—the *dynamis*—causing each particular motion. Thus, Oresme was able to show how the idea of impetus could explain why the earth's atmosphere was not displaced by terrestrial rotation, or why an object falling to earth did not descend at an angle rather than on a plumb line, thereby disarming certain classic objections to the hypothesis of a moving world. He also argued that the apparent rotation of the heavens and stability of the earth might be simply a matter of relative perspective: a point reiterated by Nicholas of Cusa (1401–1465) in the next century. Most importantly, these scholars did not regard impetus as a finite resource that drains away over time but conceived of it as a constant motive power that is corrupted or halted only when it encounters some force of resistance. This made it possible to set aside the perplexing question of the efficient cause of celestial motions, and to reimagine the invariable uniformity of celestial motions as expressions of the same physical laws that govern the variable and corruptible movements of things here below (so long, that is, as one was willing to consider the possibility of a vacuum above the atmosphere).

In any event, Copernicus was heir to a long mathematical tradition and—if he cared to make use of it—a tradition of physical theory that had opened the way to new models of the cosmos. And Copernicus's contribution, to be honest, must be reckoned rather small, in terms at least of *scientific* progress. Indeed, his treatise was not a work of science, in the modern sense, at all: it proposed nothing that might be tested, it did not prove its case either in terms of observation or theory, and it made few conspicuous advances upon Ptolemy's calculations. It is true that Copernicus was perhaps the first theorist since Aristarchus of Samos (c. 110–c. 130 B.C.) who had dared so openly to place the sun at the center of the "universe," but his reasoning was more suppositious than empirical. He also devised a model that dealt somewhat more economically than the Ptolemaic with certain ancient questions, such as why Mercury and Venus remain always near the sun. This very problem had already prompted various reflective souls over the centuries to depart in their cosmological reflections from *strict* geocentrism: in the fourth century B.C. Heracleides Ponticus apparently claimed that Mercury and Venus revolve not directly around the earth but rather around the sun; the fifth-century encyclopedist Martianus Capella concurred (not on his own authority: he was not a scientist); and, in the ninth century, John Scotus Eriugena seems to have added Mars and Jupiter to the list of planets circling the sun. After Copernicus, in fact, Tycho Brahe (1546–1601) devised a system in which all the planets above revolve around the sun, while only the sun revolves directly around the earth; and by the time of Galileo's trial, many of the greatest astronomers of the time (who were mostly to be found among the Jesuits) had come to conclude that the superterrestrial planets move in heliocentric orbits and had tended to adopt Tycho's model (though they were willing to consider the Copernican, as an unproven hypothesis).

Yet, for all the distinction Copernicus may deserve for having ventured a purely heliocentric description of the heavens, one should appreciate why his theory would not have been particularly compelling to all of his contemporaries. For one thing, the physical arguments he made were no great improvement upon those of the scholastics and so did no more than suggest that terrestrial movement is a conceptual possibility; and, for another thing, his mathematical model was wrong. Copernicus did manage to purge his system of equants, which his professors at the University of Krakow had taught him to disdain, but he still assumed, in good classical fashion, that heavenly revolutions must be circular (else they would not be "perfect") and that the planets were fixed within separate spheres. Thus, in the end, he too was forced to resort to a system of epicycles—nearly fifty, in fact, including nine for the earth—with little appreciable advantage in predictive power over Ptolemy's system. Tycho's later model, it is arguable, is preferable as science, inasmuch as it better reconciles theory with the evidence. Tycho undertook (as Copernicus did not) minute investigations of the heavens, including an observation of a comet moving above the moon, where there were supposed to be only changeless planetary spheres. Moreover, one of the oldest objections to the idea of a moving earth was the absence of any observable alteration in the position of stars relative to one another (that is, "parallax" motion). Copernicus guessed that the distance between earth and the "sphere of the fixed stars" was far greater than was commonly assumed, but Tycho's model offered a seemingly more plausible explanation. None of which detracts from Copernicus's real achievements, such as they were, any more than it diminishes the far greater achievements of Galileo (1564–1642), Johannes Kepler (1571–1630), and Isaac Newton (1643–1727); but it does mean, certainly, that Copernicus was not some isolated visionary gazing back through the centuries, across a vast chasm of Christian darkness, to the pale flickering flame of a forgotten Hellenistic wisdom.

It is, needless to say, something of an embarrassment that Galileo was forced to renounce the Copernican theory and to end his days comfortably confined to a villa in the hills outside Florence, but not because of what this tells us about Christianity's relation to science.[3] A single instance of institutional purblindness and internal dissension, which was entirely anomalous within the larger history of the Catholic Church's relation to the natural sciences, reveals nothing significant about Christian culture or Christian history as a whole but demonstrates only how idiotic a conflict between men of titanic egotism can become. Rather, the case is an embarrassment because, in serving for some as a convenient epitome of some supposedly larger truth about Catholicism or Christianity (despite its being the only noteworthy example of that truth they can adduce), it has tended to obscure the rather significant reality that, in the sixteenth and seventeenth centuries, Christian scientists educated in Christian universities and following a Christian tradition of scientific and mathematical speculation overturned a pagan cosmology and physics, and arrived at conclusions that would have been unimaginable within the confines of the Hellenistic scientific traditions. For, despite all our vague talk of ancient or medieval "science," pagan, Muslim, or Christian, what we mean today by science—its methods, its controls and guiding principles, its desire to unite theory to empirical discovery, its trust in a unified set of physical laws, and so on—came into existence, for whatever reasons, and for better or worse, only within Christendom, and under the hands of believing Christians.

Unfortunately, Galileo's career happened to coincide with a period of institutional crisis in the Catholic Church. When he appealed to the church fathers, to Augustine in particular, in defense of his claim that the scriptures ought not to be regarded as a resource for scientific descriptions of reality, he was entirely in the right. The ancient and mediaeval church had always acknowledged that the Bible ought to be read allegorically in many instances, according to the spiritual doctrines of the church, and that the principal truths of scripture are not confined to its literal level, which often reflects only the minds of its human authors. Origen, Basil of Caesarea, Gregory of Nyssa, Augustine—all denied that, for instance, the creation story in Genesis was an actual historical record of how the world was made (Augustine did write what he called a "literal" interpretation of Genesis, but it was not literal in any sense a modern fundamentalist would recognize). And figures as distant from one another in time as Augustine and Aquinas cautioned against exposing scripture to ridicule by mistaking the Bible for a scientific treatise. In the seventeenth century, however, in response to Protestant critique, the Catholic Church had become considerably more diffident in the latitude with which it interpreted the Bible, and views that a century or two earlier could have been expressed without exciting even very much institutional notice began to look to some eyes profoundly dangerous.

That said, in the years leading up to his trial, Galileo had enjoyed the amity and support of a number of important men within the church. He was respected—even revered—by some of the most brilliant Jesuit astronomers of his time, who confirmed many of his observations, such as the uneven quality of the moon's surface, the existence of sunspots, and the phases of Venus; this last observation, in fact, convinced many of them to abandon the Ptolemaic system for the Tychonic. Even when Galileo had more or less confessed himself a Copernican in 1613, he was not repudiated by his friends or censured by the church, and he even acquired new allies. Tommaso Campanella (1568–1616), the tirelessly controversial Dominican, wrote in his defense in 1616 and 1622; and the Carmelite Paolo Antonio Foscarini (c. 1562–1616) argued that Galileo was correct to deny the irreconcilability of Copernican cosmology and scripture; and both men championed the church fathers' approach to scripture over the novel and rigid literalism of some of their contemporaries. Even after his trial, Galileo was taken in for half a year by the archbishop of Siena before retiring for good to his villa. Of Galileo's friends, none was of greater consequence than Cardinal Maffeo Barberini (1568–1644), who became Pope Urban VIII. Barberini was a man of enormous culture, whose admiration of Galileo was so great that it even prompted him to compose verse in Galileo's honor, and who, as pope, lavished upon Galileo the sort of attentions—private papal audiences, public accolades, costly gifts, a pension for Galileo's son—that most men could scarcely have hoped for. In fact, he gave Galileo every support within reason, and did not so much as rebuke him for his Copernican sympathies when they first became obvious. This is not really surprising, as Copernicus's book was many decades old by that time; and, while it had both its detractors and admirers among the church hierarchy, it had never caused any great scandal. Indeed, the book's dedicatee—Pope Paul III—quite liked it. Even in Galileo's day, Kepler was championed and protected by the Jesuits. With Urban and Galileo, however, a particularly combustible combination of volatile personalities was introduced into the affair.

Galileo, it must be said, squandered good will with remarkable abandon. He was, not to put too fine a point on it, selfish, irascible, supercilious, and mildly vindictive. He could not abide rivals, resented the discoveries of others, refused to share credit with astronomers who had made observations of the same celestial phenomena as he had, and belittled those whose theories differed from his own (his attitude toward Kepler, for instance, was frightful). Incensed that the Jesuit astronomer Horatio Grassi had presumed, in 1618, to describe the movement of comets beyond the lunar sphere without mentioning Galileo—who had, as it happens, done absolutely nothing to merit such mention—Galileo chose to deny that such comets were anything but optical illusions, and for good measure even attacked Tycho's observations of comets. He provoked public controversy where none was necessary, once on the rumor that his theories had been deprecated in the course of someone else's private dinner conversation. And his uncompromising demand for an absolute vindication of his theories precipitated the ecclesial consultation of 1616 that—when it turned out that Galileo was unable to provide a single convincing proof of Copernicanism—resulted in an injunction (of great gentleness, actually) admonishing Galileo against teaching the Copernican system. As for Galileo's decisive trial in 1633, it was, as Arthur Koestler has noted, "not in the nature of a fatal collision between opposite philosophies of existence . . . but rather a clash of individual temperaments aggravated by unlucky coincidences."[4] Urban VIII himself had encouraged Galileo to write his *Dialogue concerning the Two Chief World Systems, the Ptolemaic and Copernican* (1632), enjoining only that it include a statement to the effect that Copernican theory was just a hypothesis and that no scientist could pretend to know perfectly how God had disposed the worlds. Galileo did include such a statement in the dialogue, at its conclusion in fact, but decided to place it on the lips of a ponderously obtuse character whom he tellingly named Simplicio, a doctrinaire Aristotelian placed in the dialogue so as to provide a foil for the wise Copernican Salviati and a comical contrast to Sagredo, the clever scientific novice; and, to heap one insult upon another, Simplicio attributes the formula to an "eminent and erudite personage, before whom one must needs fall silent." This was, to all appearances, an unwarranted and tasteless affront to a cultured and generous friend, and Urban—an Italian gentleman of his age, a prince of the church, and a man of enormous personal pride—took umbrage.[5]

More importantly, though, and too often forgotten, Urban was entirely right on one very crucial issue: the Copernican model *was* in fact only a hypothesis, and a defective one at that, and Galileo did not have either sufficient evidence to support it or a mathematical model that worked particularly well. Though Galileo was far and away the greatest *physicist* of his age (and indeed of human history to that point), he was not an astronomer in the fullest sense—he was more a brilliant stargazer—and seems to have been little interested in the laborious observations and recondite calculations of those who were. Hence, he seems not to have cared how impossibly complicated and unconvincing Copernicus's model of the heavens was. It is not even certain that by 1632 he clearly recalled how the Copernican system worked. He did not avail himself (though he was perfectly and resentfully aware) of Kepler's elliptical planetary orbits, which were encumbered by none of the inconsistencies and internal corrections and physical impossibilities of the Ptolemaic and Copernican systems. Instead, he insisted along with Copernicus upon the circular movement of the planets, with all the mathematical convolutions this entailed. He had no better explanation than Copernicus for the absence of any observable stellar parallax, even when the stars were viewed through a telescope. And his most cherished proof of terrestrial rotation—the motion of the tides—was manifestly ludicrous and entirely inconsistent with the observable tidal sequences (he dismissed Kepler's entirely correct lunar explanation of the tides as a silly conjecture concerning occult forces). Galileo elected, that is, to propound a theory whose truth he had not demonstrated, while needlessly mocking a powerful man who had treated him with honor and indulgence. And the irony is, strange to say, that it was the church that was demanding proof, and Galileo who was demanding blind assent—to a model that was wrong. None of which exculpates the Catholic hierarchy of its foolish decision or its authoritarian meddling. But it is rather ridiculous to treat Urban VIII as a man driven by religious fanaticism—there is good reason to doubt that he even believed in God with any particular conviction—or Galileo as the blameless defender of scientific empiricism. And Christians certainly are under no obligation to grant, on account of this ridiculous squabble, that the church or their faith was somehow a constant impediment to early modern science, when the historical evidence indicates exactly the opposite. Measured against centuries of ecclesial patronage of the sciences, and considering that in Galileo's day (and long after) many of the world's greatest and most original scientists (often in fields that had not even previously existed) were to be found among the Jesuits, one episode of asinine conflict among proud and intemperate men does not exactly constitute a pattern of Christian intellectual malfeasance.[6]

Clearly, at any rate, to return to the topic at hand, any claim that the history of Western science comprises two epochs of light—the Hellenistic and the modern—separated by a long, dark interval of Christian ignorance and fanaticism is altogether absurd. The very notion that there was ever such a thing as ancient Greek or Roman "science" in the modern sense is pure illusion. There was certainly never a continuously progressing, analytical, systematic tradition of inquiry, testing and correcting hypotheses by observation and experiment, and creating stores of "data." Hellenistic astronomy was fairly sophisticated and produced one extremely useful invention (the astrolabe). Late Roman medicine, even at its most advanced (as with Galen), was more anatomically descriptive than effectively prescriptive, but it did evolve some therapies that were more beneficial than harmful and did create a foundation for the later advances (such as they were) made by Christian and Muslim physicians. Hellenistic science could boast some real accomplishments in the geometry of optics, especially in the late work of Ptolemy, and it kept alive (though just barely) the ancient Greek tradition of natural philosophy and higher mathematics. But the sort of claims that were once part of the homiletic repertoire of, say, Arthur C. Clarke or Carl Sagan—that the tradition of Greek science to which the rise of Christianity supposedly put an end was progressing inexorably toward modern physics, modern technology, and space travel—are sheer fantasy. To quote David C. Lindberg, "It is agreed by most historians of ancient science that creative Greek science was on the wane, perhaps as early as 200 B.C., certainly by A.D. 200. Science had never been pursued by very many people; it now attracted even fewer. And its character shifted away from original thought toward commentary and abridgment. Creative natural science was particularly scarce in the Roman world, where scholarly interests leaned in the direction of ethics and metaphysics; such natural science as Rome possessed was largely confined to fragments preserved in handbooks and encyclopedias." And, as Lindberg also notes, there is no historical warrant for the belief "that the advent of Christianity did anything to diminish the support given to scientific activity or the number of people involved in it."[7]

By the time of Constantine, the greater Roman world had endured centuries of scientific and technological stagnation. The Rome of the first century A.D., as Jacques Le Goff bluntly observes, created nothing: "No technical innovation had occurred since the Hellenistic age."[8] In fact, during the three centuries between Hipparchus and Ptolemy, there were no significant advances even in astronomy, and the "late flowering" of the Ptolemaic system was of a somewhat orchidaceous variety, exotic and spectacular perhaps, but incapable of surviving outside the conservatory conditions of the purest sort of theoretical abstraction. Ptolemy was in no sense an impartial empirical astronomer; his interest in celestial motions was largely that of a committed astrologer who needed trustworthy planetary tables for his divinations. To this end he produced an elaborate mathematical fantasia, meant not as a description of any physically possible reality (no one, it is fairly certain, "believed" in such things as equants) but as a sort of geometric mythology that could, on the one hand, help to conceal the scandal of the heavenly bodies' flagrant disobedience to the principles of higher philosophy and, on the other, provide fortune-tellers with accurate predictions of celestial alignments. So entirely indifferent was Ptolemy to the actual observable physical realities of celestial motion that, according to his model, the apparent size of the moon should exhibit vast variations in the course of the lunar cycle, which it obviously does not. Ptolemy's was a magnificent achievement of mathematical choreography, without question, and one of astonishing intricacy; it was also a prodigy of intellectual decadence, an almost perfect coincidence of cerebral vigor and spiritual torpor. And it had precious little to do with anything we would call "science."

The late antique vision of reality was shaped and determined by Aristotle's cosmology and physics. The heliocentrism proposed by Aristarchus in the third century B.C.—which the Stoic Cleanthes (c. 231 B.C.–c. 131 B.C.) thought worthy of an indictment for blasphemy—was a curiosity, which bore no fruit and for which Aristarchus clearly could present no persuasive evidence; the Pythagorean belief that the sun and all the planets revolved around the "central fire" was a mystical doctrine, not a scientific theory. It was the wondrous cosmic machine of the Aristotelian universe, and the system of causes it presumed, that developed Greek thought elaborated upon, preserved, and passed on to Islamic and Christian culture. Lest we forget, the birth of modern physics and cosmology was achieved by Galileo, Kepler, and Newton breaking free not from the close confining prison of faith (all three were believing Christians, of one sort or another) but from the enormous burden of the millennial authority of Aristotelian science. The scientific revolution of the sixteenth and seventeenth centuries was not a revival of Hellenistic science but its final defeat. A person of perverse temperament might even be tempted to argue that, had there actually been a great conflagration in Alexandria in which some vast inheritance of Greek scientific texts had been consumed, or if indeed "ancient Greek science" had come to a peremptory halt some time in the fifth century, the cause of science might have been considerably advanced.

After all, no pagan theorist ever put forward a critique of the principles of ancient Greek natural philosophy as thorough or as ingenious as that of the sixth-century Christian John Philoponus. He not only argued against the immutability of the stars, but (even more outrageously) denied that the terrestrial and celestial regions possessed distinct natures. That the heavens above the moon are eternal, that their substance is the incorruptible "quintessence" ether, that the stars possess spiritual intelligence, and that all the celestial bodies belong to a divine realm immune to the decay, imperfection, and transience of the world here below—all of this was part of the firm and unalterable picture of reality to which practically every Greek scientist, philosopher, or educated layman devoutly adhered. In fact, even as late as 1572, when Tycho observed a nova in the constellation of Cassiopeia, the realization that the heaven of the fixed stars could suffer change was a severe probation of the settled convictions of most educated men. Philoponus, however, argued that one could deduce from certain variances among the known stars themselves that they are mutable objects, composed not of imperishable ether and divine intellect but of corruptible matter, and that they once came into existence and one day will perish like other material objects; the sun, he said, consists in fire, of the same basic substance as earthly fire; and he argued that the appearance of changelessness in the heavens is the effect merely of the immense temporal and spatial intervals of cosmic movement. For him—being a Christian—the entire universe was the creature of God, and the terrestrial and celestial realms alike were part of one natural order governed by the same rational laws. And so it was no great trial of faith (as it would have been for a pagan philosopher) to deny the divinity of the night sky: which is to say, Philoponus was able to cast off metaphysical dogma and apply himself to a rigorous reconsideration of the science of his time not despite but because of his Christianity and his consequent impatience for any "superstitious" confusion between material objects and gods. He also hypothesized that the space above the atmosphere might be a vacuum. He argued, against Aristotle, that light moves, and that the eye receives it simply according to the rules of optical geometry. And, most important perhaps, he rejected the Aristotelian dynamic theory of motion and proposed in its place a theory of kinetic impetus.

Philoponus's reflections on motion were, in fact, considered by (without having much effect upon) Islamic thinkers such as ibn Bajja (c. 1095–1138), and then were passed on to Christian scholastic thought, where they were taken up, defended, or corrected by the likes of Bradwardine, Swineshead, Buridan, and Oresme. Indeed, if one is really passionately attached to the idea of alternating ages of intellectual light and darkness, one might well argue that in the sixth century in Alexandria a scientific revolution in physics and cosmology had begun to stir, taking the form of a skeptical Christian reappraisal of Aristotelian science and of the "divine cosmos" of pagan thought; and when Olympiodorus, the pagan head of the Alexandrian Academy, was succeeded by Christian commentators on Aristotle, this revolution seemed set to continue indefinitely; but then the seventh-century Muslim conquest of Egypt brought an end to the Alexandrian academic tradition and plunged science into six centuries of an Islamo-Hellenistic "dark ages." And one might further argue that this Christian tradition of scientific skepticism began to reemerge in the West only during the later Middle Ages, resumed the inherently "Christian" task of preparing a way for a new paradigm of cosmic reality, and reached its final consummation in the thought of Galileo (a good Catholic), Kepler (whose chief desire as a scientist was to discover how the life of the Trinity was reflected in the beautiful harmonies with which God had marked every level of his creation), and Newton (an ardent, if radically heretical, Christian). All of this would of course be a gross oversimplification of history, an unjust denigration of Greek and Muslim natural philosophy, and in the final analysis rather silly—but no sillier than historically illiterate blather about the Christian "closing of the Western mind."

As for the old claim that, prior to the thirteenth century, scientific and medical innovation was confined to the Islamic world, while Christian scholars of the East and West were no more than sterile archivists, it is of course false. But one can concede at least this much: a few centuries after the collapse of the Western empire, and during the early centuries of the Byzantine East's cultural and military struggle to preserve its borders against the relentless advance of Muslim armies, the still nascent Islamic empire was expanding, and was able—like all great empires—to produce a synthesis of the cultures it absorbed. It had access at once to Greek,

Indian, and Babylonian astronomy and mathematics. It wholly assumed into itself the great Persian Empire, and with it the entirety of Near Eastern Christian, Jewish, and Persian scholarship and medicine. So, most assuredly, from the end of the ninth century to the middle of the thirteenth the Islamic world enjoyed a genuine measure of scientific superiority over Western and even perhaps Byzantine Christendom. But, that said, one ought not to exaggerate what that superiority amounted to. There were some improvements in those few fields where late Hellenistic science had still been somewhat active, such as optics, the astronomical calculation of the calendar, and the configuration of the astrolabe. But there were no improvements upon Aristotelian science, nor was there any real break with the Ptolemaic system. Medicine, thanks to the Nestorian Christian tradition, was well developed and in some ways may have surpassed that of the Byzantine Empire (though that is debatable). But of technological development there was practically none. A few astronomical observatories were built in the Muslim empire, late in the Middle Ages, but only two of them were not destroyed within a few years of their construction for supposedly religious reasons. The Islamic world could boast four and a half centuries of scientific preeminence, it is true, but no more progress than a moderately clever undergraduate today could assimilate in less than a single academic year. In large part, this was merely the consequence of the condition of the Hellenistic science that the Muslim world inherited: its vitality long exhausted, its inventiveness all but nonexistent, its methods (to the degree that it had any) practically useless.

Even so, as the remains of that science were reassumed into Western European culture, over a few centuries, they inspired movements of scientific theory and discovery so profuse, substantial, and constant that Western Europe ultimately surpassed every other civilization in the degree, variety, and rapidity of its scientific, technical, and theoretical accomplishments. This was largely attributable, it seems safe to say, to the institution of the medieval Christian university. The universities of Western Christendom were plentifully endowed establishments, where astonishing freedom of inquiry and debate was not only tolerated but encouraged. They were to a large extent legally and financially independent of the cities where they were situated, and were wholly integrated with one another across all of Western Europe; and they enjoyed an existence largely free from the vicissitudes of war. There could scarcely have been a more favorable climate for a critical reception, examination, and collective reassessment of ancient texts and teachings. From the time when the Cathedral School of Chartres reached its radiant zenith, in the eleventh and twelfth centuries, Western Christendom produced natural philosophers at least the equals of any of their classical predecessors: Robert Grosseteste (c. 1175–1253), for instance, a man of huge erudition and the first known expositor of a systematic method for scientific experimentation; or St. Albert the Great (c. 1200–1280), perhaps the father of biological field research, whose mastery of "all sciences," natural and speculative, was genuinely encyclopedic in scope.

In some signal areas of accomplishment, moreover, portions of the Christian world were, at least at first, measurably more sophisticated than Islamic culture. I have already mentioned the Syrian Christian physicians of Persia during the early centuries of the Islamic conquests; but Byzantine medical care was also, in notable ways, far in advance of what was available in Muslim culture for many centuries. It was once fashionable among historians of medicine to claim that, until quite recently, hospitals were little more than hospices and shelters, offering nothing like systematic medical treatment and making no particular effort to heal their patients. It is clear now, though, that in the Eastern Christian Roman world, at least as early as the sixth century, and probably earlier, there were free hospitals served by physicians and surgeons, with established regimes of treatment and convalescent care, and with regular and trained staffs. In their developed form, the hospitals of Byzantium came in a variety of specializations: some cared for the ill and injured, some were homes for the aged and infirm, some were devoted to foundlings, some were shelters for the homeless poor, and some were principally orphanages. In later centuries, Muslim society and, after the First Crusade, Latin Christian society established hospitals of their own on the Byzantine model, the most famous of which was the massive Hospital of St. John created in Jerusalem by the Hospitallers in 1099, in imitation of which hospitals were built all over Western Europe throughout the later Middle Ages.[9] And, midway through the thirteenth century, almost all major municipalities in Western Christendom employed trained physicians for the care of the poor.

And in certain other areas, the Christian world was always well ahead of the Islamic, even during the so-called Dark Ages, most particularly in the realm of technological innovation. In architecture, engineering, machinery, agronomy, and the exploitation of new sources of power, the Middle Ages were marked by periods of invention far more prolonged, creative, and diverse than any known to Hellenistic, Roman, or Islamic culture. We may find it somewhat difficult now to appreciate the revolutionary implications of devices like the heavy saddle with stirrups, the wheeled plow, the rigid horse collar, heavy armor, and the nailed horseshoe, but they allowed for the cultivation of soils that had never previously been genuinely arable, helped initiate a long period of Western military security, and did much to foster the kind of economic and demographic growth for want of which the Western Roman Empire had fallen into ruin. It requires no great labor of imagination, however, to grasp the significance of medieval developments in the use of water, wind, and coal to generate power. Waterwheels appeared at the dawn of the High Middle Ages, for instance, first as simple watermills but then, with the ever more sophisticated use of gears, as engines of mechanized industry, most particularly in the Cistercian monasteries of the twelfth century and after. In these monasteries, waterpower was used not only to grind and sift grain but also to drive hammers on camshafts for the fulling of wool, to prepare leather for tanning, to run oil presses and wood saws and the bellows of furnaces, and so on. The abundant production of wrought iron and finally of cast iron; the manufacture of cannon; constant improvements in the technology of mining, such as methods of pumping water, the trolley transport of ore, and more stable mineshafts; the invention and refinement of the windmill; the development of sophisticated earthenware and glass glazing; the flying buttress and the Gothic arch; discoveries in the geometry of refraction and the consequent perfection of magnifying lenses for eyeglasses; the birth and continuous refinement of the mechanical clock; the development of large seafaring vessels with rudders supported on sternposts and sails so rigged as to allow complete exploitation of the winds; the invention of the magnetic compass—all of these, among many more, were special achievements of Western medieval culture. And no previous culture had ever boasted technological advances of such scope and variety.[10]

Perhaps these are principally achievements of practical science, but theory rarely advances very far without some practical impulse behind it. Aristotle, for instance, for all his genius and epochal importance, was in some ways the victim of his own good fortune. Beneficiary as he was of a well-established slave economy, he naturally held the artisanal class in contempt, thought all invention exhausted, and believed science to be a realm entirely of theory and passive observation. Perhaps it was in part the persistence of this prejudice and of a slave economy that rendered both the Hellenistic and the Islamic scientific cultures so technologically static. Perhaps it required a society that had in part forgotten—not suppressed, but honestly forgotten—certain of the more barren principles of ancient "science" to produce such marvels of invention and imagination and pragmatic inspiration. And perhaps only a society that delighted in things mechanical and practical, and that had ceased to think of the sciences as purely contemplative endeavors, indifferent to the discoveries of craftsmen and farmers and sailors, could have evolved a truly experimental scientific method or arrived ultimately at the physical theories of Galileo and Newton. All of that is purely conjectural, of course; but, if even partially true, it is an exquisite example of what Hegel called the "master-slave dialectic," that law of historical necessity that dictates (among other things) that, in a slave society, the aristocratic class remains insulated by its "contemplative leisure" from practical knowledge, while those who are so debased as to work with their hands acquire a genuine consciousness of the intrinsic structure of concrete reality. It was on account of centuries of economic and social necessity, and continued demographic distress, and the general disappearance of slavery during the Middle Ages, that Western European culture became the first genuinely technological society; and, perhaps as a consequence, science was able, slowly, to descend from a largely ineffectual realm of indolent aristocratic privilege to the level of material actuality. Whether one can accept this explanation or not, though, it is certainly the case that there are times when a measure of forgetfulness can be a blessing. It would not be entirely fanciful, for instance, to date the birth of modern medicine from 24 June 1527, when Paracelsus (1493–1541)—an alchemist, but also the father of modern chemical therapy and a tireless scourge of injurious traditional remedies—burned copies of the medical treatises of Avicenna and Galen in public (a genuine case of book burning, though solely in the cause of science). One can hardly imagine what else Western European society might have accomplished had it succeeded in forgetting slightly more.

CHAPTER SEVEN

Intolerance and Persecution

AT THE END OF THE DAY, the most splendid and engrossing of modernity's self-aggrandizing fables is that of Western humanity's struggle for liberation, of the great emancipation of Western culture from political tyranny, and of Europe's deliverance from the violence of religious intolerance. Certainly it is true that, at the dawn of the modern age, European society suffered convulsions of cruelty and bloodshed, chronic and acute, that rent Western Christendom apart, that claimed untold thousands of lives, and that were haunted by the symbols and rhetoric of religion. It was the age of the great witch hunt, of the so-called wars of religion, of relentless persecution of "heretics," and of the disintegration of the old Catholic order. And we have been taught to remember that time as the culmination of the entire history of Christendom's alliance between religious absolutism and the power of the secular state—centuries, that is, of hieratic despotism, inquisitions, witch burnings, and Crusades—an alliance that has now mercifully been dissolved and replaced by a moderate regime of secular government and chartered rights. Whether, however, this tale is particularly trustworthy can be determined only if one first takes care to make certain distinctions between the medieval and modern periods of "religious" violence, and then in either case tries to make a reasonable assessment of the relative guilt of church and state.

Certain charges are more easily dismissed than others. As entertaining as it might be, for instance, to think of the Middle Ages as a time of inquisitors burning thousands of witches at the stake, it was not until the early modern period—especially from the late sixteenth century through the middle of the seventeenth—that a great enthusiasm for hunting out and prosecuting witches sprang up in various regions of Western Europe and, over three centuries (say, from the middle of the fifteenth century to the middle of the eighteenth), claimed anywhere from thirty thousand to sixty thousand lives, though not generally at the prompting or with the approval of the Catholic Church. As far as the church's various regional inquisitions are concerned, their *principal* role in the early modern witch hunts was to suppress them: to quiet mass hysteria through the imposition of judicial process, to restrain the cruelty of secular courts, and to secure dismissals in practically every case. It is true, admittedly, that belief in sorcery and magic persisted from the antique through the early modern periods, and true also that there were practitioners of folk magic, and even a few of "maleficent" magic (those who sold curses, coercive or lethal spells, abortifacients, and poisons). But during the better part of the Middle Ages most magic practices were largely ignored or treated with lenience—a sentence of penance and reconciliation with the church, for instance, such as one finds in early "penitentials"—and belief in the real efficacy of magic was treated as a heathen superstition. St. Patrick's Synod in the fifth century, for instance, anathematizes those who believe in the existence of witches with real magical powers. The Capitulary for Saxony, promulgated by Charlemagne (c. 742–814) as part of his campaign to Christianize the pagan north, made it a crime for anyone, acting on some heathen belief in magic, to burn or (grimly enough) to devour the flesh of accused sorcerers. The *Canon episcopi,* written about the same time, assumes that women who claim to have taken to the air in Diana's train are suffering from diabolical fantasies, and it prescribes expulsion from the congregation of those who insist on the reality of witches. When St. Agobard (d. 840), archbishop of Lyons, discovered that certain rustics of his diocese believed in Burgundian witches who destroyed crops with hailstones and colluded with men from the mysterious land of Mangonia —who sailed ships through the skies to steal farmers' harvests—he was not merely obliged to instruct his flock that men could not govern the weather, sail upon the wind, or in fact wield any magic powers at all; he even had to intervene to save four hapless souls from being stoned to death as captured Mangonians. The *Ecclesiastical Discipline* ascribed to Regino von Prüm (d. c. 915) enjoins clergy to warn their congregations against crediting wild tales of covens of witches flying through the night skies and worshipping Diana. Bishop Burchard of Worms (d. 1025) prescribed penance for those so timidly faithless as to believe in the power of witches. Pope Gregory VII (c. 1022–1085) forbade the courts of Denmark to execute persons accused of using witchcraft to influence the weather or spread disease or cause crop failure. The great Dominican encyclopedist Vincent of Beauvais (c. 1190–1264), in order to disabuse a woman visitor of the delusion that she was a witch who could pass through keyholes, resorted to the exquisitely simple expedient of locking his door and chasing her about with a stick while exhorting her to escape if she could.

Precisely why a new fascination with sorcery and demonolatry arose in the twilight of the Middle Ages and became so epidemic in the early modern period it is difficult to say; certain traditional explanations concern such things as the "emotional" effects of the Black Death in the mid-fourteenth century, or the "anxiety" created by the once unthinkable erosion of the religious unity of Catholic Europe, or other vague social pathologies impossible to quantify. Perhaps, one might say, even more imprecisely, it belonged to the tenor of the times to desire some outsider or other to fear and hate. It was just at the end of the eleventh century, for instance, that the condition of Jews in Western Europe suddenly began to worsen. During the earlier Middle Ages there was certainly prejudice against Jews, but no popular passion for persecutions or massacres. In 1096, however, citizen "soldiers" who had gathered for the First Crusade, putatively on their way to deliver Christians in the East from their Seljuk Turk oppressors, began robbing and murdering Rhineland Jews by the thousands, and even attacking local bishops who attempted to protect the Jews within their diocesan boundaries. The Benedictine monk and historian Hugh of Flavigny (c. 1065–1140) marveled that such atrocities could be committed, despite popular revulsion, ecclesiastical condemnation, excommunications, and threats of severe legal punishments. And surely the direst time for Europe's Jews during the whole of the High Middle Ages was the period when the demand for scapegoats was greatest: the plague years of 1348 and 1349, when Jews were accused in many areas of poisoning the wells from which Christians drank. Pope Clement VI (c. 1291–1352) was even obliged to issue a decree in 1348 in defense of the

Jews, pointing out that they too were victims of the plague (he also, to his everlasting credit, continued to offer Jews the hospitality of his court in Avignon, despite the suspicion with which they were viewed).

Another line of reasoning connects the late medieval belief in secret diabolistic cults to the rise of new heresies in Western Europe during the age of the Crusades, and especially to the rise of the Cathar Church in the south of France and in Italy during the twelfth and thirteenth centuries. This was arguably, after all, the gravest crisis the political and ecclesiastical institutions of medieval Europe ever suffered. The Cathars (or Albigensians, as they were also called) were a sect of Gnostics: that is, they held the flesh in contempt, forswore procreation, believed the material cosmos to be the creature not of God but of Satan, thought this world a prison house in which spirits are incarcerated through successive incarnations, and preached salvation through inner enlightenment and escape from the fetters of birth and death. The Cathars lived, by all accounts, ascetical, sober, and peaceful lives, and the initial attitude of Pope Innocent III (1160–1216) toward them was remarkably gentle and tolerant; the original policy of the Catholic Church in regard to the Albigensian movement was, in fact, one of peaceful persuasion through theological debate. So things might have continued until the Cathars themselves had, through their abhorrence of the childbed, brought about their own quiet extinction. But certain noble houses in the Languedoc region of France began to embrace the Cathar cause, in very large part as an excuse for seizing Catholic Church property. In the late decades of the twelfth century, the comte de Foix forcibly evicted monks from their abbey in Pamiers, desecrated the chapel, and seized the property for himself; and the vicomte de Béziers plundered and burned monasteries, imprisoned a bishop and an abbot, and, after the abbot had died in his chains, made a whimsical display of the corpse in a public pulpit. In the last decade of the century, the comte de Toulouse, Raymond VI, the most powerful of the southern barons to lend his support to the Cathars, began not only to abuse and persecute certain Catholic monks but also to despoil and burn churches; and in 1208 he apparently conspired in the assassination of a papal legate. And Catharism continued to spread. To Innocent it seemed obvious that the otherworldly creed of the Cathars had begun to breed certain very worldly (and very dire) consequences and was rapidly becoming the source of a social calamity that threatened the very foundations of Western

Christendom; so—taking counsel of his fears—he reversed his own policy of irenic dialogue and actively promoted the French crown's "crusade" against the south.

All that this turned out to be, however, was an excuse for the king of France to subdue Toulouse and the rest of the south, and for the nobles of the Norman north to steal southern fiefs for themselves from the noble houses of the Languedoc, Albigensian and Catholic alike. More effective in suppressing the Cathars was the decision of Pope Innocent IV (d. 1254) —dependent as he was, in his struggles with the Holy Roman Emperor, upon the protection of King Louis IX of France (1214–1270)—not only to institute the first inquisition to deal with the heresy, but (in 1252) to permit the occasional limited use of torture to obtain evidence. The use of torture was an ancient, common provision of Roman law, contrary to centuries of Christian legal usage but recently revived by the civil courts of the Holy Roman Empire. These same courts also—like the courts of the pagan empire of old—viewed heresy as a form of treason against the state, punishable by death, and although the church itself could not take life, an inquisition could at its discretion hand over impenitent heretics to be tried and perhaps executed by the secular authority. It was in this way that the church became complicit, in the most intimate way, in the violence of the state against perceived agents of social disorder. And, while ecclesiastical inquisitions were concerned principally with heresy, they did occasionally deal with cases of witchcraft, even though such cases properly belonged to the realm of secular jurisprudence. And thus—even though the number of witches actually tried or surrendered to the state by ecclesiastical inquisitions was minuscule—the hierarchy of the medieval church helped to lay the ground for the witch hunts of early modernity. That said, certain things should be kept in mind.

It is true, obviously, that the church was not immune to the general alarm regarding maleficent magic and cults of cannibalistic Satanists, especially during the late fifteenth century. It was, for instance, two Dominicans who, around 1486, produced the titillatingly ghastly *Malleus maleficarum,* the infamous manual of witch-hunting that convinced so many of its readers of the reality of diabolic magic. One should note, however, that the book's principal author, Heinrich Kramer, was recognized as a demented imbecile by many of his contemporaries; in Innsbruck, for instance, the local bishop not only thwarted his attempts to convict certain local women of witchcraft but even forced him to leave the city. And the same year that the *Malleus* appeared the Carmelite Jan van Beetz published his *Expositio decem catalogie praeceptum,* an icily skeptical treatment of tales of black magic. Of course, in the sixteenth and seventeenth centuries, there were popes who—whether or not they believed in magic—still believed popular tales of a rising tide of Satanism, and who consequently charged inquisitors to seek out the malefactors. Nevertheless, it was the Catholic Church, of all the institutions of the time, that came to treat accusations of witchcraft with the most pronounced incredulity. Where secular courts and licentious mobs were eager to consign the accused to the tender ministrations of the public executioner, ecclesial inquisitions were prone to demand hard evidence and, in its absence, to dismiss charges. Ultimately, in lands where the authority of the church and its inquisitions were strong—especially during the high tide of witch-hunting—convictions were extremely rare. In Spain, for example, in the whole of the fourteenth and fifteenth centuries, we have evidence of only two prosecutions going to trial. In the middle of the sixteenth century, the Catalonian Inquisition set the precedent (imitated by other inquisitions soon after) of arguing against all further prosecutions for witchcraft. In or around 1609, during an eruption of witch-hunting panic in Basque country, the Spanish Inquisition went so far as to forbid even the discussion of witchcraft; and more than once, in the years following, Iberian inquisitions were obliged to intervene when secular courts renewed prosecutions.[1]

The rather disorienting truth about the early modern fascination with witchcraft and the great witch hunts is that they were not the final, desperate expressions of an intellectual and religious tradition slowly fading into obsolescence before the advance of scientific and social "enlightenment"; they were, instead, something quite novel, modern phenomena, which had at best a weak foreshadowing in certain new historical trends of the late Middle Ages, and which, far from occurring in tension with the birth of secular modernity, were in a sense extreme manifestations of it. In many cases, it was those who were most hostile to the power of the church to intervene in secular affairs who were also most avid to see the power of the state express itself in the merciless destruction of those most perfidious of dissidents, witches. Thomas Hobbes (1588–1679), for instance, the greatest modern theorist of complete state sovereignty, thought all religious doctrine basically mendacious and did not really believe in magic; but still he thought witches should continue to be punished for the good of society. The author of *De la démonomanie des sorciers* (1580), perhaps the most influential and (quite literally) inflammatory of all the witch-hunting manifestos of its time, was Jean Bodin (c. 1530–1596), who believed witches should be burned at the stake, that nations that did not seek them out and exterminate them would suffer famine, plague, and war, that interrogation by torture should be used when sorcery was so much as suspected, and that no one accused of witchcraft should be acquitted unless the accuser's falsity be as shiningly apparent as the sun. But Bodin was also the first great theorist of that most modern of political ideas, the absolute sovereignty of the secular state, and he was certainly not an orthodox Catholic but an adherent to his own version of "natural" religion. British laws making sorcery a capital offense were passed only in 1542 and 1563, well after Crown and state had been made supreme over the English church, and the later act was not repealed until 1736. In 1542, the Concordat of Liège, promulgated under the Holy Roman Emperor Charles V (1500–1558), placed the prosecution of sorcery entirely in the hands of secular tribunals. This was also, perhaps not coincidentally, precisely the time at which the great witch hunt began in earnest.

More significantly, perhaps, some of the great early theorists of modern science and scientific method were believers in magic, and consequently were often willing to prescribe the prosecution of those who used it for maleficent ends. Rodney Stark is not overstating his case when he declares, "The first significant objections to the reality of satanic witchcraft came from Spanish inquisitors, not from scientists."[2] One might even argue that an interest in magic (though not of the maleficent variety) was one of the essential ingredients in the evolution of modern scientific thought. Certainly the Renaissance rediscovery of the *Corpus hermeticum*—the splendid late antique anthology of Neoplatonic, Gnostic, alchemical, magical, astrological, and devotional texts—was of immense importance in shaping the ethos of modern science. Francis Bacon (1561–1626), who did so much to define the inherent rationality of modern scientific method, and who was so vigorous an advocate of the human "mission" to know and to conquer the material world, was an heir at the very least to the hermetic revival's emphasis upon humanity's godlike prerogatives over the lower orders of material creation, and to the alchemical tradition of wracking elemental nature to force it to yield up its deepest secrets.

Robert Boyle (1627–1691), one of the founders of the Royal Society, perhaps the most accomplished experimental scientist of the seventeenth century and a pioneer in the study of air pressure and vacuums, was a student of alchemy and was firmly convinced of both the reality of witches and the need for their elimination. Joseph Glanvill (1636–1680), also of the Royal Society and chief apologist for its experimental methods, thought the reality of sorcery to be scientifically demonstrable.[3] Even Newton devoted far greater energy to his alchemy than to his physical theories.

In truth, the rise of modern science and the early modern obsession with sorcery were not merely contemporaneous currents within Western society but were two closely allied manifestations of the development of a new post-Christian sense of human mastery over the world. There is nothing especially outrageous in such a claim. After all, magic is essentially a species of materialism; if it invokes any agencies beyond the visible sphere, they are not supernatural—in the theological sense of "transcendent"—but at most preternatural: they are merely, that is to say, subtler, more potent aspects of the physical cosmos. Hermetic magic and modern science (in its most Baconian form at least) are both concerned with hidden forces within the material order, forces that are largely impersonal and morally neutral, which one can learn to manipulate, and which may be turned to ends fair or foul; both, that is to say, are concerned with domination of the physical cosmos, the instrumental subjection of nature to humanity, and the constant increase of human power. Hence, there was not really any late modern triumph of science over magic, so much as there was a natural dissolution of the latter into the former, as the power of science to accomplish what magic could only adumbrate became progressively more obvious. Or, rather, "magic" and "science" in the modern period are distinguishable only retrospectively, according to relative degrees of efficacy. There never was, however, an antagonism between the two: metaphysically, morally, and conceptually, they belonged to a single continuum.

As for the widespread obsession with maleficent magic and Satanism in the sixteenth and seventeenth centuries, when treatises on demonolatry, possession, evil spirits, and monsters of the night proliferated as fast as the presses could produce them,[4] it would almost be tempting simply to write it off as one of those irritating and inexplicable popular enthusiasms—like the fascination with UFOs, Yeti, the Loch Ness monster, and the Bermuda

Triangle that was so vital a part of the special idiocy of the 1970s—had its consequences not been rather more tragic and protracted. A better analogy might be the panic that seized Roman society in the second century B.C. in response to the migration into Italy of the Dionysian or Bacchic cult: Rumors spread of orgies in the dead of night, of women poisoning their husbands, of children of noble houses participating in ritual murder; the Bacchanal was banned; accusations were secured through rewards and confessions through torture; and thousands of executions were ordered. All analogies aside, however, it is perhaps no great marvel that the early modern fascination with diabolists and witches should have arisen in those centuries when the Christian order of Western Europe was slowly disintegrating, the authority of the church in the affairs of nations was weakening, and the old faith could no longer offer a sufficient sense of security against the dark and nameless forces of nature, history, and fate. Just as the Christian faith in a transcendent creator God had once stripped magic of any appearance of religious or philosophical seriousness and reduced it to mere superstition and folk craft, so the fragmentation of Christian Europe perhaps encouraged a certain kind of magical thinking to reassert itself and insinuate itself into the anxieties of a tragic and chaotic age. Whether this in any sense constitutes an adequate "explanation" of the special cruelties and fanaticisms of early modernity, however, is impossible to say.

This is not, incidentally, to exonerate the institutional Catholic Church of its complicity in the violence of early modernity, or of its increasing harshness and paranoia, such as they were. All powerful institutions fear the decay of their power. Nor is it to deny that the late medieval and early modern periods were marked by a passion to extirpate heresy unmatched since the days of Justinian. One can scarcely ignore, for instance, the Spanish Inquisition, which occupies so privileged a place among Western culture's collective nightmares. There are, however, some facts that need to be taken into account even here. For one thing, four decades of scholarship have made it clear that many of our images of the Inquisition are wild exaggerations and lurid fictions, that over the three centuries of its existence the Inquisition was far more lenient and far less powerful than was once assumed, and that in many instances—as any Spaniard accused of witchcraft had cause to know—it operated as a benign check upon the cruelty of secular courts. That said, however, I think we can all agree that an inquisition is always in principle—and frequently in practice—a disagreeable institution; that the first two decades of the Inquisition in Spain were especially brutal; and that the relative infrequency of torture or of burning at the stake renders neither practice any less heinous. What should also be remembered, though, is that the Spanish Inquisition was principally a matter of Crown policy and an office of the state.

True, it was Pope Sixtus IV (1414–1484) who authorized the early Inquisition, but he did so under pressure from King Ferdinand (1452–1516) and Queen Isabella (1451–1504), who—with the end of centuries of Muslim occupation of Andalusia—were eager for any instrument they thought might help to enforce national unity and increase the power of Castile and Aragon. Such, however, was the early Inquisition's harshness and corruption that Sixtus soon attempted to interfere in its operations. In a papal bull of April 1482, he uncompromisingly denounced its destruction of innocent lives and its theft of property (though he did not, admittedly, object in principle to the execution of genuine heretics). But Ferdinand effectively refused to recognize the bull, and in 1483 he forced Sixtus to relinquish control of the Inquisition to the Spanish thrones and to consent to the civil appointment of a Grand Inquisitor. The first man to wear this title was the notorious Tomás de Torquemada (1420–1498), a priest both severe and uncompromising, especially toward Christian converts (*conversos*) from Judaism and Islam whom he suspected of secret adherence to the teachings of their original faiths. Before he was finally reined in by Pope Alexander VI (1431–1503), Torquemada was responsible for the expulsion of a good number of Jews from Spain and for perhaps two thousand executions of "heretics." Even after Sixtus had surrendered his authority over the Inquisition, however, he did not entirely relent in his opposition to its excesses. In 1484, for instance, he supported the city of Teruel after it forbade the Inquisition entry—a revolt that Ferdinand suppressed the following year by force of arms. And Sixtus and his successor Innocent VIII (1432–1492) continued to issue sporadic demands that the Inquisition exercise greater leniency, and continued to attempt to intervene on behalf of the conversos when the opportunity arose. Over the next century, the Inquisition was often involved in the nauseating national politics of "blood purity," *limpieza de sangre*, from which no one—not even a monk, priest, or archbishop—was safe. Within Spain itself, there was some resistance to the new Spanish racialism, none more honorable and uncompromising than that of St. Ignatius of Loyola (1491–1556), founder of the Jesuits. But from racialist harassments often only the papacy's interventions could provide relief, however small or infrequent.[5]

What is one to make of any of this history? Ought one to draw some sort of conclusion regarding the lethal nature of religion or the intolerance that naturally attaches to "ultimate convictions"? Should one see this history as testament to some sort of cruelty inherent in Christianity itself? Certainly no period in Western Christian history looks, on its surface, more inviting to the anti-Christian polemicist questing after damning evidence. To me, though, it seems obvious that the true lesson to be learned is just the opposite: the inherent violence of the state, and the tragedy that the institutional church was ever assumed into temporal politics, or ever became responsible for the maintenance of social order or of national or imperial unity. It was perfectly natural for pagan Roman society to regard piety toward the gods and loyalty to the empire as essentially inseparable, and for Roman courts to institute extraordinary inquisitions and to execute atheists as traitors. But when, in 385, a Roman emperor (or pretender, really) executed the Spanish bishop Priscillian for heresy, Christians as eminent as St. Martin of Tours and St. Ambrose of Milan protested, recognizing in such an act the triumph of a pagan value and of a special kind of pagan brutality; and none of the church fathers ever promoted or approved of such measures. During the so-called Dark Ages, in fact, the only penalty for obdurate heresy was excommunication. In the twelfth and thirteenth centuries, however—when the liaison between the church and temporal power was unbreakable, and the papacy was a state unto itself, and the Holy Roman Empire was asserting its claims to the prerogatives of the old imperial order, and new religious movements seemed ever more openly subversive of both ecclesiastical and secular power, and the pillars of society seemed to be trembling as never before, and chaos seemed poised to come again—heresy once again became a capital crime throughout Western Europe. To its credit, perhaps, the Catholic Church did not actually lead the way in this matter; when, for instance, the frequently beleaguered Holy Roman Emperor Henry III (1017–1056) hanged a number of Cathars (or "Manichees") in 1051, he had to endure the rebukes of the bishop in Liège. To its everlasting *discredit*, however, the church did soon follow the fashion. When the Holy Roman Emperor Frederick II (1194–1250) passed laws dictating the surrender of all convicted heretics to the secular arm, for burning at the stake, the institutional church's compliance was encumbered by no obvious signs of unquiet conscience. And in the Iberia of the sixteenth century, it required little effort to alienate the newly instituted inquisitorial office from direct papal control and openly to transform it into an instrument for advancing the political, religious, and social unity of the emerging national powers of the peninsula.

The long history of Christendom is astonishingly plentiful in magnificent moral, intellectual, and cultural achievements; and many of these would never have been possible but for the conversion of the Roman Empire to a new faith. But it has also been the history of a constant struggle between the power of the gospel to alter and shape society and the power of the state to absorb every useful institution into itself. If it really were the case, however, that the injustices and violences of late medieval and early modern Western Christendom were the natural consequences of something intrinsic to Christian beliefs, and if it were really true that the emergence of the secular state rescued Western humanity from the rule of religious intolerance, then what we should find on looking back over the course of Western European history is a seamless, if inverted, arc: a decline from the golden days of Roman imperial order, when the violence of religion was moderated by the prudent hand of the state, into a prolonged period of fanaticism, cruelty, persecution, and religious strife, and then—as the church was gradually subdued—a slow reemergence from the miserable brutality of the "age of faith" into a progressively more rational, more humane, less violent social arrangement. This, though, is precisely what we do not find. Instead we see that violence increased in proportion to the degree of sovereignty claimed by the state, and that whenever the medieval church surrendered moral authority to secular power, injustice and cruelty flourished. We find also that early medieval society, for all its privations, inequities, and deficiencies, was in most ways far more just, charitable, and (ultimately) peaceful than the imperial culture it succeeded, and, immeasurably more peaceful and even more charitable (incredible as this may seem to us) than the society created by the early modern triumph of the nation state. Nor, in this last instance, am I speaking merely of the violence of the "transitional" period of early modernity, on the eve of the so-called Enlightenment. The Age of Enlightenment—considered in purely political terms—was itself merely the transition from one epoch of nationalist warfare, during which states still found it necessary to use religious institutions as instruments of power, to another epoch of still greater nationalist warfare, during which religious rationales had become obsolete, because the state had become its own cult, and power the only morality.

This, however, belongs to the argument of the next chapter.

CHAPTER EIGHT

Intolerance and War

THE VIOLENCE OF early modernity was expressed nowhere more purely or on a grander scale than in the international and internecine conflicts of the period, which custom dictates should be called "the wars of religion." Given, though, the lines of coalition that defined these conflicts, and given their ultimate consequences, they ought really to be remembered as the first wars of the modern nation-state, whose principal purpose was to establish the supremacy of secular state authority over every rival power, most especially the power of the church.

They were certainly not, at any rate, some sort of continuation of the "tradition" of the Crusades (the only "holy wars" in Christian history). The Crusades, after all, began as a perfectly explicable—albeit, in the event, brutal and frequently incompetent—response to tales of atrocities committed against Eastern Christians and Western Christian pilgrims by the Seljuk Turks, and to the appeals of the Byzantine emperor Alexius I (1081–1118) for military aid in resisting Seljuk aggressions in the Eastern Christian world and at the periphery of Western Christendom. When Pope Urban II (c. 1035–1099) called for the First Crusade, there was nothing insincere in the indignation with which he recited tales of Christians robbed, enslaved, and murdered, or in his dire forebodings of Christendom conquered by an enemy that had held many Christian lands and peoples in thrall for four centuries. And, in fact, a great number of the

Christian nobles who answered Urban's call were earnest, pious, and self-sacrificing men, who saw themselves as faring forth to succor the oppressed, set the bondsman free, and rescue the holy places from desecration. Unfortunately, riding the crest of the wave of enthusiasm that initiated the First Crusade, a considerable number of louts, brigands, and killers came along as well, at least for the first leg of the journey (as I shall discuss later). Thereafter, the Crusades—sporadic, limited, inconclusive, and often pointless—became at once the last great adventure of a fading warrior caste, an occasionally bloody but ultimately profitable cultural and mercantile embassy from late Western Frankish civilization to the Byzantine Christian and Islamic civilizations, and a great ferment of cultural and intellectual interaction between East and West. They were driven by high ideals and by low motives, perhaps in equal measure. But they were entirely of their time. They were episodes within a conflict between Islam and Christendom that began in the seventh century, with the rapid and brilliant Muslim conquest of vast reaches of the Christian world. They certainly had no basis in any Christian tradition of holy war. They were more truly the last gaudy flourish of Western barbarian culture, embellished by the winsome ceremonies of chivalry.

The European wars of the sixteenth and seventeenth centuries were something altogether different. They inaugurated a new age of nationalist strife and state violence, prosecuted on a scale and with a degree of ferocity without any precedent in medieval history: wars of unification, revolutions, imperial adventures, colonialism, the rebirth of chattel slavery, endless irredentism, ideologically inspired frenzies of mass murder, nationalist cults, political terrorism, world wars—in short, the entire glorious record of European politics in the aftermath of a united Christendom. Far from the secular nation-state rescuing Western humanity from the chaos and butchery of sectarian strife, those wars were the birth pangs of the modern state and its limitless license to murder. And religious allegiances, anxieties, and hatreds were used by regional princes merely as pretexts for conflicts whose causes, effects, and alliances had very little to do with faith or confessional loyalties.[1]

This should not, all things considered, be a particularly controversial claim. Early modernity was the age of the new secular ideologies of "absolute monarchy" and "divine right," and the age consequently of the great political struggle of the independent nation state to emancipate itself from all the religious, legal, moral, and sacramental bonds that had ever in any way confined or constrained its total sovereignty over its subjects. Older medieval models of overlapping and subsidiary spheres of authority and fealty, and of a realm of spiritual authority transcendent of the rule of princes, gave way to the idea of a monarch in whom the full power and legitimacy of the state, in its every institution, was perfectly concentrated. The monarch was now a tautology: a king was king because he was king, not because he was liege of his nation's estates, charged with reciprocal responsibilities to his vassals, and subject to the church's law. This meant that the church—the only universally recognized transnational authority that could possibly rival or even overrule the power of the monarch—had to be reduced to a national establishment, an office of the state, or a mere social institution. This was the principal reason, after all, for the success of the Reformation, which flourished only where it served the interests of the secular state in its rebellion against the customs and laws of Christendom, and in its campaign against the autonomy of the church within its territories. The French monarchy remained Catholic in the sixteenth and seventeenth centuries, rather than imitate England's Anglican establishment, in part because the church in France had already effectively been reduced to a Gallican establishment, first in 1438 with the Pragmatic Sanction of Bourges (which severely restricted papal jurisdiction in France, reserved the rights of episcopal appointment and the distribution of benefices to the French Crown, and withheld all future annates from Rome), then in 1516 with the Concordat of Bologna (which confirmed and extended the power of the French Crown over the Gallican church and all ecclesial appointments), and finally in 1682 with the enactment of the four Gallican Articles (which rejected all papal claims of secular authority, asserted the primacy of ecumenical councils over the pope, and affirmed as inviolable such special French practices as the Crown appointment of bishops). Much the same was true in the case of the Iberian states. Especially after 1486, for instance, the authority of the Spanish Crown over the church in its territories was all but absolute. Where, however, the church could not be so easily subdued, separation from Rome proved necessary. And where the ambitions of one state, or of one faction within a state, came into conflict with the ambitions of another, war was inevitable, and religion was as good an excuse as any for the extension of one or another prince's rule.[2]

Admittedly, it would have provided no excuse at all had there not been a great deal of religious hatred to exploit in the first place. Consider, for instance, the most notorious atrocity of the French "religious" wars, the St. Bartholomew's Day Massacre of 1572, in the course of which thousands of Huguenot Protestants were slaughtered in and about Paris. This was not, as it happens, a spontaneous popular assault upon a despised minority. Many Huguenot nobles and commoners had come from Navarre to celebrate the nuptials of their king, Henri de Bourbon (1553–1610), to Princess Marguerite de Valois (1553–1615), sister of the French king Charles IX (1550–1574). Four days after the wedding, however, Charles's mother, Catherine de Médicis (1519–1589), in league with the Guises, attempted but failed to have a confidant of her son, the Huguenot admiral Gaspard de Coligny, assassinated; and so she staged the massacre as a desperate second measure, in order to kill Coligny along with any Huguenot witnesses and then to conceal the entire affair behind a veil of blood. But, even if the proximate cause of the massacre was not religious, it would not have come to pass had hatred of the Huguenots not been sufficiently fierce to make the massacre a, so to speak, plausible cover for Catherine's crime. Reports of the event inspired celebrations in the royal court of Spain and in the papal court in Rome, where the political threat of the Protestant cause was a perpetual source of anxiety; the pope reputedly even had a commemorative medal struck to honor the occasion. As I have said, human beings frequently disappoint.

Nonetheless, no matter how shameful it may have been, all the religious hatred, fear, or resentment of the period taken together was impotent to move battalions or rouse nations to arms, and no prince of the time waged war against another simply on account of his faith. The first of the early modern "religious" wars in Europe were waged by the Habsburg Holy Roman Emperor Charles V to shore up his power in his various demesnes: wars that ended in 1555 with the Peace of Augsburg, which established in imperial law the principle that the faith of a people would be determined by its prince (*cuius regio, eius religio*—"whosoever's region, his religion"—to use the phrase of the time). While it is certainly true that Charles saw the embrace of Lutheranism by various German princes as a very real challenge to his authority over his vassal states, before 1547 it was only Catholic blood that he spilled in any appreciable quantity: not only was he simultaneously involved, from 1521 to 1522, in a war with Francis I of France and in another to suppress sedition among his subjects in Spain, in 1527 he turned his forces against the pope, and that same year his soldiers entered Rome and sacked the city. As for the wars he fought from 1547 to 1548 and again (after the revolt of the Protestant elector of Saxony) from 1552 to 1555, these were hardly campaigns to impose the "true faith" upon peoples struggling for religious liberty. They were conflicts between, on the one hand, principalities seeking complete sovereignty over their own lands and subjects—without interference from either Rome or the Habsburgs—and, on the other, a corrupt and dying imperial order striving to preserve itself against its inevitable demise. This is why the Catholic German princes of the empire made no effort to assist Charles in his German wars; they were as eager as their Lutheran counterparts for the settlement of Augsburg. And it is worth noting, perhaps, that after Augsburg the only places where anything resembling religious liberty was to be found within the empire was not in the principalities themselves but in the free cities of the imperial jurisdiction, where no national sovereignty was at stake.

As for the so-called religious wars fought in France during the latter half of the sixteenth century, they were principally struggles among a number of noble families for the French Crown. From at least 1560, when the penultimate Valois king Charles IX (1550–1574) acceded to the throne at the age of ten and his mother, Catherine de Médicis, became regent, the Houses Guise, Montmorency, and Bourbon were all engaged in intrigues to control the monarchy. Some of the Montmorencies were supporters of the Protestant Huguenots when it served their interests, while the Bourbons were leaders of the Huguenot cause, though both houses were predominantly Catholic. The Guises identified their cause exclusively with the interests of France's Catholic majority. Needless to say, the French Catholic Church, in the denatured form it had assumed definitively in 1516, was one of the stoutest pillars of Valois rule; but this did not prevent Catherine, early in her regency when her fear of the Guises was particularly pronounced, from seeking to cultivate a Huguenot alliance: not only did she rather absurdly propose in 1561 the institution of a Gallican church that would encompass both Catholic and Calvinist congregations, in 1562 she—the very woman who would a decade later orchestrate the St. Bartholomew's Day Massacre—issued the first edict of toleration for Protestants in France, allowing them to worship openly

outside municipal purlieus. Unfortunately, such overtures to the Protestant faction were too suggestive of a rise in Bourbon power and led to an
alliance of the Guises and Montmorencies. The Guises' (Catholic) forces
seized Paris and the (Catholic) royal family, but the alliance was unable
to defeat the Huguenots in the provinces decisively, and the war ended
after a year with another, more limited grant of toleration. War resumed
five years later, on account of a Huguenot plot to seize power with the
aid of the German Palatinate, and dragged on till 1570 brought another
inconclusive armistice—as was also the result in 1576, at the end of the
conflicts ignited by the St. Bartholomew's Day Massacre.

The wars of the next two decades were, as much as anything else,
ideological conflicts. Among those disposed to fight for France's future,
there were some who sought to preserve the old feudal order of limited
monarchy and subsidiary powers, and there were some who desired an
absolute monarchy with control over all institutions within its boundaries.
The Politiques, a loose party of moderate Catholics, were champions of
"divine right" and of the supremacy of the Crown over the church; this
fitted well with the official Calvinist position on earthly government,
and the Politiques were natural supporters of the Huguenot cause. They
sought toleration for French Protestants, though a Gallican Catholic establishment, but they were also believers in a kind of state absolutism that
recognized no "contractual" obligation of the monarch to his subjects. By
contrast, the Catholic Holy League, formed in the days of the last Valois
king, Henri III (1551–1589), was devoted to the cause of the old order that
had recognized the rights, liberties, and powers of the provinces and estates of France. But the league was also a creature of the Guises and served
as a clandestine embassy of Philip II of Spain (1527–1598). Philip desired
the throne of France for his daughter Isabella Clara Eugenia (1566–1633),
who was a Valois on her mother's side; when, in 1583, Henri III's brother
died and his brother-in-law Henri de Bourbon—the Huguenot king of
Navarre—became heir to the throne of France, the league instigated in-
surrections against the Crown, secured an agreement with the king in
1585 to exclude the Bourbon pretender from succession, and then in 1588
drove the king himself out of Paris. Thus the (Catholic) Valois king and
his (Protestant) Bourbon heir, who had been at war with one another only
a year earlier, were now allies against the House of Guise and the Spanish
Crown. But the duc de Guise and his brother were assassinated in 1588, as

was Henri III in 1589, and Henri de Bourbon became Henri IV of France. The war continued, however, for nine more years. In 1593, Henri converted to Catholicism, with no great perturbation of spirit, which allowed many towns and families that had resisted his sovereignty to withdraw from the fight without shame. Thereafter the war became principally a struggle for the throne between, on the one side, the (Catholic) Bourbon king and, on the other, the (Catholic) Spanish king. In 1598, finally, hostilities ceased, Spain recognized Henri IV as France's king, Henri promulgated the Edict of Nantes, which granted full toleration to the Protestants of France, and Philip of Spain had the good grace to die of cancer.

Of all the princes involved in the French wars, only Philip could possibly be suspected of any great surfeit of principle. At least, he styled himself a defender of the Catholic faith against its enemies, Turk and heretic alike, and certainly invoked the cause of the church whenever he plausibly could. And yet it is hard not to notice that there was always a happy coincidence—if one followed Philip's arguments—between his interests and those of the church, even apparently when the pope did not recognize it. True, Philip sent armies to the Netherlands, but only because he was the ruler of the Netherlands and was seeking to suppress a rebellion; in 1576, the Protestant provinces of the northern Netherlands and the Catholic provinces of the south even entered into alliance (though the south soon made a separate peace with Spain). As for Philip's war with England, such as it was, few would be so foolish as to suggest that either side fought for religious reasons.

The last and worst of the "wars of religion" was, of course, the Thirty Years' War, which began in 1618 when King Ferdinand of Bohemia (1578–1637) attempted to consolidate his rule by enforcing Catholic uniformity in his dominions, and thereby provoked an uprising of Protestant houses in Bohemia and, in 1619, a Bohemian and Moravian invasion of Austria. Ferdinand—who in 1619 was made Holy Roman Emperor Ferdinand II—was a pious Catholic by all accounts, but in his campaign to retake Austria and Bohemia he certainly had no objection to the military assistance of the Lutheran elector of Saxony John George I (1585–1656). It is true that, during the first half of the wars that followed in Austria and the German states, there were distinct Catholic, Lutheran, and Calvinist parties, and that, when foreign Protestant powers—Denmark and Sweden, principally —entered the fray, they did so as enemies of the Habsburg Empire; but

Denmark and Sweden were actually at war with one another for much of the period, and the humiliating defeat of the former in 1645 was at the hands of the latter. More significantly, the wars in Germany were in time absorbed into the struggle between Bourbon France and Habsburg Spain. Indeed, the Swedish king Gustav II Adolf (1594–1632) was able to send troops into Germany in 1630 only because France's Cardinal Richelieu (1585–1642) provided such handsome subventions—an alliance, incidentally, encouraged and assisted by Pope Urban VIII. And, in 1635, France entered directly into the war on the side of the Protestant powers. There is nothing surprising in this, really, given both the pope's and Richelieu's desire to preserve their respective states against a resurgence of Habsburg power. Religious affiliations may have determined the tribal loyalties of some of the combatants in these wars, but the great struggle of the time was one between the old imperial order of the Habsburgs and the new "Europe of nations." For Habsburg emperors, the Roman Church was an indispensable instrument of state unity; for the papal state, the ideal situation was that of a united church and a fragmented empire; and for princes who sought to extend their own sovereignty, it was necessary either to sever ties to Rome through reformation or to reduce the Catholic Church to an office of state within their territories (in either case producing a subservient ecclesial establishment). Moreover, from the mid-fifteenth century on, the French monarchy had succeeded not only in subjugating the church upon its soil but in misappropriating the church's symbols to promote the idea of itself as a sacred monarchy.[3] It was in the French interest, therefore, both to preserve a Gallican Catholic establishment and to oppose the empire. Hence, from 1635 to 1648, the years of greatest devastation, the Thirty Years' War was principally a struggle between two Catholic houses: the Bourbons (along with their Protestant allies), who were champions of the new state absolutism, and the Habsburgs (along with their Catholic League allies), who were the defenders of the old imperial system. Alliances, that is to say, naturally followed lines of political interest, not confessional adherence.

None of which is to deny, again, that Catholics and Protestants often hated one another quite sincerely and ferociously, or that religious passion was a splendidly effective weapon when wielded adroitly by canny statesmen. But there is something inherently absurd in persistently speaking of these Habsburg wars and nationalist wars and wars of succession as "wars of religion," as though they were fought principally over matters of doctrine by parties whose chief concern was the propagation of one or another version of the "true faith," or as though it were obviously the case that, say, the rebellious German principalities sought independence from the empire because they were Protestant, rather than that they had become Protestant because they sought independence. The mercenary armies whose predatory brutality to the towns and villages of the German states was part of the special horror of the Thirty Years' War were scarcely motivated by disputes over papal primacy or transubstantiation.

There is, moreover, something extravagantly—even obscenely—absurd in the fiction that the new secular order of state supremacy rescued Europe from conflicts prompted by religious faith and thereby, at long last, brought peace to the Continent. The final adoption of the Peace of Westphalia, which ended the Thirty Years' War in 1648 by reaffirming the principles of Augsburg, was not a rational settlement to an irrational argument, imposed by the prudent hand of a benevolent political system; rather, Westphalia represented the victory of one side of the conflict, the very end for which many states had been fighting all along: its decisive confirmation of the rule of cuius regio, eius religio, and its grant to the empire's member principalities of independence in foreign affairs and affairs of state consigned the ideal of a united Christendom to the past and ushered in the new age of the nation-state. The empire was preserved formally for a time, but its power had been broken. The struggle for the future of Europe between the old imperialism and the new nationalism had been decided in the latter's favor, for better or worse. Thus Westphalia was not merely the end of the early wars of modern Europe: in a very real sense, it was their cause. In the words of Henri Daniel-Rops, "The Treaties of Westphalia finally sealed the relinquishment by statesman of a noble and ancient concept . . . which had dominated the Middle Ages: that there existed among the baptized people of Europe a bond stronger than all their motives for wrangling—a spiritual bond, the concept of Christendom. Since the fourteenth century, and especially during the fifteenth, this concept had been steadily disintegrating. . . . The Thirty Years' War proved beyond a shadow of a doubt that the last states to defend the ideal of a united Christian Europe were invoking the principle while in fact they aimed at maintaining or imposing their own supremacy."[4]

As for the "peace" upon which this Europe of nations rested, it was, to say the least, of a strangely sanguinary kind. The slow, convulsive, miserable, violent death of the Holy Roman Empire, both before and after Westphalia, belonged to the first phase of a new age of territorial and (ultimately) ideological wars, nationalist and (then) imperialist wars, wars prompted by commerce, politics, colonial interests, blood and soil, and (at the last) visions of the future of Europe and even of humanity: England's wars with the Netherlands, Spain, Portugal, and France, Sweden's wars with Poland, Russia, and Denmark, France's wars with Spain, the Netherlands, and the League of Augsburg; the war of the Spanish succession, the war of the Polish succession, the two Silesian wars of Austrian succession, the third Silesian war; revolutionary France's wars with Britain, Holland, and Spain, the wars of the First, Second, and Third Coalitions, and all the Napoleonic wars; the wars of Italian unification, the wars of German unification, the Franco-Prussian War; the first and second Balkan wars, the First World War, the Second World War . . . (to name just the most obvious examples). Never in European history had there been so many standing armies, or large armies on campaign, or so many men endowed with the power to send other men to kill and die.

Every age, obviously, has known wars and rumors of wars, and cruelty, injustice, oppression, murderous zeal, and murderous indifference; and men will obviously kill for any cause or for none. But, for the sheer scale of its violences, the modern period is quite unsurpassed. The Thirty Years' War, with its appalling toll of civilian casualties, was a scandal to the consciences of the nations of Europe; but midway through the twentieth century, Western society had become so inured to the idea of war as a total conflict between one entire people and another that even liberal democracies did not scruple to bomb open cities from the air, or to use incendiary or nuclear devices to incinerate tens of thousands of civilians, sometimes for only the vaguest of military objectives. Perhaps this is the price of "progress" or "liberation." From the late tenth through the mid-eleventh centuries, various church synods in France had instituted the convention called the "Peace of God," which used the threat of excommunication to prevent private wars and attacks upon women, peasants, merchants, clergy, and other noncombatants, and which required every house, high and low, to pledge itself to preserving the peace. Other synods, over the course of the eleventh century, instituted the "Truce of God," which forbade armed aggression on so many days of the year—penitential periods, feasts, fasts, harvests, from Wednesday evening to Monday morning, and so on—that ultimately more than three-quarters of the calendar consisted in periods of mandatory tranquility; in the twelfth century, the Truce's prohibitions became fixed in civil law. The reason such conventions could actually serve (even partially) to limit aggression is that they proceeded from a spiritual authority that no baptized person, however powerful or rapacious, could entirely ignore. And, while we might be disposed to think such things as the late medieval code of chivalry, or the church's teachings on just causes for and just conduct in war, or the church's bans upon the use of certain sorts of military machinery rather quaint and ineffectual, they did actually exercise—in the days when men and women still had souls to consider—a moral authority greater than the ambitions or sovereignty of any lord, monarch, or state. With the advent of modernity, however, and the collapse of Christian unity in the West, the last traces of that authority were effectively swept away. To compensate for the loss, devout Christian scholars of law, such as Francisco de Vitoria (c. 1483–1546), the Dominican champion of the cause of the New World Indians, and the Dutch Reformed jurist Hugo Grotius (1583–1645), laid the foundations for conventions of international law regarding "human rights" and justifiable warfare, derived from Christian traditions concerning natural law. But, of course, it was the sovereign state alone that determined to what extent those conventions would be adopted; they were grounded, after all, in theological tradition, and the "irrational" dictates of faith could no longer command assent. The special—indeed, unique—contribution of the newly emancipated secular order to the political constitution of Western society was of another kind altogether; it can be reduced to two thoroughly modern, thoroughly post-Christian, thoroughly "enlightened" principles: the absolute state—and total war.

CHAPTER NINE

An Age of Darkness

ONE COULD GO ON indefinitely, really, adducing one example after another of false or distorted history and then attempting to correct the record. But, in the great "struggle for the past," these engagements amount to mere local skirmishes, at the end of which we have accomplished little more than to confirm what we already knew: that men are rarely as good as we might hope, though not always as bad as we might fear, and that powerful institutions are as often as not gardens of ambition and injustice. It is far better, ultimately, to try to gain a perspective upon the whole: to attempt, that is, to see Christianity in itself, rather than in the fragmentary form of a series of apologetic refutations. More important, perhaps, there comes a point past which the effort to refute an accusation begins to legitimate the terms in which it has been made. It is not difficult, for instance, to demonstrate the absurdity of the claim that the rise of Christianity impeded the progress of science; but if one thereby seems to concede that scientific progress is an absolute value, upon which Christianity's "respectability" somehow depends, one grants far too much. To be honest, I would not be especially bothered if I thought the triumph of Christianity *had* in fact delayed the advance of some scientific achievements in the West. The value of the true influence of Christian convictions upon culture ought not to be calculated according to the modern ideology of "pure science," which has given us at once effective therapies for cancer, atomic weaponry, astrophysics, and new varieties of neural toxins; for this ideology, I think it safe to assert, is morally rather ambiguous. That Christendom fostered rather than hindered the development of early modern science, and that modern empiricism was born not in the so-called Age of Enlightenment but during the late Middle Ages, are simple facts of history, which I record in response to certain popular legends, but not in order somehow to "justify" Christianity. And I would say very much the same thing in regard to any of the other distinctly modern presuppositions—political, ethical, economic, or cultural—by which we now live. My purpose in these pages is not (I must emphasize) to argue that Christianity is essentially a "benign" historical phenomenon that need not be feared because it is "compatible with" or was the necessary "preparation for" the modern world and its most cherished values. Christianity has been the single most creative cultural, ethical, aesthetic, social, political, or spiritual force in the history of the West, to be sure; but it has also been a profoundly destructive force; and one should perhaps praise it as much for the latter attribute as for the former, for there are many things worthy of destruction.

Naturally, a Christian should wish that the first Christian emperor had not been a violent, puritanical, ponderous, late Roman brute like Constantine, or that all his successors had been men of exemplary holiness, or that ancient, medieval, or modern Christians had never betrayed the law of Christian mercy. But that same Christian need not therefore yield to excessive sentimentality over empty pagan temples or vanished cults. We may be prone—commendably—to lament the loss of fascinating artifacts, barbaric or beautiful, and the disappearance of exotic or dignified rituals. We can all share the disdain of the pagan rhetorician Libanius (c. 314–c. 394) for the roving gangs of Egyptian and Syrian "monks" who, in the late fourth century, lived off the temples they despoiled and the pagans they robbed. And I, for one, wish the Serapeum had been preserved (even if Serapis himself was a somewhat grotesque and factitious hybrid of gods with more respectable pedigrees). But, when considering the passing of the old cults, we should make some attempt to understand the social and religious realities of late antiquity, and to remember that, however passionately we today may believe in the sanctity of ornament and in the inviolability of "local charm," to the Christians and pagans of the time something more was at stake. Simply said, it was time for the gods of that age to withdraw: for too long they had served as the terrible and beautiful guardians of an order of majestic cruelty and pitiless power; for too long they not only had received oblations and bestowed blessings but had presided over and consecrated an empire of crucifixions and gladiatorial spectacle and martial terror. The real reproach that should be brought against the victorious church is not that it drove out the old gods but that it did not succeed in driving them or their ways sufficiently far off.

Above all, I am anxious to grant no credence whatsoever to the special mythology of "the Enlightenment." Nothing strikes me as more tiresomely vapid than the notion that there is some sort of inherent opposition—or impermeable partition—between faith and reason, or that the modern period is marked by its unique devotion to the latter. One can believe that faith is mere credulous assent to unfounded premises, while reason consists in a pure obedience to empirical fact, only if one is largely ignorant of both. It should be enough, perhaps, to point to the long Christian philosophical tradition, with all its variety, creativity, and sophistication, and to the long and honorable tradition of Christianity's critical examination and reexamination of its own historical, spiritual, and metaphysical claims. But more important in some ways, it seems to me, is to stress how great an element of faith is present in the operations of even the most disinterested rationality. All reasoning presumes premises or intuitions or ultimate convictions that cannot be proved by any foundations or facts more basic than themselves, and hence there are irreducible convictions present wherever one attempts to apply logic to experience. One always operates within boundaries established by one's first principles, and asks only the questions that those principles permit. A Christian and a confirmed materialist may both believe that there really is a rationally ordered world out there that is susceptible of empirical analysis; but why they should believe this to be the case is determined by their distinctive visions of the world, by their personal experiences of reality, and by patterns of intellectual allegiance that are, properly speaking, primordial to their thinking, and that lead toward radically different ultimate conclusions (though the more proximate conclusions reached through their research may be identical). What distinguishes modernity from the age of Christendom is not that the former is more devoted to rationality than was the latter but that its rationality serves different primary commitments (some of which—"blood and soil," the "master race," the "socialist Utopia"—produce prodigies of evil precisely to the degree that they are "rationally" pursued). We may, obviously, as modern men and women, find certain of the fundamental convictions that our ancestors harbored curious and irrational; but this is not because we are somehow more advanced in our thinking than they were, even if we are aware of a greater number of scientific facts. We have simply adopted different conventions of thought and absorbed different prejudices, and so we interpret our experiences according to another set of basic beliefs—beliefs that may, for all we know, blind us to entire dimensions of reality.

Certainly we moderns should not be too quick to congratulate ourselves, or to imagine ourselves as having embraced a more rational approach to the world, simply because we are less prone than were ancient persons to believe in miracles, or demons, or other supernatural agencies. We have no real rational warrant for deploring the "credulity" of the peoples of previous centuries toward the common basic assumptions of their times while implicitly celebrating ourselves for our own largely uncritical obedience to the common basic assumptions of our own. Anyway, even in modern Western society a great many of us apparently find it sublimely easy to revert to the perspective of "primitive" peoples on these matters; and there are still today entire cultures that—on irreproachably rational grounds—find the prevailing prejudices of Western modernity almost comically absurd. I know three African priests—one Ugandan and two Nigerian—who are immensely educated and sophisticated scholars (linguists, philosophers, and historians all) and who are also unshakably convinced that miracles, magic, and spiritual warfare are manifestly real aspects of daily life, of which they themselves have had direct and incontrovertible experience on a number of occasions. All three are, of course, creatures of their cultures, no less than we are of ours; but I am not disposed to believe that their cultures are somehow more primitive or unreasoning than ours. It is true they come from nations that enjoy nothing like our economic and technological advantages; but, since these advantages are as likely to distract us from reality as to grant us any special insight into it, that fact scarcely rises to the level of irrelevance. Truth be told, there is no remotely plausible reason—apart from a preference for our own presuppositions over those of other peoples—why the convictions and experiences of an African polyglot and philosopher, whose pastoral and social labors oblige him to be engaged immediately in the concrete realities of hundreds of lives, should command less rational assent from us than the small, unproven, doctrinaire certitudes of persons who spend their lives in supermarkets and before television screens and immured in the sterile, hallucinatory seclusion of their private studies.

There is, after all, nothing inherently reasonable in the conviction that all of reality is simply an accidental confluence of physical causes, without any transcendent source or end. Materialism is not a fact of experience or a deduction of logic; it is a metaphysical prejudice, nothing more, and one that is arguably more irrational than almost any other. In general, the unalterably convinced materialist is a kind of childishly complacent fundamentalist, so fervently, unreflectively, and rapturously committed to the materialist vision of reality that if he or she should encounter any problem—logical or experiential—that might call its premises into question, or even merely encounter a limit beyond which those premises lose their explanatory power, he or she is simply unable to recognize it. Richard Dawkins is a perfect example; he does not hesitate, for instance, to claim that "natural selection is the ultimate explanation for our existence."[1] But this is a silly assertion and merely reveals that Dawkins does not understand the words he is using. The question of *existence* does not concern how it is that the present arrangement of the world came about, from causes already internal to the world, but how it is that anything (including any cause) can exist at all. This question Darwin and Wallace never addressed, nor were ever so hopelessly confused as to think they had. It is a question that no theoretical or experimental science could ever answer, for it is qualitatively different from the kind of questions that the physical sciences are competent to address. Even if theoretical physics should one day discover the most basic laws upon which the fabric of space and time is woven, or evolutionary biology the most elementary phylogenic forms of terrestrial life, or palaeontology an utterly seamless genealogy of every species, still we shall not have thereby drawn one inch nearer to a solution of the mystery of existence. No matter how fundamental or simple the level reached by the scientist—protoplasm, amino acids, molecules, subatomic particles, quantum events, unified physical laws, a primordial singularity, mere logical possibilities—existence is something else altogether. Even the simplest of things, and even the most basic of principles, must first of all *be,* and nothing within the universe of contingent things (nor even the universe itself, even if it were somehow "eternal") can be intelligibly conceived of as the source or explanation of its own being.

Many philosophers, admittedly, in both the Continental tradition and the Anglo-American analytic tradition have argued otherwise, seeking to conjure away the question of being, as something lying beyond rational scrutiny, or as an illusion generated by language, or as an improper understanding of what "being" is. But none has ever succeeded at overcoming the perplexity that the enigma of our existence occasions in us, in those moments of wonder that we all from time to time experience and that are (according to Plato and Aristotle) the beginning of all true philosophy. In the terms of Thomas Aquinas, a finite thing's essence (*what* it is) entirely fails to account for its existence (*that* it is); and there is a very venerable and coherent Christian tradition of reflection that holds that this failure, when considered with adequate rigor, points toward an infinite and infinitely simple actuality transcendent of all material, composite, or finite causes and contingencies, a "subsistent act of being" (to use one of Aquinas's most entrancing names for God), in whom essence and existence are identical. This, obviously, is not the place to argue such matters; it is enough simply to remark that reason leads different minds to disparate and even contradictory conclusions. One can, I imagine, consider the nature of reality with genuine probity and conclude that the material order is all that is. One can also, however, and with perhaps better logic, conclude that materialism is a grossly incoherent superstition; that the strict materialist is something of a benighted and pitiable savage, blinded by an irrational commitment to a logically impossible position; and that every "primitive" who looks at the world about him and wonders what god made it is a profounder thinker than the convinced atheist who would dismiss such a question as infantile. One might even conclude, in fact, that one of the real differences between what convention calls the Age of Faith and the Age of Reason is actually the difference between a cogent intellectual and moral culture, capable of considering the mystery of being with some degree of rigor, and a confined and vapid dogmatism without genuine logical foundation. Reason is a fickle thing.

All of this, however, is really of only secondary importance. The modern period has never been especially devoted to reason as such; the notion that it ever was is merely one of its "originary" myths. The true essence of modernity is a particular conception of what it is to be free, as I have said; and the Enlightenment language of an "age of reason" was always really just a way of placing a frame around that idea of freedom, so as to portray it as the rational autonomy and moral independence that lay beyond the intellectual infancy of "irrational" belief. But we are anything but rationalists now, so we no longer need cling to the pretense that reason was ever our paramount concern; we are today more likely to be committed to "my truth" than to any notion of truth in general, no matter where that might lead. The myth of "enlightenment" served well to liberate us from any antique notions of divine or natural law that might place unwelcome constraints upon our wills; but it has discharged its part and lingers on now only as a kind of habit of rhetoric. And now that the rationalist moment has largely passed, the modern faith in human liberation has become, if anything, more robust and more militant. Freedom for us today is something transcendent even of reason, and we no longer really feel that we must justify our liberties by recourse to some prior standard of responsible rationality. Freedom—conceived as the perfect, unconstrained spontaneity of individual will—is its own justification, its own highest standard, its own unquestionable truth. It is true, admittedly, that the modern understanding of freedom was for a time still bound to some concept of nature: many Enlightenment and Romantic narratives of human liberation concerned the rescue of an aboriginal human essence from the laws, creeds, customs, and institutions that suppressed it. Ultimately, though, even the idea of an invariable human nature came to seem something arbitrary and extrinsic, an intolerable limitation imposed upon a still more original, inward, pure, and indeterminate freedom of the will. We no longer seek so much to liberate human nature from the bondage of social convention as to liberate the individual from all conventions, especially those regarding what is natural.

There is, of course, no obvious reason why we should not choose to conceive of freedom in ways unknown to our distant ancestors; but it is wise to be cognizant of the fact. It is, at the very least, instructive to realize that our freedom might just as well be seen—from certain more antique perspectives—as a kind of slavery: to untutored impulses, to empty caprice, to triviality, to dehumanizing values. And it can do no harm occasionally to ask where a concept of freedom whose horizon is precisely and necessarily nothing—a concept that is, as I have said, nihilist in the most exact sense—ultimately leads. This is not a question, I would add, simply for the conservative moralist, pining nostalgically for some vanished epoch of decency or standards, but a question that should concern anyone with any consciousness of history. Part of the enthralling promise of an age of reason was, at least at first, the prospect of a genuinely rational ethics, not bound to the local or tribal customs of this people or that, not limited to the moral precepts of any particular creed, but available to all reasoning minds regardless of culture and—when recognized—immediately compelling to the rational will. Was there ever a more desperate fantasy than this? We live now in the wake of the most monstrously violent century in human history, during which the secular order (on both the political right and the political left), freed from the authority of religion, showed itself willing to kill on an unprecedented scale and with an ease of conscience worse than merely depraved. If ever an age deserved to be thought an age of darkness, it is surely ours. One might almost be tempted to conclude that secular government is the one form of government that has shown itself too violent, capricious, and unprincipled to be trusted.

It is, at the very least, no longer possible to believe, in naive Enlightenment fashion, that moral truth is something upon which all reasonable persons can agree, or that it is something that, in being grasped, exercises an irresistible appeal upon the will; nor is it possible any longer to deceive ourselves that humanity free from religious authority must inevitably advance toward higher expressions of life rather than retreat into pettiness or cruelty or barbarism. Either human reason reflects an objective order of divine truth, which awakens the will to its deepest purposes and commands its assent, or reason is merely the instrument and servant of the will, which is under no ultimate obligation to choose the path of mercy, or of "rational self-interest," or of sympathy, or of peace. When Nietzsche—the most prescient philosopher of nihilism—pondered the possibilities that had opened up for Western humanity in the age of unbelief, the grimmest future he could imagine was a world dominated by the "Last Men," a race of empty and self-adoring narcissists sunk in banality, complacency, conformity, cynicism, and self-admiration. For him, the gravest danger confronting a nihilist culture was the absence of any great aspirations that could prompt humanity to glorious works and grand achievements and mighty deeds. There is much to be said for Nietzsche's prophetic gifts, certainly: contemporary culture does after all seem so to excel at depressing mediocrity and comfortable conventionality, egoistic preciosity and mass idiocy. But, honestly, Nietzsche's fears seem almost quaint now, given how much more nihilistic we know a truly earnest nihilism can be. Christian society certainly never fully purged itself of cruelty or violence; but it also never incubated evils comparable in ambition, range, systematic precision, or mercilessness to death camps, gulags, forced famines, or the extravagant brutality of modern warfare. Looking back at the twentieth century, it is difficult not to conclude that the rise of modernity has resulted in an age of at once unparalleled banality and unprecedented monstrosity, and that these are two sides of the same cultural reality.

And why should this not be so? If the quintessential myth of modernity is that true freedom is the power of the will over nature—human or cosmic—and that we are at liberty to make ourselves what we wish to be, then it is not necessarily the case that the will of the individual should be privileged over the "will of the species." If there is no determinate human nature or divine standard to which the uses of freedom are bound, it is perfectly logical that some should think it a noble calling to shape the fictile clay of humankind into something stronger, better, more rational, more efficient, more perfect. The ambition to refashion humanity in its very essence—social, political, economic, moral, psychological—was inconceivable when human beings were regarded as creatures of God. But with the disappearance of the transcendent, and of its lure, and of its authority, it becomes possible to *will* a human future conformed to whatever ideals we choose to embrace. This is why it is correct to say that the sheer ruthlessness of so much of post-Christian social idealism in some sense arises from the very same concept of freedom that lies at the heart of our most precious modern values. The savagery of triumphant Jacobinism, the clinical heartlessness of classical socialist eugenics, the Nazi movement, Stalinism—all the grand utopian projects of the modern age that have directly or indirectly spilled such oceans of human blood—are no less results of the Enlightenment myth of liberation than are the liberal democratic state or the vulgarity of late capitalist consumerism or the pettiness of bourgeois individualism. The most pitilessly and self-righteously violent regimes of modern history—in the West or in those other quarters of the world contaminated by our worst ideas—have been those that have most explicitly cast off the Christian vision of reality and sought to replace it with a more "human" set of values. No cause in history—no religion or imperial ambition or military adventure—has destroyed more lives with more confident enthusiasm than the cause of the "brotherhood of man," the postreligious utopia, or the progress of the race. To fail to acknowledge this would be to mock the memory of all those millions that have perished before the advance of secular reason in its most extreme manifestations. And all the astonishing violence of the modern age—from the earliest European wars of the emergent nation-state onward—is no less proper an expression (and measure) of the modern story of human freedom than are the various political and social movements that have produced the modern West's special combination of general liberty, material abundance, cultural mediocrity, and spiritual poverty. To fail to acknowledge *this* would be to close our eyes to the possibilities for evil that have been opened up in our history by the values we most dearly prize and by the "truths" we most fervently adore. To these matters, though, I shall return in the third part of this book.

Now, though, I want to retreat from the present to the dawn of Christian civilization, in order to consider the sort of freedom the church proclaimed when it first entered the world of late antiquity, and to consider as well the world that was born from that proclamation. It is my governing conviction, in all that follows, that much of modernity should be understood not as a grand revolt against the tyranny of faith, not as a movement of human liberation and progress, but as a counterrevolution, a reactionary rejection of a freedom which it no longer understands, but upon which it remains parasitic. Even when modern persons turn away from Christian conviction, there are any number of paths that have been irrevocably closed to them—either because they lead toward philosophical positions that Christianity has assumed successfully into its own story, or because they lead toward forms of "superstition" that Christianity has rendered utterly incredible to modern minds. A post-Christian unbeliever is still, most definitely, for good or for ill, post-*Christian*. We live in a world transformed by an ancient revolution—social, intellectual, metaphysical, moral, spiritual—the immensity of which we often only barely grasp. And it is this revolution (perhaps the only true revolution in the history of the West) to which I want now to turn.

CHAPTER TEN

The Great Rebellion

WE ARE FAR REMOVED from the days when one's baptism could be said to be the most momentous event—and perhaps the most dramatic, terrifying, and joyous experience—of one's life. Most Christians today, at least in the developed world, are baptized in infancy; and even those whose traditions delay the rite until adulthood are, for the most part, children of Christian families and have grown up in the faith, and so their baptisms merely seal and affirm the lives they have always lived. This was obviously not the case, however, for most of the Christians of the earliest centuries; for them, baptism was of an altogether more radical nature. It was understood as nothing less than a total transformation of the person who submitted to it; and as a ritual event, it was certainly understood as being far more than a mere dramaturgical allegory of one's choice of religious association. To become a Christian was to renounce a very great deal of what one had known and been to that point, in order to be joined to a new reality, the demands of which were absolute; it was to depart from one world, with an irrevocable finality, and to enter another.

A convert to Christianity from paganism somewhere in, say, the greater Byzantine world, within the first few decades after the Edict of Milan, would not in most circumstances have been granted immediate entry into the community of the faith. Catechetical and liturgical customs varied greatly from place to place, but certain aspects of Christian baptism were very nearly universal. In general, if one sought to be received into the church, one had first to become a catechumen, a student of the church's teachings, and during the period of one's catechumenate one participated only imperfectly in the life of the community; not only did one not yet enjoy access to the "mysteries" (that is, the sacraments), but one might typically be required to depart from the congregation on Sundays after the liturgy of the word, before the Eucharist was celebrated. And one could remain in this liminal state, in many cases, for years, receiving instruction, submitting to moral scrutiny, learning to discipline one's will, and gradually becoming accustomed to the practice of the Christian life. Whether brief or protracted, however, the period of one's preparation for baptism could not conclude until one had been taught the story of redemption: how once all men and women had labored as slaves in the household of death, prisoners of the devil, sold into bondage to Hades, languishing in ignorance of their true home; and how Christ had come to set the prisoners free and had, by his death and resurrection, invaded the kingdom of our captor and overthrown it, vanquishing the power of sin and death in us, shattering the gates of hell, and plundering the devil of his captives. For it was into this story that one's own life was to be merged when one at last sank down into the "life-giving waters": in the risen Christ, a new humanity had been created, free from the rule of death, into which one could be admitted by dying and rising again with Christ in baptism and by feeding upon his presence in the Eucharist.

Ideally—again, making allowances for variations in local customs and for the unpredictability of particular circumstances—one's baptism would come on Easter eve, during the midnight vigil. At the appointed hour, the baptizand (the person to be baptized) would depart the church for the baptistery, which typically housed a large baptismal pool or (if possible) flowing stream. There, in the semidarkness of that place, he or she would disrobe and—amid a host of blessings, exhortations, unctions, and prayers—descend naked into the waters, to be immersed three times by the bishop, in the name first of the Father, then of the Son, and finally of the Holy Spirit. The newly baptized Christian would then emerge from the waters to be anointed with the oil of chrismation, the seal of the Holy Spirit, and to don a new garment of white, and would return to the church to see the Eucharist celebrated—and to partake of it—for the first time. On that night, the erstwhile catechumen would have died to his or her old life and received a new and better life in Christ.[1] Perhaps the most crucial feature of the rite, however—at least, for understanding what baptism meant for the convert from paganism—occurred before the catechumen's descent into the font: at the bishop's direction, he or she would turn to face the west (the land of evening, and so symbolically the realm of all darkness, cosmic and spiritual), submit to a rather forcibly phrased exorcism, and then clearly renounce—indeed, revile and, quite literally, spit at—the devil and the devil's ministers. Then he or she would turn to face the east (the land of morning and of light) to confess total faith in, and promise complete allegiance to, Christ. This was by no means mere ritual spectacle; it was an actual and, so to speak, legally binding transference of fealty from one master to another. Even the physical posture and attitude of the baptizand was charged with a palpable quality of irreverent boldness: pagan temples were as a rule designed with their entrances to the east and their altars at their western ends, while the arrangement of Christian churches was exactly the reverse. In thus turning one's back upon, rejecting, and abusing the devil, one was also repudiating the gods to whose service one had hitherto been indentured, and was doing so with a kind of triumphant contempt; in confessing Christ, one was entrusting oneself to the invincible conqueror who had defeated death, despoiled hell of its hostages, subdued the "powers of the air," and been raised up the Lord of history.

We today are probably somewhat prone to forget that, though the early Christians did indeed regard the gods of the pagan order as false gods, they did not necessarily understand this to mean simply that these gods were unreal; they understood it to mean that the gods were deceivers. Behind the pieties of the pagan world, Christians believed, lurked forces of great cruelty and guile: demons, malign elemental spirits, occult agencies masquerading as divinities, exploiting the human yearning for God, and working to thwart the designs of God, in order to bind humanity in slavery to darkness, ignorance, and death. And to renounce one's bonds to these beings was an act of cosmic rebellion, a declaration that one had been emancipated from (in the language of John's Gospel) "the prince of this world" or (in the somewhat more disturbing language of 2 Corinthians) "the god of this world." In its fallen state, the cosmos lies under the reign of evil (1 John 5:19), but Christ came to save the world, to lead "captivity captive" (Ephesians 4:8), and to overthrow the empire of those "thrones, dominions, principalities, and powers" (Colossians 1:16, 1 Corinthians 2:8, Ephesians 1:21, 3:10) and "rulers on high" (Ephesians 6:12) that have imprisoned creation in corruption and evil. Again, given the perspective of our age, we can scarcely avoid reading such language as mythological, thus reducing its import from cosmic to more personal or political dimensions. In so doing, however, we fail to grasp the scandal and the exhilaration of early Christianity. These thrones and powers and principalities and so forth were not merely earthly princes or empires (though princes and empires served their ends); much less were they vague abstractions; they were, according to Jewish Apocalyptic tradition, the angelic governors of the nations, the celestial "archons," the often mutinous legions of the air, who—though they might be worshipped as gods, and might in themselves be both mighty and dreadful—were only creatures of the one true God. It was from the tyranny of these powers on high that Christ had come to set creation free. And so the life of faith was, for the early church, before all else, spiritual warfare, waged between the Kingdom of God and the kingdom of this fallen world, and every Christian on the day of his or her baptism had been conscripted into that struggle, on the side of Christ. From that point on, he or she was both a subject of and a co-heir to a "Kingdom not of this world," and henceforth no more than a resident alien in the "earthly city."

However greatly tempted we may be to view beliefs of this sort as either touchingly quaint or savagely superstitious (depending on the degree to which we deceive ourselves that our vision of reality surpasses all others in sanity), we should recall that, in late antiquity, practically no one doubted that there was a sacral order to the world, or that the social, the political, the cosmic, and the religious realms of human existence were always inextricably involved with one another. Every state was also a cult, or a plurality of cults; society was a religious dispensation; the celestial and political orders belonged to a single continuum; and one's allegiance to one's gods was also one's loyalty to one's nation, people, masters, and monarchs. One could even say (to indulge in a very large generalization) that this was the sacred premise of the whole of Indo-European paganism: that the universe is an elaborate and complex regime, a hierarchy of power and eminence, atop which stood the Great God, and below whom, in a descending scale, stood a variety of subordinate orders, each holding a place dictated by divine necessity and fulfilling a cosmic function—greater and lesser gods and daemons, kings and nobles, priests and prophets, and so on, all the way down to slaves. This order, moreover, though it was at once both divine and natural, was also in some ultimate sense precariously poised and strangely fragile. It had to be sustained by prayers, sacrifices, laws, pieties, and coercions, and had to be defended at all times against the forces of chaos that threatened it from every side, whether spiritual, social, political, erotic, or philosophical. For cosmic, political, and spiritual order was all one thing, continuous and organic, and its authority was absolute.

In such a world, the gospel was an outrage, and it was perfectly reasonable for its cultured despisers to describe its apostles as "atheists." Christians were—what could be more obvious?—enemies of society, impious, subversive, and irrational; and it was no more than civic prudence to detest them for refusing to honor the gods of their ancestors, for scorning the common good, and for advancing the grotesque and shameful claim that all gods and spirits had been made subject to a crucified criminal from Galilee—one who during his life had consorted with peasants and harlots, lepers and lunatics.[2] This was far worse than mere irreverence; it was pure and misanthropic perversity; it was anarchy. One can see something of this alarm in the fragments we still possess of *On True Doctrine* by the second-century pagan Celsus (preserved in Origen's treatise *Against Celsus*, written many decades later). It is unlikely that Celsus would have thought the Christians worth his notice had he not recognized something uniquely dangerous lurking in their gospel of love and peace. He would have naturally viewed the new religion with a certain patrician disdain, undoubtedly, and his treatise contains a considerable quantity of contempt for the ridiculous rabble and pliable simpletons that Christianity attracted into its fold: the lowborn and uneducated, slaves, women and children, cobblers, laundresses, weavers of wool, and so forth. But, at that level, Christianity would have been no more distasteful to Celsus than any of those other Asiatic superstitions that occasionally coursed through the empire, working mischief in every social class, and provoking a largely impotent consternation from the educated and well bred. It would hardly have merited the energetic attack he actually wrote.

What clearly and genuinely horrified Celsus about this particular superstition was not its predictable vulgarity but the novel spirit of rebellion that permeated its teachings. He continually speaks of Christianity as a form of sedition or rebellion, and what he principally condemns is its defiance of the immemorial religious customs of the world's tribes, cities, and nations. The several peoples of the earth, he believed, were governed by various gods who acted as lieutenants of the Great God, and the laws and customs they had established in every place were part of the divine constitution of the universe, which no one, high born or low, should presume to disregard or abandon. It was appalling to him that Christians, feeling no decent reverence for these ancient ordinances and institutions, should refrain from worship of the gods, should decline to venerate the good daemons who served as intermediaries between the human and divine worlds, and should even refuse to pray to these ancient powers for the emperor. These Christians were so depraved as to think themselves actually *above* the temples and traditions and cults of their ancestors; they even—ludicrously enough—imagined themselves somehow to have been raised above the deathless emissaries of God, the divine stars and all the other celestial agencies, and to have been granted a kind of immediate intimacy with God himself. And in thus claiming emancipation from the principalities and powers, the thrones and dominions, they had also renounced their spiritual and moral ties to their peoples and to the greater cosmic order. To Celsus, this was all too clearly an unnatural and deracinated piety, something unprecedented and even somewhat monstrous, a religion like no other, which—rather than providing a sacred bond between the believer and his nation—sought to transcend nations altogether.

And, of course, he was entirely correct. The Christians were indeed a separate people, or at least aspired to be: another nation within each nation (as Origen liked to say), a new humanity that (according to Justin Martyr) had learned no longer to despise those of other races but rather to live with them as brothers and sisters. The church—governed by its own laws, acknowledging no rival allegiances—aimed at becoming a universal people, a universal race, more universal than any empire of gods or men, and subject only to Christ. No creed could have been more subversive of the ancient wisdom of the world, and no movement more worthy of the hatred of those for whom that wisdom was the truth of the ages.[3]

One of the more diverting ironies of contemporary anti-Christian polemic is the recrudescence of this same line of critique—or, rather, the development of something very similar, though with a more modern inflection. Today, obviously, it is not the "seditiousness" of the gospel that offends us (we are scarcely conscious of it), much less its "vulgarity" (which for us is a word almost devoid of any connotation of disapproval), but its "intolerance." At least, in certain circles, this has become a favorite complaint. It is, needless to say, a charge redolent of certain distinctly modern concerns. The early Christians rarely would have had the leisure to think in such terms, even had those terms been intelligible to them. As theirs was for centuries the weaker position within society, they tended to think of the faiths of their ancestors not simply as rival creeds but as a tyranny from which they had escaped. They understood their rejection of all gods but their own as the very charter of their spiritual freedom, their writ of emancipation from the malign cosmic principalities that enslaved the nations. To judge from some of the recent popular literature on the topic, however, there are some who view this attitude on the part of the early Christians not only as unreasonable, nor only as a little wicked, but as Christianity's principal and most damning fault.

This is not, strictly speaking, an entirely new line of attack. It was Gibbon who first ventured it, by proposing a general opposition between monotheist bigotry and polytheist magnanimity—between, that is, the inflexible spirit of intolerance supposedly typical of faith in the One God and the allegedly more hospitable and eclectic openness of religions that expect their gods to come in a variety of forms and in indefinite quantities: "The devout polytheist, though fondly attached to his national rites, admitted with implicit faith the different religions of the earth . . . nor could the Roman who deprecated the wrath of the Tiber, deride the Egyptian who presented his offering to the beneficent genius of the Nile. . . . Such was the mild spirit of antiquity, that the nations were less attentive to the difference than to the resemblance of their religious worship."[4] This is a positively charming portrait of antique piety, without doubt. Certainly one must feel that, by contrast, a spirit far bitterer and more severe had taken possession of the Roman world by the time that the Christian emperor Gratian (359–383) decided to impose Nicene Christianity upon the empire, to withhold state patronage from all other cults, and to remove the altar of the goddess Victory from the Senate. And one can hardly fail to be moved by the words of the "noble pagan" Symmachus (c. 345–402), who—in arguing for that same altar's restoration—admonished his hearers not to care "by which road each man pursues the truth," because "so great a mystery" cannot be reached by one approach alone. In fact, one cannot deny that Christianity entered the ancient world as a faith strangely incapable of alloy with other creeds, a characteristic it shared with the Judaism from which it sprang. Though the Christianity of the first several centuries was merely one among many mystery religions—that is, cults involving rites of initiation and regeneration, sacramental meals, promises of personal enlightenment or salvation, myths of mystical death and rebirth, and so on—it differed from all other devotions in requiring of its adherents a loyalty not only devout but exclusive. The votaries of Dionysus, Cybele and Attis, Isis and Osiris, Sabazius, Mithras, or any of the other pagan savior deities were not obliged to derogate or deny the power or holiness of other gods, or to remain totally aloof from their rites or temples; they merely acquired a new, perhaps dominant, but in no sense solitary god or goddess to adore. Only the Christian mystery demanded of the convert an absolute commitment to one God and a denial of all others. All of this is true. Even so, the notion that with the triumph of the church a relaxed and expansive polytheism was overthrown by a pitilessly narrow monotheism is simply false; more to the point, it is a complete confusion of categories.

To begin with, to attribute "pluralistic values" to a culture that had neither any concept of pluralism nor any commitment to "diversity" or to freedom of worship is simply anachronistic. The polytheism of the Roman Empire may have had enormous patience for a remarkable diversity of *cults*, but it certainly had none for any great diversity of *religions*. This may seem an overly subtle distinction, but it is in fact one so elementary that unless it is taken into account nothing of importance can be said of the relations between pagan and early Christian culture. The larger Indo-European and Near Eastern pagan world was often quite welcoming, within reason, of new gods—one could never really have too many—but only so long as those gods were recognizably inhabitants of a familiar mythic and religious universe, who could be integrated into a variegated and ramifying network of licit devotions without any turmoil. In this sense, and in this sense only, was the greater Roman world religiously "tolerant": it was tolerant of creeds that were simply different expressions of its own religious temper and that were, in consequence, easily absorbed. It was tolerant, that is to say, of what it found tolerable. When, however, it encountered beliefs and practices contrary to its own pieties, alien to its own religious sensibilities, or apparently subversive of its own sacral premises, it could respond with extravagant violence.

This was true even in cases of other pagan devotions that seemed dangerously or perversely exotic. A perfect example, already mentioned above, would be the reaction of the staid and pious Romans of 186 B.C. to the appearance of the Bacchanalia in Etruria, and the harsh measures they undertook to suppress it (for, as the consul Postumius reminded his fellow Romans, only the gods of Rome were true gods). And this was anything but an aberration. The Roman Senate often, before and well into the imperial age, undertook to drive foreign cults out of the city, or out of Italy altogether, by destroying their temples, forbidding their rites, and even—if necessary—deporting or executing their adherents. The attempts made to expel the cult of Isis from Rome, from the middle of the first century B.C. through the reign of Tiberius, involved not only state coercion but a good deal of interreligious strife as well (the worshippers of Cybele being especially hostile to this Nilotic parvenue). Atheism, moreover, was always something abhorrent to good god-fearing polytheists, and in certain times and places was even a capital offense (in the tenth book of Plato's *Laws*, if one is interested, quite a thorough case is made for imprisoning and, if necessary, executing those who deny the gods). When, moreover, polytheistic culture came into contact with the Jews—a people intransigent in their religious particularity, who refused either to have their God numbered among the gods of other peoples or to submit to the invasion of their devotions by foreign deities—pagan "tolerance" occasionally dissolved with alarming abruptness. And even worse than Jewish "particularism," with its obstinate insistence upon creedal and ritual purity, was Christian "universalism," with its promiscuous indifference to local customs and cultic loyalties.

The very notion that polytheism is inherently more tolerant of religious differences than is "monotheism" is, as a historical claim, utterly incredible. Proof to the contrary, in fact, is so plentiful that any selection of particular examples is necessarily somewhat arbitrary. Even if one confines oneself, just for the sake of convenience, to the ancient societies from and within which Christianity arose, one suffers an embarrassment of riches. There was, for example, the reign of the Seleucid emperor Antiochus IV Epiphanes (c. 215–164 B.C.) and his monstrously brutal murders of devout Jews who resisted his desecration of their faith—recounted in rather unpleasant detail in the books of the Maccabees. Or one might mention the unrest in Alexandria in A.D. 38, when pagan mobs installed idols of the "divine" Caligula in the city's synagogues, Jews were stripped of their municipal citizenship and forced to retreat into a sequestered quarter of the city, hundreds of Jewish homes were destroyed, and Jews who ventured out of their ghetto were murdered or beaten in the streets. Or—not to disdain the obvious—one might just want to mention the persecutions of Christians under various Roman emperors. These last were certainly inspired by more than mere political pragmatism; they were expressions of a great deal of pagan religious sentiment, and were often prompted by unambiguously religious motives. In Alexandria, for instance, late in 248 or early in 249, before the imperial edicts of late 249 that inaugurated the Decian persecutions, there was an eruption of violence against the city's Christians apparently initiated by a pagan "prophet." And the last and most savage of the imperial persecutions were instigated, at least in part, by the words of a god: Diocletian, so the story goes, was told by the prophet of Apollo in Didyma that the great number of "the Just in the earth"—meaning the empire's Christians—had made it difficult to obtain the god's oracles, which convinced the emperor to issue a series of decrees for the spiritual purification of his dominions. One could go on, but suffice it to say that large generalizations about the relative "tolerance" of monotheism and polytheism are best avoided. At different times and in different places, Jews and pagans persecuted Christians, pagans persecuted Christians and Jews, and Christians persecuted Jews and pagans; in fact, pagans persecuted other pagans, Jews other Jews, and Christians other Christians (and, of course, in the modern period certain atheists proved themselves by far the most ambitious, murderous, and prolific persecutors of all—but that is neither here nor there).

In another sense, though, the critics are right: in many notable respects, pagan religious culture was immeasurably more "tolerant" than Christianity ever was—indeed, it could tolerate just about anything. Admittedly, many of the more spectacular depravities of pagan cult, such as human sacrifice, were actively discouraged by Rome wherever it encountered them, whether in northern Europe, Asia Minor, North Africa, Gaul, or even Italy. As early as 97 B.C., in fact, the Senate had made such sacrifices a crime. But ancient traditions do not vanish easily; as late as the time of the emperor Hadrian (A.D. 76–138) it was still necessary to pass laws forbidding the oblation of human victims, in order to suppress certain local festal customs (such as, perhaps, the yearly immolation of a single man to the Cyprian Jupiter at Salamis). In a larger sense, though, human sacrifice of a sort—or, at any rate, its logic—was never entirely absent from Roman religious culture. Whether or not one should credit dubious tales of human lives offered up to the gods, on very special occasions, by emperors as conservative as Augustus or as degenerate as Commodus (A.D. 161–192)—rather more plausible in the latter case than in the former, one would think—it was always the case that the sacred order of Roman society was nourished and sustained by certain acceptable forms of human sacrifice. The execution of a criminal, for example, was often quite explicitly an offering made to the god against whose laws the criminal had offended (hence Julius Caesar, in 46 B.C., could understand his execution of two mutinous soldiers as a sacrifice to Mars). And surely there was no grander sacrificial spectacle, and no more satisfying celebration of sacred order, than the entertainments provided during lunch on game days in the arena, between the morning's slaughter of wild beasts and the afternoon's gladiatorial matches, when condemned criminals of the lower classes, slaves, or foreign prisoners were executed by crucifixion, torture, or burning, or were committed to the mercy of wild animals. For that matter, the gladiatorial competitions themselves were originally understood as *munera mortis,* tributes paid to the manes, the spirits of the dead. And, of course, there are some forms of "human sacrifice" that require an offering different from—but not necessarily any less grave than—the victim's life, such as the ecstatic self-castration and regular self-mutilation required of the priests of the Anatolian Great Mother, Cybele, or of the "Syrian Goddess" Atargatis. Examples are numberless.

Quite apart from their more revolting ritual observances, however, the religions of the empire were—to a very great degree—contemptible principally for what they did not do, and what in fact they never considered worth doing. Occasional attempts have been made by scholars in recent years to suggest that the paganism of the late empire was marked by a kind of "philanthropy" comparable in kind, or even in scope, to the charity practiced by the Christians, but nothing could be further from the truth (as I discuss below). Pagan cult was never more tolerant than in its tolerance—without any qualms of conscience—of poverty, disease, starvation, and homelessness; of gladiatorial spectacle, crucifixion, the exposure of unwanted infants, or the public slaughter of war captives or criminals on festive occasions; of, indeed, almost every imaginable form of tyranny, injustice, depravity, or cruelty. The indigenous sects of the Roman world simply made no connection between religious piety and anything resembling a developed social morality. At their best, their benignity might extend as far as providing hostelry for pilgrims or sharing sacrificial meats with their devotees; as a rule, however, even these meager services were rare and occasional in nature, and never amounted to anything like a religious obligation to care for the suffering, feed the hungry, or visit prisoners. Nor did the authority of the sacred, in pagan society, serve in any way to mitigate the brutality of the larger society—quite the contrary, really—and it would be difficult to exaggerate that brutality. To take an example more or less at random (one I choose, I have to say, only because reading about it affected me so forcibly when I was a boy): Tacitus relates the tale of the murder of Pedanius Secundus in A.D. 61 by one of his own slaves, which brought into effect the ancient custom that in such cases all the slaves of the household should be put to death—a custom that meant, on this occasion, the execution of approximately four hundred men, women, and children. There was, commendably enough, considerable public protest against the killing of so many innocents, but the Senate concluded that the ancient ways must be honored, if only for the example the slaughter would set, and nowhere in the course of the debate, it appears, was any concept of divine justice or spiritual virtue invoked.[5] That might seem a rather irrelevant anecdote here, admittedly, but the points to note are that the social order that the imperial cults sustained and served was one that rested, not accidentally but essentially, upon a pervasive, relentless, and polymorphous cruelty, and that to rebel against those cults was to rebel also against that order.

This, above all, must be remembered when assessing the relative openness or exclusivity of ancient creeds. We may recall with palpable throbs of fond emotion how the noble Symmachus pleaded for a greater toleration of pagan practices, and we may generally be disposed to endorse his view that the roads to truth are many; but we would do well to avoid excessive sentimentality all the same. We should remember not only that his broad "tolerance" involved imposing the cult of Victory upon Christian senators but also that his religious perspective was one almost entirely devoid of any discernibly ethical angles. This was the same man, after all, who complained of having been, as it were, defrauded of an enormous sum he had spent on public entertainments when twenty-nine of the Saxon prisoners he had purchased for the arena killed themselves before they could be made to perform.[6] I do not wish to make any exorbitant claims for the record of institutional Christianity in ameliorating the society to which it found itself attached; indeed, I cannot. If, for instance, it is true that, as Theodoret of Cyrus (c. 393–c. 457) reports, the emperor Honorius (384–423) finally brought an end to gladiatorial combat only in 404, and then only after a monk had been killed by spectators at an arena when he had attempted to bring the battle to a halt, that would mean that such games persisted for more than a decade after the empire had become officially Christian, and nearly ninety years after Constantine had first attempted to make them illegal.[7] That said, it was, after all, a monk whose death brought this change about, and it was only because such spectacles were by their nature repellant to Christian faith, and contrary to the laws of the church, that they were finally brought to an end. This in itself marks a vast and irreconcilable difference (and necessary antagonism) between the moral sensibilities of Christianity and those of the religions it displaced. It should probably neither surprise nor particularly disturb us, then, to discover that Christians of the late fourth century were not very inclined to agree with Symmachus that all religious paths led toward the same truth, given that one could walk so many of those paths quite successfully without ever turning aside to bind up the wounds of a suffering stranger, and without even pausing in alarm before unwanted babies left to be devoured by wild beasts, or before the atrocities of the arena, or before mass executions. If, as Christians believed, God had revealed himself as omnipotent love, and if true obedience to God required a life of moral heroism, in service to even "the least of these," how should Christians have viewed the religious life of most pagans if not as a rather obscene coincidence of spiritual servility and moral callousness? And how should they have viewed the gods from whose power Christ had liberated them if not as spirits of strife, ignorance, chaos, fate, and elemental violence, whose cults and devotions were far beneath the dignity of creatures fashioned in the divine image?

When all is said and done, we shall understand very little about the Christianization of the Roman Empire if we approach it simply as the story of one set of spiritual devotions—on account of their intransigent and unreasoning "exclusivity"—replacing other sets of spiritual devotions, or if we simply imagine (as modern persons are particularly prone to do) that religion is by definition a matter of "private" conviction, rather than a cultural, social, spiritual, and political order of values, authorities, and ideals. Christianity was, quite unambiguously, a cosmic sedition. It may have been partially subdued by the empire in being officially embraced, but even so its ultimate triumph resulted not merely in the supplantation of one cult by another, or even of one kind of mythic consciousness by another, but in the invention of an entirely new universe of human possibilities, moral, social, intellectual, cultural, and religious. And whether these new potentialities reached fruition at once or only over the course of centuries, they would never have opened up within human experience at all had not the old order passed away, and had not the gods who presided over it, endowed it with a sort of spiritual glamor, and lent it mythic form and structure been reduced to a newly subordinate status. The old and the new faiths represented two essentially incompatible visions of sacred order and of the human good. They could not coexist indefinitely, and only a moral imbecile could unreservedly regret which of the two it was that survived. The old gods did not—and by their nature could not—inspire the building of hospitals and almshouses, or make feeding the hungry and clothing the naked a path of spiritual enlightenment, or foster any coherent concept of a dignity intrinsic to every human soul; they could never have taught their human charges to think of charity as the highest of virtues or as the way to union with the divine.

It is, I might add, discourteous to reproach the oppressed for failing to honor their oppressors. Former slaves are under no particular obligation to feel indulgent toward their erstwhile masters. When considering the record of early Christianity's "intolerance"—when recalling those exorcisms in that baptistery on Easter eve (to return to the point from which I set out)—one should also remember that the Christians of the empire were not some foreign tribe who arrived in the pagan world one long afternoon, laden with swords and colonialist prejudices, and then set about systematically eradicating the aboriginal religions of an alien people. The gods they rejected had been their gods too, their masters of old. If they came to find those gods unworthy of reverence, and the cults of those gods inherently irreconcilable with whatever the story of Christ had awakened within them, it would be rather presumptuous of us to reprehend them for their "exclusivity" or "bigotry." There are times when a kind of holy impiety, or sacred irreverence, or charitable ingratitude is not only appropriate but necessary. A rather enchanting story from the year 389—or a distressing story, perhaps, depending on one's sensitivities—tells how the Christian noblewoman Serena, wife of Stilicho (who would later become imperial regent), one day entered the Palatine Temple of the Great Mother Cybele, strode up to the idol of the goddess, removed the statue's necklace, and placed it around her own throat; she then departed with her spoils while the lone priestess present, the last of the Vestal Virgins, hurled curses at her back.

I like this story, I should say, only for its symbolic significance. Obviously I have no insight into Serena's actual motives. She may simply have fancied the necklace and thought a needlessly provocative display of triumphalist derision a convenient cover for her theft. And, to be honest, this was somewhat after the period when Christians could still be said to be suffering much residual anxiety from their ill treatment at the hands of the old state religion, or even at the hands of the emperor Julian; within two years, in fact, Serena's uncle, the emperor Theodosius, would close all the temples of the old gods. But there is a kind of emblematic purity in Serena's gesture that, however ill mannered, merits at least a moment's admiration, or at least a moment's sympathy. It was, so to speak, a final, pleasingly gratuitous act of defiance, a grandly dismissive display of confident contempt toward an old, discredited fable, and an elegantly brash demonstration of a defeated tormenter's impotence. There is always something distasteful in vengeful mockery, I admit—the newly enfranchised citizen merrily reviling the deposed queen as she is carried by in the tumbrel, and so on—but there is also something quite understandable in it too. The gods had from the beginning been sacred accomplices in the cruelties of a culture that was boundlessly cruel and, quite often, cheerfully sadistic (and Cybele was a more grievous offender than many); not only had they failed in any signal respect to alleviate the sufferings of their worshippers, or to instruct them in how to care for one another, they had in fact provided divine legitimation for the practices, institutions, and prejudices of a society in which the law of charity was not only an impossibility but an offense against good taste.

None of which is to deny that many pagans were sincerely devoted to the gods; much that was lovely, consoling, and ennobling attached to their worship, some of which the church would appropriate for itself in later centuries. The gods invaded the hideous mundanity of human existence with intimations of transcendence, they mitigated human dread before nature's impersonal violences and vastitudes by filling the organic world with innumerable personal agencies whom one could propitiate and adore, and (perhaps most important) they kept boredom at bay by imparting to those who believed in them some sense of an abiding and irreducible mystery dwelling deep in the heart of things. But the benignity of their rule, such as it was, is visible to us now only because they were put in their place centuries ago by the triumph of Christian "atheism." So long as it still stood intact, the pagan spiritual order was circumscribed by certain permanent boundaries, at which the old gods stood as wardens. As much as the gods gave to the human imagination a world to inhabit, and stories to tell about it, they also confined the imagination within that world and within its moral and intellectual possibilities, which were nowhere near so immense or demanding as those that entered human culture with the advent of the gospel. And it required a willingness to rebel against beliefs of immeasurable antiquity and authority to cross those boundaries without a sense of transgression or a fear of divine retribution.

It is perhaps somewhat curious, then, that from the time of the apostolic church to the conversion of Constantine, as decades lengthened into centuries, so great a number of persons (at least by any sound statistical estimate) chose to forsake old allegiances and to "join the revolution"; and perhaps it would be wise to ask why this was so. How had so many become disenchanted with the ancient order and lost their fear of the old gods? What was it in the experience of Christian faith that prompted them to shed their former adherences? And why, in time, would all of Western culture submit to this baptism? At first, as the church spread, it invited a few Jews to assert their freedom from the powers and principalities, a few pagans to renounce their ancestral gods; and there will always be, at any given time or place, a select company of the brave, the reckless, or the eccentric willing to break with tradition, forsake old certitudes, and chase after exotic fads. But Christianity continued to grow relentlessly, not only throughout the empire but even past its eastern and southern frontiers and—in time—its northern and western frontiers as well, assuming into its ranks converts from every class, every cult, every faith, every race of the ancient European, Eastern, Near Eastern, and greater Mediterranean world.

Obviously, the rise to power of a Christian—or, at any rate, semi-Christian—emperor abruptly altered the course of imperial history and accelerated the decline of the indigenous religion of the empire. But to suppose that this is sufficient explanation for the ultimate triumph of Christianity, or that the new faith would have merely lingered on as an obscure and insignificant cult but for Constantine's victory at the Milvian Bridge, is to succumb to an almost magical understanding of historical processes. The very possibility of a Christian emperor—of a man able to take and maintain control of the Roman world while espousing this foreign creed—attests to the prior plausibility of Christianity in the early fourth century and suggests that the church already possessed a formidable degree of cultural stability and public acceptance (especially in the Eastern half of the empire). For that matter, much the same thing is suggested by the rather desperate and remarkably savage attempts of Constantine's almost immediate predecessors to exterminate the faith. This is not to deny that Christianity was still a minority religion when Constantine adopted it, or that it would perhaps have remained one for some time but for his conversion. The precise number of Christians in the empire at the beginning of the fourth century is impossible to determine, but it was certainly far smaller than the number of pagans. Nevertheless, the expansion of Christianity had by that time shown itself to be relentless, and it seems clear (even if only in retrospect) that its ultimate eclipse of the weaker, more diffuse, more fragmentary cults and devotions of the pagan world was something on the order of a historical inevitability. One might even regard Constantine's conversion as an interruption of the natural course of Christianity's gradual ascendancy: if nothing else, the slow, cumulative, inexorable increase of the church in earlier centuries seemed, on the whole, to produce better Christians and to keep the church free from the worst effects of worldly power and internal dissension. It is, at any rate, perfectly justifiable to assert that, when Constantine adopted the Christian faith, his conversion—for all its enormous significance—did not cause, but was merely one moment within, a movement that had already begun to conquer the empire and that had in some sense even surpassed it in scope and begun to transform the world of antiquity to its very foundations. Constantine may have hastened this process—though he also, in very profound ways, retarded it—but he was as much its crea-ture as its master.

These are, needless to say, contestable assertions, and they are ulti-mately unimportant to my argument. What, though, is beyond debate is that by the time of the last great persecution and of Constantine's ascent to the purple, Christians may have been a minority in the empire, but they were a strong minority, large enough to seem both a threat and a credible alternative to the ancient customs of the pagan world. Whatever might have happened had imperial history taken another turn at the Milvian Bridge, what did happen—what had been happening by that point for centuries—was that untold thousands of pagans chose to abandon the ways of their ancestors and to embrace a faith of so radically different a nature that they were obliged to leave almost everything proper to their old religious identities behind. This required not merely a change of habits but a total conversion of will, imagination, and desire. Why, then, did it happen? What made the new faith, and even the risks that attended it, so very preferable to a world of beliefs and practices that had endured with profuse and solemn majesty for millennia?

CHAPTER ELEVEN

A Glorious Sadness

THE PAST IS ALWAYS to some extent a fiction of the present. In our more melancholy hours, it is soothing to surrender to wistful "memories" of those better worlds that we have as a race or a people forsaken; and, in our moments of complacency and self-congratulation, we take pleasure in "recalling" the darkness from which we have now emerged, or the barbarisms of which we have long since taken leave. There is nothing necessarily unseemly in this: it is all part of what Nietzsche called the uses of history for the purposes of life. And during the early centuries of Christendom's long decline—say, from the Renaissance through the early industrial age—these purposes were usually served, among the educated classes of Europe, by two grandly conceived (and reconceived) periods of Western history: it became fashionable to cultivate both a kind of mordant disdain for the long night of a largely mythical Middle Ages and a kind of moony nostalgia for an antiquity that never was. The temperate atmosphere of a new and admirably confident humanism nurtured a very particular vision of pagan antiquity: a sort of lost paradise, a culture of superabundant vitality, beauty, and creativity, erected upon the foundation of a sane harmony between body and mind, and animated by an exuberant embrace of this world in all its fecundity, destructiveness, and inextinguishable power. The Greeks of the Periclean age, especially, acquired a (not wholly undeserved) reputation for intellectual vigor, wisdom, spiritual equilibrium, and spontaneous happiness; theirs came to be seen as Europe's "golden age," which could not be mourned vociferously enough.

Making allowance for the lushly picturesque medievalism of certain of the Romantics, one can say that, in general, this Hellenophilia was the great aesthetic and intellectual passion of whole generations of European scholars, philosophers, poets, and artists, a largely benign fever, reaching its warmest intensity from the middle of the eighteenth to the late nineteenth centuries, and infecting minds as splendid as Goethe's and Hölderlin's or as ridiculous as Algernon Swinburne's. Even Nietzsche, however much he sought to expose the darker subterranean streams nourishing ancient Greek culture, could not resist the contagion. The sublime genius of the Greeks of the age of Attic tragedy, he claimed, lay in their ability to gaze without illusion into the depths of life and into all the chaos and terror of the world, and to respond not with fear, resignation, or despair but with joyous affirmation and supreme artistry; the pagan world as a whole, he believed, possessed a kind of vital power now impossible for us, one born from a ruthless willingness to subordinate all values to aesthetic judgments and so to discriminate, without any pangs of conscience, between the good—that is, the strength, elation, bravery, generosity, and harshness of the aristocratic spirit—and the bad—the weakness, debility, timorousness, ignobility, squalor, and vindictive resentfulness of the slavish soul. Nietzsche's principal charge against Christianity, in fact, was that it constituted a slave revolt in values: a new and sickly *moral* vision of reality, judging all things, noble or base, according to the same pernicious and vindictive categories of good and evil. It was, Nietzsche claimed, this monstrous sedition against greatness and beauty that ultimately caused both the heroic joy of the Greeks and the stern grandeur of the Romans to sink beneath the flood of Christian spitefulness, pusillanimity, and otherworldliness. The gospel has robbed us of the health of our pagan forebears and reduced us all to spiritual invalids.

All nonsense, of course. Most of us are inheritors of this bracingly fabulous vision of the Attic past, but most of us also probably know that it is more romance than history. It is, however, a captivating romance, one that continues to operate in many of us at an almost unconscious level. Something of the old classicist nostalgia lingers on even in popular culture today, if in a somewhat more imprecise and untutored form, despite that general oblivion of all historical consciousness that condemns most late modern persons to a perpetual present. Most of us, I think, have some vague sense that *homo paganus* was a livelier specimen than the moralizing spiritual cripples who succeeded him, living as he did nearer than they to the natural, erotic, sensual, and mystical wellsprings of life; and so we like to imagine him as paradoxically both more attached to this world and more indifferent to death (or, at any rate, heroically reconciled to its inevitability). We even like to imagine, absurdly enough, that paganism is the name of a way of life more attentive to nature, more at home in the earth, more at ease in the flesh. Gore Vidal, for example, in his slightly adolescent and clumsy novel *Julian,* portrays the apostate emperor as a kind of champion of earthly life, courageously attempting to restore for his age an appreciation of the goodness of this world, before it is lost forever to the bloodless antisensualism of the Christians. Actually, there could scarcely be a more implausible candidate for such a role, given the real Julian's "philosophical" contempt for the material world and his longing for an ultimate escape from the prison of the body; but, in Vidal's universe, paganism is a kind of higher worldliness, an exalted attachment to the power and frailty of corporeal life, while Christianity is a diseased detestation of this world, and so of course—how could one doubt it?—Julian's was a campaign to rescue the overflowing vigor of pagan culture from Christianity's icy and withering embrace. And I suspect that most of us, even though we really know that this image of a world of wise innocence across which the deadening shadow of Sinai had not yet fallen is little more than an Arcadian fantasy, nevertheless cannot help but associate pagan culture with some indistinct ideal of spiritual health or guiltless happiness.

The story can, however, be told very differently. It is impossible to paint a psychological portrait of a people, a culture, an epoch, or—as in this case—an immense cross section of peoples, cultures, and epochs; and it is useless to try. That said, one could just as plausibly choose to see the pagan world as one of unremitting melancholy. Over the years, in fact, there have been historians or classicists who have preferred to call attention to the pervasiveness of the "tragic" element in the culture of antiquity: the darkness haunting much of its mythology, the capriciousness and brutality of the pagan divine, the morbidity of certain philosophical schools, the misery and despair with which death was contemplated, the fear of occult forces within nature, the religious reliance upon sacrifices of appeasement and impetration, the violence of many sacral practices, and above all a nearly universal acquiescence to the law of fate. The great Jacob Burckhardt (1818–1897), for instance, inveighed against the Romantic image of the ancient Greeks as an irrepressibly cheerful folk and proposed in its place a picture of a positively self-torturing people, almost unimaginably resigned to unrelenting pain and hopelessness. And it is certainly the case that, in a larger sense, ancient pagan culture—Asian or European, Greek or Roman, early or late—was marked by a kind of omnipresent dejection that seems simply absent from the Christian culture of the Middle Ages. This is, of course, a generalization susceptible of so many qualifications and exceptions that it may be no more than a personal impression, and it certainly runs contrary to many of our prevailing pictures of medieval squalor and misery. But, taking everything into account, it would not be entirely outlandish to characterize the *spiritual* ethos of antiquity (which is to say its religious and philosophical temper) as a kind of glorious sadness.

At least, viewed as a religious or cultic continuum, pagan society as a whole never succeeded—in its creeds, philosophies, or laws—in escaping that immemorial Indo-European mythos according to which the cosmos was a sort of perpetual sacrifice: a closed system within which gods and mortals occupied places determined by inscrutable necessity, inseparably dependent upon one another. This system was in every sense an economy, a finite cycle of creation and destruction, order and chaos, stability and violence, which preserved life through elaborate religious and cultural transactions with death. Nature was a thing at once endlessly bountiful and endlessly terrible, whose powers had to be exploited and propitiated simultaneously. The gods required our sacrifices—we fed them, so to speak—and in return they preserved us from the very forces they personified and granted us some measure of their power, in order to preserve the regime of city or empire, to give sacral legitimacy to the hierarchy of society, to grant victory in war, and to bless us with good harvests and profitable commerce. The dimensions of such a world were not, perhaps, as spacious as we might sometimes like to imagine in long retrospect. There was precious little hope for the average person, in this world or beyond it; social fluidity was small, and social aspirations were correspondingly meager; and even those who enjoyed social or political power could do very little to delay the approach of death or render it less terrifying. The greatest literary artifacts of antiquity (not wholly excluding the comedies and satires) are pervaded by a certain, consistently recognizable pathos: the majestic sadness of the *Iliad,* the sublime fatalism of Attic tragedy, the pensive lugubriousness of Horace's poetry, and so on. It is even arguable that all the major philosophical schools of antiquity reflect something of this same pathos, in varying registers; certainly none of them (with the occasional and imperfect exception of certain Platonisms) could lift its gaze beyond the closed universe of necessity, whether it embraced an ultimate monism that merely equated the divine with nature or an ultimate dualism that placed this world in a sort of tragic tension with divine reality. None, at any rate, could imagine a divine source of reality fully transcendent of the world, freely creating and sustaining all things out of love.

If, however, all of these seem like excessively ambitious generalities, I would still want at the very least to suggest that the particular pagan culture within which Christianity evolved was one of widespread moral or spiritual decline, however difficult it may be to measure such things. One cannot, at any rate, imagine the Athenians of the tragic age—or even, for that matter, the Romans of the republic—taking such guileless and persistent delight in the sort of public diversions that became common fare in the imperial age and that provoked such revulsion from Christian moralists. It was, for instance, fashionable in the time of Nero and after to make condemned criminals perform parts in plays written on mythic themes, in the roles of certain doomed characters, so that the audience could enjoy the rare amusement of watching an actor actually killed on stage (which at least, I suppose, accorded the poor man a somewhat more refined audience than he would have attracted at midday in the arena). Of course, every culture has its theaters of cruelty, where the emotionally diseased can enjoy the torments of others at leisure (ours are the cinema and the video game, since our technology permits us to produce the spectacle without the inconvenience of having to dispose of the corpses afterward); and most ancient peoples were quite frank in the pleasure they derived from the public humiliation, torture, and execution of captured enemies, or criminals, or outsiders. But, both in scale and nature, the entertainments favored by the late Romans suggest a sensibility nourished by something more monstrous than just the common human appetite for playful malice. They speak of the very special sadism of the disinterested voyeur, and it is far from unreasonable to think that a culture that accepted such cruelty as a matter of course—and in fact as one of its principal sources of public or private entertainment—suffered from a fairly extreme degree of spiritual ennui or decadence.

It seems, moreover, to have been a period of intense religious curiosity and yearning, of a sort that certainly does not suggest anything like a climate of general spiritual equilibrium and peace, much less any broad cultural inclination toward affirmation or celebration of life in the flesh. The late antique world within which Christianity arose was—if religion is any indicator—more than a little burdened by a sort of cosmic disenchantment, and the spiritualities it incubated within itself were pervaded by a profound and often almost desperate otherworldliness. It was not merely a time when Eastern esoterica, magic, the occult, and exotic sects flourished; all of that was to be expected in the cosmopolitan atmosphere of a great empire. It was also a time when religion and philosophy alike were increasingly concerned with escape from the conditions of earthly life, and when both often encouraged a contempt for the flesh more absolute, bitterly unworldly, and pessimistic than anything found in even the most exorbitant forms of Christian asceticism. Various mystery religions provided sacramental rites and imparted secret knowledge that could grant eternal life, leading the soul out of the dark prison house of this world and carrying it beyond the reach of the material order's endless cycles of birth and death. The longing for salvation often took the form of a quest after secret knowledge or mystical power and sometimes fixed itself upon "saviors" like Simon Magus, the sorcerer and Gnostic messiah, or Apollonius of Tyana, the Neo-Pythagorean sage and miracle worker; in every case, salvation was understood as emancipation from the bondage of the material universe. Not only is it wrong, in fact, to say that Christianity imported a prejudice against the senses into the pagan world; one should really say that, if the Christianity of the early centuries was marked by any excessive anxiety regarding the material world or life in the body, this was an attitude that had migrated from pagan culture into the church.

Perhaps the best evidence of a prevailing mood of cosmic disquiet in the culture of late antiquity would be the rise of certain Gnostic sects, in both the Eastern and Western halves of the empire, during the second and third centuries: not because these sects were necessarily very populous (they almost certainly were not) but because they reflect a very special sort of religious tendency and because they were sufficiently numerous, diverse, and widespread to suggest that this tendency was in some sense characteristic of their age. One has to tread cautiously, however, when discussing the Gnostics these days, because certain contemporary scholars—noting that many Gnostic sects understood themselves as Christian—would prefer to dispense altogether with the category of Gnosticism and speak instead of "alternative Christianities," which—through historical misfortune or evolutionary disadvantage—were unable to compete with the "orthodox" or "Great Church" Christianity that ultimately extinguished them. In the view of some, what came in time to be regarded as Christian orthodoxy was originally no more than one among innumerable, equally plausible Christian variants, and achieved the status of "genuine" Christianity only by using the power of an enfranchised institutional church to eliminate its rivals and to alter the record in such a way as to make it seem that these other Christianities were merely small, aberrant factions. Some argue that even the attempts of early champions of the orthodox position, such as Tertullian and Irenaeus of Lyon (c. 130–c. 203), to portray the Gnostics as tiny splinter groups ought to be treated with suspicion. The churches of the second century were marked by such a bewildering diversity of beliefs and scriptural canons, some now suggest, that one should really regard Gnostic and orthodox parties as merely distinct and somewhat accidental crystallizations within a great sea of religious possibilities.

In reality, the early apologists characterized the Gnostics as marginal, eccentric, and novel almost certainly because, in relation to the Christian community at large, that is precisely what they were. At least, that is what any unprejudiced examination of the historical evidence should lead one to conclude. That said, it is a matter of indifference to me whether one prefers to speak of Gnostic factions or of alternative Christianities, so long as all the proper qualifications are made. Before all else, one should emphasize that Gnosticism as an identifiable religious phenomenon was not found only among those who called themselves Christians, but took in a number of communities and philosophies that were clearly extra-Christian. The Naassene sect, for instance, may have worshipped Christ, but it also worshipped God under other names as well, such as Dionysus or Attis. Many of the Gnostic sects were in fact audaciously syncretistic and drew freely on Persian, Jewish, Mesopotamian, Greek, Syrian, and

Egyptian thought simultaneously, some even to the complete exclusion of any overt Christian symbolism. All the Gnostic schools, that is to say, belonged to a larger religious movement whose origins were not indigenous to Christian tradition. More to the point, standing over against all of these Gnostic Christianities was what any disinterested historian would have to call the dominant and mainstream Christian tradition, whose arguments for its own authenticity and authoritativeness were sound and attestable in a way that Gnostic claims were not. Not that Christian Gnostics did not share many themes, concerns, and ideas with the orthodox, not least the rejection of the rule of the cosmic powers; and there are certainly places within Christian tradition (such as parts of the fourth Gospel, for instance) where the distinction between Gnostic and orthodox forms of thought is more a matter of degree than of kind. There was, moreover, considerable theological variety within the ranks of the orthodox, and certainly Gnosticism was not an intentionally subversive movement. But, even so, the orthodox were all bound to certain affirmations that the Gnostics were equally bound to reject: that this world is the good creature of the one God, who is both the God of the Jews and the Father of Jesus of Nazareth; that it was this same God who sent Christ for the redemption of the world; that all men and women are called to be sons and daughters of God; that, in dying and rising again, Christ overthrew the power of death for all humankind; and that, while God frequently imparts wisdom to those who seek it, Christ did not come to save only the wise. These were the beliefs held by the vast majority of those who called themselves Christians, and the only beliefs that we can attribute to the apostolic church without violently distorting the historical evidence; these are also the very beliefs whose rejection distinguishes the Gnostics from the Christians of the Great Church. Moreover, as Irenaeus correctly argued, this larger tradition was the only form of Christianity that could claim any sort of universal scope or any historical continuity with the apostles themselves that was not patently fictitious.

Even, then, if one doubts the initial strength or authenticity of the Great Church position, the category of "Gnosticism"—as distinct from Christianity "proper"—remains valid. Even pagan observers seemed able to tell the difference. When Neoplatonists like Plotinus (205–270) and Porphyry attacked Gnosticism, they did not treat it as a species of Christianity but recognized it as a philosophy in its own right, one whose most peculiar features set it apart from any other school of thought.[1] And, for our purposes, it is enough to recognize that Gnosticism was a distinct style of speculation—a distinct kind of religious consciousness and longing—which, though it may frequently have taken up residence in Christian circles or adopted Christian garb, was essentially a sort of transreligious theosophy, neither specifically Jewish, nor Pagan, nor Christian but typical in a more general way of many of the spiritual longings of its age. The nature of these longings, however, is difficult to appreciate unless one disentangles one's understanding of the Gnostics from the often quite seductive misrepresentations found in most of the available popular literature on their teachings, much of which gives the impression that they were spiritual egalitarians, environmentalists, feminists, mystical pantheists—indeed, practically anything but what they actually were.

The divergence between the orthodox and Gnostic styles of speculation is obvious from a very early point in the evolution of Christian scripture, even in instances where orthodoxy shows itself hospitable to Gnostic motifs. A very profitable contrast can be drawn, for example, between the "orthodox" Gospel of John and the "proto-Gnostic" Gospel of Thomas (which is actually just a collection of one hundred and fourteen *logia* or sayings attributed to Jesus). The Gospel of John is a composite text, admittedly, probably incorporating earlier Gnostic or semi-Gnostic texts within itself, and so it is difficult to pronounce upon it as a whole; its style is, moreover, frequently dark and disturbing; and it definitely portrays Christ as a divine savior who descends from the world above into a cosmos ruled by evil, which is the classically Gnostic picture of the savior. That said, it also quite explicitly states that Christ is the Logos, the original principle of this world's existence, that he is the light that enlightens all persons, that the world he enters is his own world, created in him, that he came not to judge the world but to save it, and that the Father so loves the world that he gave even his only-begotten Son to deliver it from evil and death. By contrast, the Jesus of the Gospel of Thomas is a mysterious and obviously otherworldly messenger, in no way properly attached to the order of the material cosmos, who comes to lead a very select company of men—men, not women (except in an equivocal sense)—away from this world. And, as a whole, Thomas's Gospel appears to presume the standard Gnostic doctrine that within certain men there dwells a kind of divine spark, held captive in a universe of which it is no true part. Only these men possess immortal spirits, and only they are truly alive; all other persons are already really dead and will—like this world and the one who presides over it—pass away (*logion* 11). The blessed are those few men who came into existence before they came into existence (19),[2] whose true home is the divine Kingdom of light, from which they fell into this world, and to which they will one day return (49); they are the elect of the Living Father, but only because they originally came from his light (50). This world is merely a corpse, and he who knows it as such has risen above it (56; cf. 80). The spirit, on the other hand, is a great treasure that has somehow, tragically, come to be housed in the immense poverty of the body (29). One logion (37), in fact, seems to liken the body and perhaps the soul to garments that must be shed before one's immortal spirit can truly see the Son of the Living One (assuming this passage is not just an exhortation to some kind of sacramental nudism). And the path of true wisdom for the elect, once they have recalled their true home, is not to fast, pray, or give alms, for these things are actually deleterious to the spirit; rather, they should heal the sick in exchange for food (14), but otherwise become mere "passers-by" in this world (42). The Jesus of Thomas's Gospel, it should be noted, is not entirely devoid of magnanimity toward those outside the circle of the elect: though he agrees with his disciples, for instance, that Mary Magdalene, being a woman, is unworthy of life, he nevertheless goes on to promise that he will change her into a man, so that she also—like his male disciples—may become a living spirit (114).

In truth, it would be difficult to imagine any creeds less egalitarian and less well disposed toward the material cosmos than those of the major Gnostic schools: Valentinian, Basilidean, Sethian, or other. The constant premise in all these systems was an uncompromisingly radical dualism: however much their mythological schemes may have differed from one another in particular details, they all taught that the God who acts to rescue his elect is not in any sense the God of this world; and that the material cosmos is the evil or defective creation either of inferior gods (the archons or "rulers" who reign in the planetary spheres above) or of the chief archon (the wicked or incompetent demiurge or "world maker," often identified with the God of the Old Testament), who out of either ignorance or envy claims to be the sole true God, beside whom there is no other. Most men and women are the creatures of these gods or this god, but a very few are actually—in the inmost cores of their beings—mere sojourners in this world, scintillae of the godhead who have come this way by mischance, or on account of a kind of divine sabotage of the demiurge's work, and who consequently are now trapped here below, forgetful of their true homeland.

It would be impossible, as well as crushingly boring, to attempt to describe the wildly elaborate and rather silly mythologies by which various schools explained how these divine sparks came to fall into this world. Many spoke of a divine Pleroma—that is, Plenitude—of light, a sort of precosmic community of divine beings called the "aeons," generated in eternity by a divine Father who himself nevertheless remained hidden from them in the inaccessible heights of his transcendence. It was in this divine world, it seems, that the primordial catastrophe occurred. According to some systems, the lowest of the aeons, Sophia or Wisdom, conceived an unlawful longing to know the hidden Father, and in this way fell—in whole or in part—from the fullness of the godhead. Then, in one way or another, in the course of her fall or of her rescue, she generated the demiurge and the lower powers that govern this cosmos (at times, the physiological imagery employed to describe this process is quite revolting). Then, as a further consequence of the original divine tragedy or as a result of divine cunning, sparks of divine spirit were seeded within the machinery of the demiurge's cosmos. But, again, I am anxious to avoid too detailed a précis of any single system. The complications and involutions are endless and often pointless, the quality of invention is rather puerile, and the mythic sensibility frequently rises no higher than the level of comic books or Scientology. Nothing so dilutes one's sympathy for the Gnostics as an encounter with their actual writings. There are some notable exceptions: *The Acts of Thomas,* for instance, possesses a rare dramatic unity and power, and it would be difficult to deny the haunting occult splendor of the related *Hymn of the Pearl;* and the "Hymn of Jesus" from the *The Acts of John* is fetchingly cryptic. In general, though, whatever moments of beauty or profundity can be found among the literary remains of the Gnostics are insufficient to alleviate the surpassing dreariness of the whole. The only real virtue of these texts is their historical interest: they tend to confirm, in a diffuse but sufficient way, the reports of early Christians regarding the Gnostic understanding of salvation; they may qualify our acceptance of those reports in some measure, but not drastically.

According to the most developed Gnostic systems, the fallen man is an unhappy amalgamation of body (*soma*), soul (*psyche*), and spirit (*pneuma*). The first two aspects are part of the demiurge's creation and so fall under the sway of the archons and of that iron law of fate—*heimarmene*—by which this world is guided; the last aspect, however, is a pure emanation of the divine world beyond and has no natural relation to this cosmos, and so can, when recalled to itself, free itself from the tyranny of the cosmic principalities. Most human beings, however, are composed of only one or two of these elements: there are the *somatikoi*, soulless brutes for whom death is simply dissolution, and the *psychikoi*, who possess higher faculties of will and intellect in addition to their physical nature but are nonetheless subjects of the demiurge (according to some sects, orthodox Christians belong in this latter class). Salvation, properly speaking, inasmuch as it is a divine rescue of fallen spirits, is reserved solely for the *pneumatikoi*, those who are "spiritual" by nature—though, at least in some systems, certain of the psychikoi might also be granted eternal life, if they are willing to submit themselves to the pneumatikoi. Salvation itself consists principally in an inner awakening, for—until it is roused by its savior—the spirit slumbers in the deepest depths of the fallen man, wrapped not only in the flesh but also in the soul—or, in fact, the souls—created for it by the rulers of this cosmos. In some systems, the spirit is enfolded within a separate soul garment for each of the heavens through which it fell in the beginning; to be saved from rebirth here below, it must reascend through the spheres, leaving the body behind and then shedding the appropriate psychic sheath at each of the heavens through which it passes. For some systems, this means the decortication of only seven souls, one for each of the seven spheres of the planetary archons, but the number is not fixed: Basilidean mythology, for instance, sets the number of heavens and of souls at three hundred and sixty-five. And this ascent will be fraught with perils, for the archons are jealous of their plunder and will strive at each sphere to prevent the pneumatikos from returning to the Pleroma. Both the self and the cosmos are, as it were, labyrinths in which the spirit is lost and wandering, until Christ or some other savior brings it knowledge of itself, and stirs it from the drugged sleep in which it languishes as it drifts from one life to another. This savior, being divine, is often understood to possess no real terrestrial body; he appears in the form of a man, but only in order to deceive the archons. He requires no real terrestrial body, however, since the saving gift he brings is "gnosis," knowledge, and his mission is simply to instruct his charges in the secrets that will guide them safely home. And this knowledge often consists not only in spiritual awareness but also in the names, magical incantations, or forms of address that the spirit will need to know after death, in each planetary sphere, in order to elude that sphere's reigning archon.[3]

The incorrigibly distasteful features of a great deal of Gnostic thought and literature are difficult to ignore: the vapid obscurantism, the incontinent mythopoesis, the infantile symbolism, the sickly detestation of the body, the profound misanthropy, and so on. Especially difficult to endure is the occasional cruelty and callous triumphalism of the Gnostic vision of reality. In *The Second Treatise of the Great Seth*, for instance, the Gnostic Christ, speaking in the first person, relates how he deceived the powers of this world by causing Simon of Cyrene to take on his appearance and to be crucified in his place, while he watched from above, laughing at the spectacle. The sufferings of Simon, a mere creature of the demiurge apparently, are no more than an occasion for divine mirth at the expense of the cretinous archons. At such moments, one cannot help but feel that the Gnostic sensibility is especially suited to persons of arrested development. But behind the crassness and childishness of many Gnostic beliefs there lies a more pardonable conviction, and even an understandable pathos: a profound sense that somehow one is not truly at home in this world, and a deep longing for escape. In this respect, the Gnosticism of the second and third centuries was simply a particularly acute and colorful expression of a spiritual yearning that was omnipresent in the empire.

One finds, after all, a very similar morphology of salvation in the mystery religions of the time. One sought initiation into Mithraism, for instance, so that after death one's soul might reascend through the seven heavens and return to the sphere of the fixed stars whence it came, purged of all the impurities it had acquired from the planetary powers when it fell. In a wider sense, moreover, the general fascination of the age with astrology, alchemy, Egyptian and Chaldean ritual magic, occultism, necromancy, demonology, and so forth sprang not merely from a desire to master the secret technologies of the unseen world, for the purpose of personal gain, but also from a devout yearning for deliverance from the bondage of the material world and for an intimate encounter with the divine. The later Platonists, for example, especially from the time of Iamblichus (c. 250–c. 330) to that of Proclus (c. 410–485), employed these spiritual techniques in order to communicate with good daemons and deities, to prepare the soul for death, to call down divine assistance, and to thwart the malevolent daemons on high who might seek to impede the soul in its return to God.[4]

It is not hard to discern, moreover, a certain quality of desperation in many of the forms this longing for spiritual emancipation took: the willingness of some, for instance, to undertake rigors spanning the spectrum from the merely inconvenient to the genuinely dangerous; or the credulity to which even the very educated were often reduced. The mysteries of Mithras, for example, involved not only various levels of initiation but also a pitilessly enormous number of "castigations"—ordeals of fire and water, torture and endurance, abnegation and privation—which may well have killed the occasional eager postulant. Of course, Mithraism was a military sect composed exclusively of men, and one must always take into account the male appetite for needless pain and pointless trials of courage; and one cannot be entirely certain that, in many times in places, these ordeals were not as much metaphorical as actual. Even so, clearly no one sought entry into such mysteries lightly, and few would have been drawn to them and all that they required had not the desire for a life beyond the tyranny of cosmic fate been more powerful than almost any other motive. And then there was the charlatanism of the age, and the readiness of so many to be taken in by it. We know of mechanical devices, optical illusions, and combustible chemicals used to simulate miracles and divine visitations: conjurers' tricks with fire, automata used to give the impression of idols brought to life by the descent of daemons, hidden speaking trumpets for producing the voices of unseen gods, light reflected from hidden pans of water onto reflective surfaces in darkened temples' ceilings, skulls cunningly fashioned from friable wax that would "miraculously" melt away after delivering their oracles, shadowy temple vaults suddenly transformed into the starry heavens by light projected upon fish scales embedded in the masonry, temple doors designed to open on their own as the "god" passed through them, and so on. There are always, of course, especially susceptible souls ready to invest their faith in any piece of vulgar chicanery that impresses them; but, by the same token, such souls are generally rendered susceptible only by a prior and rather anxious need to believe.

Spiritual anxiety, however, was scarcely confined to the ranks of the credulous. The most refined disciplines of spiritual liberation were colored by the same dreads and melancholies. Even the philosophical schools still presumed the ancient vision of the cosmos as a closed totality. The Stoics, admittedly, sought to find a way to be at home in the great city of the universe, but this meant a serenity purchased at the price of an immense resignation: an acceptance of the limited nature of reality, of the necessity of one life supplanting another, of the ultimate extinction and eternal recurrence of the universe; and it also meant a stilling of the passions, a benign detachment from all desire, a philosophical reverence for the God whose mind pervades all things, and an indifferent acceptance of suffering and joy alike, as inseparable concomitants within the weft of destiny. The Platonists, by contrast, believed in a realm of purified vision transcendent of this world, to which the soul might ascend; but this conviction too—perhaps paradoxically—required something like the same kind of resignation on the philosopher's part. Plotinus, for example, the greatest of the early Neoplatonists, was contemptuous of the Gnostics for their denigration of the material universe, and praised the beauty of this world as the most perfect that could be produced by the workings of a divine mind upon the recalcitrant substrate of matter. But he also saw this world as the realm of fallen vision, the land of unlikeness, from which the *nous*, the spiritual soul, must detach itself in order to return to its highest nature and to the eternal vision of the heavenly forms. There is a quality of tragic leave-taking in his thought that is only partially mitigated by his affirmations of the essential goodness of all being. This world, for all its beauty, must be fled if the highest and eternal beauty is ever to be known in the purity of its own glory.

In any event, to return to my principal point, the Christianity of the early centuries did not invade a world of noonday joy, vitality, mirth, and cheerful earthiness, and darken it with malicious slanders of the senses, or chill it with a severe and bloodless otherworldliness. Rather, it entered into a twilit world of pervasive spiritual despondency and religious yearning, not as a cult of cosmic renunciation (pagan religious and philosophical culture required no tutelage in that) but as a religion of glad tidings, of new life, and that in all abundance. It was pagan society that had become ever more otherworldly and joyless, ever wearier of the burden of itself, and ever more resentful of the soul's incarceration in the closed system of a universe governed by fate. It was pagan society that seemed unable to conceive of any spiritual aspiration higher than escape—higher, that is, than the emancipation of a few select spirits from the toils of an otherwise irredeemable world—and that could imagine no philosophical virtue more impressive than resignation to the impossibility of escape. The church, by contrast, was obliged to preach a gospel of salvation that somehow embraced the entire created order. Obviously, Christianity was, no less than any other mystery religion, a way of salvation; and, just as obviously, it shared with many other creeds a belief that this world is governed to a great extent by evil. At the same time, however, it was obliged to proclaim, far more radically than any other ancient system of thought, the incorruptible goodness of the world, the original and ultimate beauty of all things, inasmuch as it understood this world to be the direct creation of the omnipotent God of love.

Far from preaching a gospel of liberation from the flesh, moreover, Christianity's chief proclamation was the real resurrection of Christ, in body and soul, and the redemption this proclamation offered consisted in an ultimate transfiguration of the flesh and the glorification of the entirety of creation (as Paul says in the eighth chapter of Romans). Christianity, uniquely, rejected the pagan morphology of salvation, and hence even the church's ascetic practices were inspired by motives and expectations unknown to pagan thought. When Christians undertook to discipline the appetites of the body through austerities and renunciations, it was not because they sought release from the "prison" or "tomb" of the body—as did those who belonged to other ascetical traditions—but because they regarded the body as God's good creature, the proper home of the soul, a worthy temple of the Holy Spirit, requiring sanctification only so as to be restored to its true dignity as a vessel of divine glory and raised to participation in the Kingdom of God. And the Kingdom itself was understood to be this world renewed, perhaps broken in order to be knit aright again, but the one creation of the one true God, set free at last from bondage to death. Robin Lane Fox is quite correct to note that, among the authors of the second century, "it is the Christians who are most confident and assured," and that the "magnificent optimism" of Irenaeus of Lyon and the almost innocent cheerfulness of Justin Martyr stand out as distinctively and unmistakably Christian characteristics.[5] Even Christian funerals took the form of triumphal processions and communal celebrations of the overthrow of death. Whatever else Christianity brought into the late antique world, the principal gift it offered to pagan culture was a liberation from spiritual anxiety, from the desperation born of a hopeless longing for escape, from the sadness of having to forsake all love of the world absolutely in order to find salvation, from a morbid terror of the body, and from the fear that the cosmic powers on high might prevent the spirit from reaching its heavenly home. As Paul had assured the Roman Christians, "neither death nor life, nor angels nor principalities nor powers, nor things present nor things to come, nor height nor depth, nor any other thing created, shall have the power to separate us from the love of God which is in Christ Jesus our Lord" (Romans 8:38–39). This is not to say that Christian culture ever wholly succeeded in resisting contamination by pagan melancholy and gravity, or even that it ever fully purged itself of this unwelcome alloy. But the "new thing" that the gospel imparted to the world in which it was born and grew was something that pagan religion could only occasionally adumbrate but never sustain, and that pagan philosophy would, in most cases, have found shameful to promote: a deep and imperturbable joy.

CHAPTER TWELVE

A Liberating Message

TWO QUESTIONS SHOULD probably be asked at this point. The first is whether it is demonstrably the case that the gospel did in fact spread through the world of late antiquity on account of the novelty of its message—which is to say, because those who first heard it preached were truly conscious of the radical originality of its ethos—or whether it prospered simply because it was the mystery cult that happened to have the most engaging myths, and that ultimately had the good fortune to be adopted by an emperor. And the second is whether any actual social effects followed from the triumph of Christianity that would corroborate the claim that the gospel substantially transformed the moral and spiritual consciousness of Western humanity. Neither is a question, of course, that yields a perfectly definitive answer. The social effects of ideas or beliefs are especially difficult to calculate, as they tend to make themselves manifest only gradually, over generations and centuries, and often in only the subtlest ways. That said, even delayed effects must follow from immediate causes; and these it should be possible, however partially, to measure.

The reason for asking these questions, incidentally, is that the current critical climate somewhat demands that one do so. In previous generations, even Christianity's detractors would generally have answered both in the affirmative, no matter what qualifications they might then have felt obliged to add. Nietzsche's entire case against the church, to take an especially obvious example, required him to believe that, from the first, the gospel exercised a unique appeal upon a certain very particular social element (the weak, resentful, and slavish) and that, as a result, the rise of Christianity had bred social and cultural consequences not only large but catastrophic. Today, however, there is something of a contrary tendency among some scholars, many of whom argue that the true social consequences of Christianity's victory over paganism were few and meager, and that the appeal of the new religion lay not in any notable novelty in its message—at least, not one of which most converts could have been acutely conscious—but in certain purely fortuitous social and political accidents of the faith. Perhaps the most influential scholar in the English-speaking world today making such an argument is the classicist Ramsay MacMullen; though his own tersely condensed accounts of the Christianization of the empire—with their huge copses of elliptical footnotes—enjoy a necessarily limited readership, they have done a great deal to shape the work of less credentialed but more popular historians. And this is important chiefly because no other reputable scholar is as uncompromising as MacMullen in his attack upon what was once the conventional view of Christianity's moral revision of pagan society. As far as he is concerned, the triumph of the church from the time of Constantine on was a matter almost entirely of social ambition and legal coercion, while the success of the church before Constantine had had nothing to do with anything intrinsically new in Christianity, intellectual or moral, but had been the result either of a general vulgar credulity (stirred into irrational enthusiasm by apparent or supposed miracles and exorcisms) or of the social pressures exercised within particular households. In MacMullen's view, at no point did any clear, generally recognized concept of Christianity's moral or spiritual precepts play a significant part in the history of conversion, and the rise of Christianity made no very conspicuous contribution to the general amelioration of conditions for the poor or of the lot of slaves, women, or the dispossessed.

Were it not for his special importance—were his books not the deep background of a surprisingly large number of anti-Christian polemics—I might not single out MacMullen for special consideration; but then again I might, as his is so thoroughly and refreshingly skeptical a picture of early Christianity's success that it tends to keep one honest. But, I also have to point out, I do not think that he can always be praised for the quality of his historical analysis: he too often seems uninterested in distinguishing between general and particular truths, or in certifying the relevance of the comparisons he draws, or in interpreting texts in terms of the traditions from which they come. Nor can I vouch for the perfect probity of his methods: his use of historical sources is too often not merely selective, but misleading. At times, in fact, his method seems to consist principally in confecting confusions by a promiscuous mixture of unrelated sources or a disorienting ramble through the labyrinths of his footnotes.

To take a simple example: early on in his *Christianity and Paganism in the Fourth to Eighth Centuries,* in discussing the emperor Justinian's religious policies, MacMullen reports that "those [Justinian] disagreed with, he was likely to mutilate if he didn't behead or crucify them."[1] What the reader is meant to conclude from this remark, it seems clear, is that these were the means Justinian adopted to suppress religious dissent; and even if one repairs to MacMullen's notes at this point, one will not—unless one is a specialist—be able to tell from the citations provided there that such a conclusion is not only unwarranted by the historical record but plainly contradicted. Now, certainly Justinian enjoys no very great reputation for gentleness, and he was quite willing to kill when it suited his purposes; but one's suspicion should be roused immediately by the mention of crucifixion, a punishment that had been abolished in 315 by Constantine and that, by the time of Justinian in the early sixth century, would have been an unthinkable form of execution, if for no other reason than the offense it would have given to Christian piety. In his note, the only evidence MacMullen cites for his extraordinary claim is a passage from the *Chronographia* of John Malalas, from which he has chosen to translate the Greek verb *ephourkisen* as "crucified" rather than (as is correct) "hanged."[2] In itself, that might be small cause for complaint (legal murder by any other name . . .); but a more important concern is that the passage cited from Malalas happens to have absolutely nothing to do with Justinian's methods for enforcing religious uniformity in the empire; in fact, it has nothing to do with Justinian himself at all. It concerns, rather, the aftermath of large Jewish and Samaritan riots in Caesarea in July of 556, during which many Christians had been killed and many churches plundered, and during which a Samaritan mob had robbed and murdered the imperial governor Stephanos. Justinian's sole part in the drama was to order an investigation of the unrest by Amantios, the "Governor of the

East"; it was Amantios who, on discovering the identities of several of the murderers, ordered their execution, by hanging or decapitation. He also, in keeping with the harsh justice of the times, had the right hands of some of the rioters cut off, presumably for acts of violence falling short of murder.[3] Mutilation, unfortunately, was a penalty long employed by Roman courts, as a supposedly humane alternative to capital punishment.

Again, however, as much as we might dislike the efficient brutality of ancient law—and criminal laws under Justinian were actually in many respects more merciful than they had been under his predecessors—this anecdote is not even remotely germane to Justinian's persecutions of pagans, Manicheans, Jews, Christian heretics, and so on. Justinian's actual measures against obdurate pagans are recounted by Malalas, briefly and precisely, and they are sufficiently discreditable to require no embellishment: in 529, there was "a large persecution of the Hellenes"—that is, pagans—during which many properties were seized and some persons even died (presumably as the result of rough treatment or of impoverishment); the emperor decreed, moreover, that those who persisted in Hellenic beliefs should be excluded from any office of state, and that "heretical" Christians had three months to convert to the "orthodox" confession or face banishment from the empire.[4] These were harsh edicts, certainly; but they were still a far cry from mass crucifixions.

In the case of Justinian, whom nobody very much liked or likes, I suppose one might argue that a little exaggeration does not amount to much of an injustice; it would be a bad argument, but understandable. But the reputations of better men than Justinian also suffer from the liberties MacMullen sometimes takes with his sources. Very early on in *Christianity and Paganism,* he raises the perfectly legitimate and interesting question of whether women found Christianity a more welcoming religious tradition than paganism (as most historians believe they did), and then attempts to answer it by comparing the written records of two fourth-century trials: the first occurred in the Egyptian Thebaid in the 380s A.D., and concerned a man who had murdered a prostitute and had, in so doing, left the poor murdered woman's mother without any means of support; and the second occurred in Liguria, and concerned a woman accused of adultery, whose forensic torture, conviction, and death sentence were vividly described by St. Jerome in his first epistle. In the former case, MacMullen reports, the judge—whom he presumes was a pagan—expressed his pity for the murdered woman, lamented the profession to which poverty had driven her and the abuse and dishonor she had suffered as a result, and awarded a tenth of her killer's property to her mother—"the laws suggesting this to me," said the judge, "and magnanimity, *philanthropia*." He then sentenced the murderer to death. In the latter case, however, at least as MacMullen tells the tale, we find that the Christian Jerome, like the "other church officers" present at the trial, "quite accepts" the "ethical tradition" that prescribes that women be "beheaded for extramarital fornication"; and this, says MacMullen, "casts further doubt on the question of . . . whether women of the empire were likely to see Christians as a more receptive community than that to which they had been used."[5]

It might cast such doubt, I shall grant, if the comparison were sound and if the account of the two trials given here were accurate; neither is the case, however. Even if one knew no more of these trials than these brief sketches, though, one would still have to note that they concern two very different crimes, committed—or said to have been committed—in two vastly different regions, and prosecuted under the scrutiny of judges about whom we know very little. As such, they simply cannot serve as epitomes of, respectively, pagan or Christian moral tradition. There is not even any good reason to suppose that the judge in the first case was a pagan; true, he is depicted as twice using the term "philanthropy," which was often favored (though hardly exclusively) by pagan moralists, and on one occasion as exclaiming "nē Dia," which is to say "By Jove!" This is hardly compelling proof of his religious adherences. But, even if the judge in question was not a Christian, or was only nominally Christian, no conclusions can be drawn from his verdict regarding the moral customs of ancient pagan society, for the simple reason that the laws to which the verdict refers and the values the judge professes had been, by the late fourth century, profoundly shaped and colored by Christian moral precepts, which had become part of the common ethical vocabulary of the empire and had entered even into pagan thought. The language the judge uses, the pity he expresses for the dead prostitute, his dismay at the life she had felt forced to live—none of this should be read as some sort of unalloyed expression of native pagan ideals. By the same token, the laws that permitted the magistrate in the second case to torture confessions from persons accused of adultery, or to execute them upon conviction, were of pagan provenance, and long antedated Christian custom in the empire. Moreover, the judge in that second case might very well not have been a Christian; a pagan magistrate, as it happens, was far more likely to be found in Italy than in Egypt. Again, though, we know almost nothing about these men.

All of this is, however, at least comparatively, of minor importance. A far greater cause for concern is that MacMullen has grossly distorted Jerome's letter, which is more than unfortunate because—when read through—that letter actually casts an altogether startling light on the difference between the pagan moral sensibilities expressed in the legal procedures of the court and the Christian moral vision that Jerome brings to bear upon them. It is simply untrue that Jerome's report of the Ligurian trial indicates an acceptance on his part of an ethical tradition that thought it right to condemn adulteresses to death by the sword, or reveals that there were other church officers present who supported the court's actions. In fact, quite the opposite is the case. Jerome's letter is a long, poignant, even somewhat mawkish denunciation of the injustice of the trial, and of the sentence passed upon the accused woman, as well as a celebration of the "miracle" by which she was ultimately spared. Jerome portrays the governor who officiated at the trial as a pitiless sadist, and the woman herself as something very like a saint, refusing even under the most dreadful torture (which Jerome describes with manifest horror) to deny her innocence. Even when her alleged paramour—also on trial—sought to escape his punishment by accusing her, says Jerome, she continued to maintain both her blamelessness and his, but to no avail: both were condemned, and the young man was promptly decapitated. When, though, the executioner attempted to kill the woman, his sword failed him three times, and the witnessing crowd attempted to come to her rescue, even threatening the executioner's life; she, however, rather than allow the poor headsman to be killed in her stead, submitted to a second executioner, who—after four laborious strokes—appeared at last to have dispatched her, and she was carried away by the attending clergy to be buried. Before she could be interred, however, she revived (or was raised) and, in order to hide her from the law, the clergy filled the grave prepared for her with the body of a pious old woman who had died that same day. When, though, word of the condemned woman's reviviscence got out, the authorities resumed their designs upon her life, and finally relented only after a Christian holy man named Evagrius, pleading her case before the emperor, secured her pardon. Far from approving of the trial, Jerome offers no moral observation on the incident other than "Where there is the most law, there also is the most injustice." It is true that, as MacMullen says, Jerome "offers no comment on the death penalty for women taken in adultery" in his letter,[6] but an argument from silence is almost always a bad argument, and in this case it is rather on a par with noting that Oedipus, in the process of tearing out his eyes, enunciates no principled objections to incest. As for the "church officers" mentioned in the letter, these are in fact the clergymen who came to give the executed woman a Christian burial, and who did all in their power to hide her from the courts after she revived; they were not passive participants in her trial, and their presence was anything but a sign of approbation.

This sort of careless misuse of textual evidence is simply unnecessary at the end of the day. MacMullen is far more interesting and effective—and poses a far more powerful challenge to certain conventional views of the early history of Christianity—in the measured skepticism with which he discusses the nature and reality of the Christian conversion of the empire. Here, at his best, he raises questions that touch upon the very essence of Christianity as a social movement. He begins, as I have noted, from the claim that conversion in the early centuries of the Christian movement was the effect neither of the example of Christian behavior nor, for the most part, of the content of Christian teachings, but almost entirely of other, accidental forces. Indeed, he asserts, the closed and exclusive nature of the Christian mysteries and of the Christian communities of the early centuries would have prevented persons not as yet converted from gaining any substantial exposure to Christian practices, religious or social. Nor does he believe that many conversions could have been won through reasoned argument or simple preaching. It is more likely, rather, that persons were for the most part "converted" in the same sense that we can say that the household of Lydia was "converted" by the apostle Paul in the book of Acts: that is, the head of the household, having adopted the faith, prescribed the new cult for the whole "family," including all children, slaves, and dependent families. But if this is so, says MacMullen, obviously such persons had never really been converted at all; they had conformed in practice to their new religion but had not actually come to believe or even to understand its tenets. In time, many of them perhaps genuinely adopted the faith as their own, through force of habit; but most of them were nominally Christian at most, and then only in order to secure social and material benefits.

As for those in whom Christian evangelism really did succeed in producing conviction, says MacMullen, we cannot understand their conversion properly until we have distinguished properly between the content of Christian teaching and the sort of proof by which it was recommended to its original audiences. The content he dismisses as largely banal, an amalgam of familiar ideas (a supreme God who confers blessings on those who worship him, the world's ultimate destruction) and of various, somewhat more exotic novelties of doctrine (the immortality of all souls, heaven for the blessed and eternal torment for the wicked, the war between the kingdoms of light and darkness, and so on). The *proof* of these things, however, he claims consisted principally in a variety of wonders, such as supposedly miraculous healings and exorcisms. These, combined with the appeal of possible supernatural blessings, the terror inspired by Christian eschatology, and the unprecedented militancy of Christian evangelism, were the chief vehicles of persuasion: not arguments, not doctrines, and certainly not ideas. And, while of course "miracles" might also be produced on behalf of gods other than the Christian, the signs and wonders wielded by Christian evangelists were associated with a cult that was unprecedentedly exclusive of all other religious loyalties; and so, uniquely, the miracles of the Christians destroyed faith even as they created faith.[7] In this way, from the first, Christianity was engaged in extinguishing all rival faiths.

Now, as it happens, there are elements of truth in much of this. Certainly there were, from the very beginning of the church, conversions to the new faith that had nothing to do with the desires or inclinations of the converts. It is almost certainly wrong, however, to suggest that such conversions were in any sense in the majority, or even particularly common. It is also true that the Christian mysteries (the sacraments, that is) were closed to non-Christians, and that many Christian teachings were unknown to the uninitiated. But, again, we know from sources both pagan and Christian that many of the essentials of Christian belief were open to all who cared to learn of them, and that the distinctive behavior of Christians—including temperance, gentleness, lawfulness, and acts of supererogatory kindness—not only was visible to their neighbors outside the faith but constituted a large part of the new faith's appeal. Even the emperor Julian, for all his hostility to the Christians, was obliged by the evidence of his eyes to acknowledge as much: "It is [the Christians'] philanthropy towards strangers, the care they take of the graves of the dead, and the affected sanctity with which they conduct their lives that have done most to spread their atheism."[8]

Admittedly, and unarguably, it is true that the early Christians placed great stock in miraculous healings and exorcisms, and that in the realm of Christian legend bold claims were often made regarding the power of their Lord over the powers of darkness. But it is just as true that the process of becoming a Christian was one of long and careful indoctrination, even for the easily convinced, and that, as Robin Lane Fox notes, "between the Apostolic age and the fourth century A.D., we know of no historical case when a miracle or an exorcism turned an individual, let alone a crowd, to the Christian faith." Even Paul's ministry, Lane Fox adds, consisted in tireless preaching, instruction, and persuasion, often carried out over a course of days. To imagine, then, that converts were made by the sight of a single wonder is to "shorten a long process" and "to misjudge the canniness of Mediterranean men"; even those convinced that they had genuinely witnessed a preternatural event would still have had no reason to see the Christian god as anything more than one powerful divine agency among many; nor would the memory of a few marvels seen years before have had the power to make men and women die terrible deaths for their faith.[9] Whatever appeal the gospel exercised on ancient persons, it certainly reached deeper springs in the soul than the native human capacity to be beguiled by a few clever tricks.

More powerful than astonishment, of course, present or remembered, is fear of the future; and here, I confess, I feel somewhat greater sympathy for MacMullen's position. The threat of eternal torment is an appeal solely to spiritual and emotional terror, and to the degree that Christians employed it as an inducement to faith, their arguments were clearly somewhat vulgar. The doctrine of hell, understood in a purely literal sense, as a place of eternally unremitting divine wrath, is an idea that would seem to reduce Christianity's larger claims regarding the justice, mercy, and love of God to nonsense. But, even here, one must take care to make proper distinctions, for it is not at all clear to what degree such an idea was central or even peculiar to the preaching of the early Christians. The earliest

Christian documents, for instance—the authentic epistles of Paul—contain no trace of a doctrine of eternal torment, and Paul himself appears to have envisaged only a final annihilation of evildoers. The evidence of the Gospels, moreover, is far more ambiguous on this point than most persons imagine; even Christ's allegorical portrait of the final judgment in Matthew chapter 25 allows considerable latitude for interpretation, and patristic theologians as diverse as Origen, Gregory of Nazianzus, Gregory of Nyssa, and Isaac of Nineveh saw in the phrase *aiōnios kolasis* (typically translated as "eternal punishment," but possible to read as "correction for a long period" or "for an age" or even "in the age to come") no cause to conclude that hell was anything but a temporary process of spiritual purification. Indeed, if the testimony of several of the church fathers is to be believed, this "purgatorial" view of hell was far from being an eccentric minority opinion among the Christians of the first few centuries, especially in the Eastern reaches of the empire. All that said, though, one must grant that the idea of eternal punishment for the wicked or for unbelievers formed part of Christian teaching from an early date. But one should also note that the idea of eternal punishment was not a uniquely or even distinctively Christian notion; its pagan precedents were many; it was an idea well established among, for instance, the Platonists; and it is not wholly fanciful to suggest that its eventual ascendency in Christian teaching was a result as much of the conventional religious thinking that Christianity absorbed from the larger culture as of anything native to the gospel. Whatever the case, it is doubtful that Christian teaching succeeded much in exacerbating fear of death or the afterlife. All the documentary evidence suggests that the special attraction of Christianity in ancient society lay elsewhere, in aspects of the faith that clearly set it apart from other contemporary visions of reality.

As a whole, I think it fair to say, MacMullen wants to place the weight in his narrative not upon the contents of Christian belief but upon the credulity of the converted, which was, he suggests, aggravated by a general decline in rationality and cultured skepticism during the first three centuries of the Christian era, even within the educated classes (a decline, to be sure, for which Christianity was not to blame, but from which it certainly profited). The evidence MacMullen supplies for the superior rationality of first-century over, say, third-century thinking is mostly anecdotal, however. For instance, he recalls that Plutarch, in the first century, argued that tales of supernatural events ought not to be immediately accepted but should first be subjected to a thoroughly naturalistic investigation; or he reminds his readers that both Plutarch and his older contemporary Pliny preferred natural rather than magical explanations for the phenomena of nature; or he notes that, in the third century, Plotinus—the last great voice of ancient philosophy—rebuked those who believed that spells or exorcisms could cure illness; and so on.[10] It was this sort of "rationalism," claims MacMullen, that was dying away just as the church was coming into its own. In truth, though, there is no sound reason to claim that rationality was either a more highly cherished value or a more refined practical impulse in the first century than in the third, or that one can simply delineate the rational from the irrational in any given period in antiquity. Even these cultured pagans of the older sort turn out to be, on nearer inspection, no less men of the ancient world than the monks of the desert or the catechumens of the church. Pliny's natural philosophy was no less hospitable to superstition than to naturalism, and encompassed certain traditional remedies that bordered on sympathetic magic; Plutarch spent his twilight years as a priest at Delphi writing treatises on religious questions, such as what kinds of punishments and rewards awaited souls after death; Plotinus objected to spells and exorcisms not because they offended against his rationalist principles but because they were incompatible with his own theology and daemonology. It may be true, of course, that ancient culture was as a rule more given to credulity than is ours (though I think not). As I have said, I wish to make no claims regarding the plausibility or truth of Christian belief, or of religious conviction in general. But the notion that the rise of Christianity coincided with or was assisted by some universal decay of the power of rational thought in late antiquity is simply insupportable; and the notion that the whole appeal of the church for ancient men and women consisted in little more than meretricious pasteboard spectacle, embellished with childish promises and threats, is contrary not only to the evidence but to plain logic. The truth of large cultural and religious movements is never so simple a thing as that.

Probably the soundest ways to ascertain what the "Christian difference" was—what set the new faith apart from other creeds, what drew converts to it, what excited the wrath of its detractors—is to attempt to assess what social or moral difference Christianity made, either for individuals or for culture as a whole. And here, for one last time, it is helpful to summon MacMullen as a kind of "negative witness"; for he, almost alone among serious scholars, wishes to argue that, on the whole, the moral consequences of Christian belief were at best nugatory, at worst malign, and that the classes that historians have generally claimed were especially likely to be attracted to Christian precepts—women, the poor, slaves—were neither particularly susceptible to conversion nor very likely to benefit from it; in fact, he argues, their lots may very well have been worsened by conversion to the new faith. After all, he observes, once Christians were established within the highest echelons of society, they were just as prone to class prejudice as the pagan aristocracy had ever been. In some cases, fully enfranchised Christians may have exhibited greater contempt for their social inferiors. Did not Pope Leo the Great (r. 440–461), asks MacMullen, prohibit the ordination of slaves to the priesthood lest they pollute the office itself? And did not pagan culture, by contrast, grant slaves almost unrestricted access to all cults and temples, and allow them to form cultic societies of their own, with their own sacerdotal hierarchies? By the same token, were not Christian women excluded from all significant ecclesiastical offices, while pagan women often served as priestesses in the cults of female deities? And, even if priestesses were nowhere near so numerous as their male counterparts, was it not the case that, in various parts of the empire, women were allowed to participate in almost the entire range of possible religious observances?[11] As for the poor, wonders MacMullen, did the Christian ideal of charity really constitute so vast an improvement over pagan ideals of philanthropy, and did it really inspire greater generosity or provide better succor for the destitute? What of those once thriving temples of which Libanius wrote so nostalgically around 380, to which the poor had once been able to repair for plenteous food and refreshment whenever a wealthy patron provided sacrificial beasts for the festal slaughters and wine for the celebrations, and in which treasure used to be stored to provide the indigent with assistance? Was the Christian Church's aid to the poor really anything more than a continuation of religious practices and an emulation of virtues already native to pagan society?[12]

To begin with the last of these questions, the concise answer would be no. The picture MacMullen presents of pagan philanthropy is positively enchanting, even idyllic, but—alas—the evidence he cites from Libanius betrays him: if anything, it reflects only the rather restricted and occasional almsgiving practices adopted by pagan temples during the Christian era, as a result of the emperor Julian's attempts to force the pagan priesthood to imitate the church's aid to the poor. If either religious tradition influenced the other in this matter, it was almost certainly the younger creed that informed the elder. Setting that to one side, though, it is perfectly fair to call attention to the failure of ancient Christians to behave as their beliefs should have dictated. Again, I will happily stipulate that the rise of Christianity did not miraculously transform ancient society from the ground up, or for that matter from the top down; nor did it rid that society of its immemorial injustices. All that being granted, however, even that stipulation needs certain qualifications, both factual and conceptual. To begin with, it is more than a touch perverse to credit the pagan cults with a religious egalitarianism greater than—or even comparable to—that of the early church. With some rare exceptions, such as the Bacchic mysteries, most organized religious societies of the ancient world admitted only one sex (generally men) and strictly excluded slaves from their memberships. Temples, of course, were by their nature open places of worship and offering, and we cannot say with certainty what social restrictions might have been observed in various places; but the sort of cultic affiliations a person could claim for himself or (more rarely) herself were most definitely determined by what he or she was, which is to say, what station he or she occupied. One of the reasons why slaves had to form their own cultic societies is that they were not allowed to join those of their masters. The Christians, by contrast, admitted men and women, free and bound, to equal membership and obliged them to worship together. This was, in many ways, the most radical novelty of their community: that it transcended and so, in an ultimate sense, annulled "natural" human divisions. Pope Leo did, it is true, forbid the ordination of slaves; or, rather, he forbade the ordination of slaves and serfs who had not been set free by their masters, lest the priesthood be stained by men who had not yet even earned the trust of those they had served for years; but the discovery that a fifth-century Roman gentleman was occasionally prone to the hauteur of his class should not divert our attention from other realities. For one thing, Leo's policy was not general: it was never adopted in the more cosmopolitan and liberal East, and even in the West, during the first half of the sixth century, various councils in Orléans declared the ordinations of slaves perfectly valid, and a Roman council of 595 declared that slaves did not have to obtain the consent of their masters to enter monastic orders.

I shall defer the issue of slavery largely to the next chapter; here I wish simply to caution against the anachronism of allowing our own cultural premises to determine our understanding of ancient society. For instance, one really cannot make sense of the position of women in pagan cultic associations in abstraction from issues of social class; one is simply thinking like a late modern bourgeois if one imagines either that the principal concern of the women of late antiquity could possibly have been one of career equality or that the existence of pagan priestesses was somehow emblematic of greater equality between the sexes within pagan religion. In point of fact, the priestly caste of cultic societies was made up of the patrons of those societies. Priesthood was not a career path, so to speak, for anyone; it was for the most part, in the pagan order, the privilege of the wealthy. So, yes, certain rich women purchased cults for themselves; and, yes, a few women of the aristocracy and a few pledged girls served as priestesses and votaries in the temples of a few goddesses. But it is impossible meaningfully to compare their vocations to those of Christian priests, who came from every social and economic quarter of society, and who served an institution in which patronage did not endow the benefactor with religious authority.[13] We today might feel a certain discomfort at the early church's adoption of a male priesthood, but no ancient person of either sex would have regarded such practices as somehow unfairly exclusive; there was simply no cultural grammar for such ideas. Moreover, it makes little sense to deny what even Christianity's pagan adversaries freely acknowledged to be the case: that this new religion was uncommonly attractive to women, and that many women found in the Church's teachings forms of solace that the old religions could not provide. Celsus, as I have noted, regarded the disproportionate number of women among the Christians as evidence of Christianity's irrationality and vulgarity. Julian, in his *Misopogon* (Beard-Hater), chided the men of Antioch for allowing their wealth to be squandered by their wives in contributions to the Galilaeans and to the poor, which had had the unhappy effect of inspiring a general admiration for the Christians' "atheism." And so on. Frankly, no survey of the documentary evidence regarding early Christianity could leave one in any doubt that this was a religion to which women were powerfully drawn, and one that would not have spread nearly so far or so swiftly but for the great number of women in its fold.

This should not really surprise us. Whether women of great privilege would have gained much by association with the Galilaeans can no doubt be debated, but there can be little question regarding the benefits that the new faith conferred upon ordinary women—women, that is, who were neither rich nor socially exalted—literally from birth to death. Christianity both forbade the ancient pagan practice of the exposure of unwanted infants—which is almost certainly to say, in the great majority of cases, girls—and insisted upon communal provision for the needs of widows—than whom no class of persons in ancient society was typically more disadvantaged or helpless. Not only did the church demand that females be allowed, no less than males, to live; it provided the means for them to live out the full span of their lives with dignity and material security. Christian husbands, moreover, could not force their wives to submit to abortions or to consent to infanticide; and while many pagan women may have been perfectly content to commit their newborn daughters to rubbish heaps or deserted roadsides, to become carrion for dogs and birds or (if fortunate) to become foundlings, we can assume a very great many women were not. Christian husbands were even commanded to remain as faithful to their wives as they expected their wives to be to them; they were forbidden to treat their wives with cruelty; they could not abandon or divorce their wives; their wives were not their chattels but their sisters in Christ. One might even argue that the virtues that Christianity chiefly valued—compassion, humility, gentleness, and so forth—were virtues in which women had generally had better training; and that it was for this reason, perhaps, that among Christians female piety was often so powerful a model of the purity of their faith. Even in the latter half of the fourth century, Christian men as prominent as Basil of Caesarea and his brother Gregory of Nyssa could look to their brilliant and pious sister Macrina as a kind of ideal of the Christian life.[14] That ancient Christians were not modern persons, and so could not yet conceive of a society in which men and women occupied the same professions or positions, is both obvious and utterly undeserving of reproach. The "social technology" of perfect sexual equality—or, at any rate, equivalence—was as far beyond their resources as was the material technology of electric light. But Christians had been instructed by Paul that a man's body belonged to his wife no less than her body belonged to him, and that in Christ a difference in dignity between male and female did not exist. And while it would be silly to imagine that the women who converted to Christianity in the early centuries had first calculated the possible social benefits of such an act, it would be just as foolish to deny that Christian beliefs had real consequences for how women fared in the Christian community, or to imagine that Christian women were entirely unconscious of the degree to which their faith affirmed their humanity.

It should also probably not go unremarked that the legal reforms instituted by a number of Christian emperors, in their attempts to bring the law into closer conformity with the precepts of their faith, betray a solicitude for the welfare and rights of women often absent from pagan legislation. Constantine's efforts in this regard, while not as radical as they might have been, and not always particularly consistent, certainly eased the hardships of widows, shielded women from prosecution in public, forbade divorce on trivial grounds, made public accusations of adultery against women illegal, and protected girls against marriage by abduction and forcible proleptic "consummation." Theodosius and his successors went further. For instance, the legal Code of Theodosius II (401–450), which incorporated and expanded upon the reforms of previous Christian emperors, included changes in divorce law from 421 that eradicated many of the disadvantages imposed upon women. A wife abandoned by her husband simply on grounds of domestic unhappiness was now entitled not only to reclaim her dowry but to retain her husband's betrothal gifts to her as well; she also acquired the right to remarry after a year of separation, while her husband was condemned to perpetual bachelorhood (if he violated this prohibition, both the dowry and the betrothal gifts of the new marriage became the property of his first wife). A husband, moreover, was prohibited from squandering or diminishing his wife's dowry, and at his death it reverted to her rather than passing into his estate. In fact, the code made inheritance law more equitable in general by assuring that the estates of deceased women passed uncontested to their children. A girl whose father prostituted her was entirely liberated from his authority, and (more remarkably) a slave girl similarly abused by her master ceased to be his property. And the emperor Justinian, encouraged in great measure by his wife Theodora, expanded the rights and protections of women in the empire to an altogether unprecedented degree.

◆ ◆ ◆

Justinian's reforms also, I should note, considerably improved the lot of slaves, and made emancipation legally less complicated; and in fact, long before Justinian's Code, Constantine had made it illegal for slaveholders to separate married slaves by selling them to different masters and had eased the legal procedures for manumission, permitting slaveholders to grant slaves their liberty simply by going to church and making the declaration of emancipation before the bishop. It is true, sadly, that the conversion of the empire to Christianity not only did not result in the abolition of the institution of slavery but did not even seem call it into serious question. Nor is there any empirical measure by which to determine whether Christian slaveholders exhibited conspicuously greater compassion or liberality than their pagan counterparts. In many cases they surely did not. The most one can say with certainty is that, under Christian emperors, the law became more humane, though not by any means ideal, and that those who aspired to genuine Christian virtue in their homes would have had cause to heed the injunctions of scripture and to regard their servants as brothers and sisters in Christ. Bonded servitude, however, was a universally accepted feature of ancient economy and of the ancient household; and, in the Roman world, it was ubiquitous, inasmuch as slaves occupied all kinds of posts and "professions": they were not only laborers but just as often craftsmen, tutors, scribes, artists, entertainers, civil servants, administrators, architects, and so forth. The slave's social station, in short, was one of the fixed realities of human existence; practically no one could envisage a society that could function without a class of bound men and women, even though there were those, like the Stoics and the Christians, who found it possible to deplore the reality of human enslavement, either in principle or in respect to its more inhumane expressions. Even the apostle Paul, if he was indeed the author of the letter to Philemon, made no explicit appeal for the emancipation of Philemon's slave Onesimus but asked only that a baptized slaveholder recognize that his baptized slave was now in fact his brother as well, whom he ought not to treat as a mere menial. That in Christ the distinction between master and slave had been abolished was at the very heart of Paul's understanding of the resurrection; that this new reality might actually result in a society from which that distinction had been fully eradicated was a thing for which Paul obviously did not presume to hope this side of God's

Kingdom. As yet, the explosive implications of the gospel remained, for him and for many generations of Christians after him, more a matter of eschatology than of social philosophy. (And, of course, he could scarcely have known that Christians would ever be in a position to shape the world they lived in.) Even granting all of this, however, those implications could not entirely fail to make themselves obvious to sincere Christians, and one should not ignore the very real differences between pagan and Christian attitudes toward slaves. If nothing else, the Christian Church admitted slaves to full membership and allowed them full access to its mysteries, and required masters and slaves to worship and pray together as equal members of the one household of faith. The demand, moreover, that Christian masters regard their slaves as kindred rather than chattels, and treat them with justice, gentleness, and charity, is a frequent refrain in the writings of some of the greatest of the church fathers—Clement of Alexandria, Gregory of Nyssa, John Chrysostom, to name a few—though, again, we can only speculate on how well individual Christian households might have closed the inevitable fissure between injunction and action.

Where I feel no need to concede any ground whatsoever is before the suggestion that there was any substantial similarity or continuity between pagan provisions for those in need and Christian charity. Even pagan critics of the church were aware of the astonishing range of Christians' exertions on behalf of others. This is not to say that there was no such thing as pagan munificence. A certain kind of theatrical lavishness was very much a part of the patrician culture of honor and good report, and rich men with any concern for their reputations could be expected to provide gifts to their client families on festal days and to win themselves renown through grand displays of public largesse. The state, moreover, made occasional attempts to improve the conditions of the poor, if not necessarily out of purely humanitarian motives. The emperors Nerva and (on a larger scale) Trajan provided supplementary supplies of food (*alimenta*) to poor children in Italy, in the hope of halting the decline of the native Italian population and of thereby reaping a greater harvest in later years of nonbarbarian recruits for the legions. Ultimately, however, one finds nothing in pagan society remotely comparable in magnitude to the Christian willingness to provide continuously for persons in need, male and female, young and old, free and bound alike.

Christian teaching, from the first, placed charity at the center of the spiritual life as no pagan cult ever had, and raised the care of widows, orphans, the sick, the imprisoned, and the poor to the level of the highest of religious obligations. Thus, in the late second century, Tertullian could justly boast that whereas the money donated to the temples of the old gods was squandered on feasts and drink, with their momentary pleasures, the money given to the churches was used to care for the impoverished and the abandoned, to grant even the poorest decent burials, and to provide for the needs of the elderly.[15] The *Didascalia,* a fascinating Christian document of the third century, describes the duties of a bishop as encompassing responsibility for the education of orphans, aid to poor widows, and the purchase of food and firewood for the destitute, as well as strict vigilance over the money flowing through the church, lest it issue from men guilty of injustice or of the abuse of slaves, or lest it find its way into the hands of persons not genuinely in need. In 251 the church in Rome alone had more than fifteen hundred dependents on its rolls, and even small local churches kept storerooms of provisions for the poor, such as oil, wine, and clothing (especially, tellingly enough, women's clothing).[16] In this way the church, long before Constantine, had created a system of social assistance that no civic or religious office of the pagan state provided; once Constantine became emperor and shifted state patronage to his new religion, storerooms became storehouses, and the church became the first large, organized institution of public welfare in Western history. It was a great repository and redistributor of goods, alms, state moneys, and bequests; it encouraged the rich to give, beyond the dictates of prudence, even in some cases to the point of voluntary poverty; it provided funds for hospitals, orphan asylums, and hostels. Even when the established church neglected or fell short of the charitable ideals it professed, it still did far more for those in need than the gods of old had ever done.

From the first century through the fourth, I think one can fairly say, no single aspect of Christian moral teaching was more consistent or more urgent than this law of charity. In the surviving Christian literature of the first five centuries, both before and after the church's transformation into the imperial cult, the refrain is ceaseless, and is most poignantly audible in the admonitions of the great church fathers of the post-Constantinian period—Basil, Gregory Nazianzen, John Chrysostom—to rich Christians: to follow Christ, one must love the poor and give to them without reserve or preference. At its very best, the Christian pursuit of charity, both before and after Constantine's conversion, was marked by a quality of the super- erogatory that pagan religious ideas could simply never have inspired. During the great pandemic plague of 251–266, for instance, at least if the perfectly credible accounts of the bishops Dionysius of Alexandria and Cyprian of Carthage are to be believed, Christians in the two great North African cities, clergy and laity alike, distinguished themselves by their willingness to care for the ill and to bury the dead, even at the cost of their own lives. And, as I say, even committed pagans acknowledged the peculiar virtues of the Galilaeans. The pagan historian Ammianus Marcellinus, for instance, who admired Julian and who harbored no rosy illusions regarding the church, still commended the faith of the Christians as a "gentle" creed, essentially just in its principles and its acts.[17]

All of this having been said, however, it seems to me that we have still touched only the surface of what set Christianity apart from the older religions of the empire.

CHAPTER THIRTEEN

The Face of the Faceless

ALL FOUR OF THE canonical Gospels tell the tale of the apostle Peter's failure on the very eve of Christ's crucifixion: Peter's promise that he would never abandon Christ; Christ's prediction that Peter would in fact deny him that same night, not once but three times, before the cock's crow; Peter's cautious venture into the courtyard of the high priest, after Christ's arrest in the garden, and his confrontation with others present there who thought they recognized him as one of Christ's disciples; and the fear that prompted Peter to do at the last just as his master had prophesied. John's Gospel, in some ways the least tender of the four, leaves the story there; but the three synoptic Gospels—Matthew, Mark, and Luke—go on to relate that, on hearing the cock announce the break of day, Peter remembered Christ's words to him earlier in the evening and, seized by grief, went apart to weep bitterly.

To us today, this hardly seems an extraordinary detail of the narrative, however moving we may or may not find it; we would expect Peter to weep, and we certainly would expect any narrator to think the event worth recording. But, in some ways, taken in the context of the age in which the Gospels were written, there may well be no stranger or more remarkable moment in the whole of scripture. What is obvious to us—Peter's wounded soul, the profundity of his devotion to his teacher, the torment of his guilt, the crushing knowledge that Christ's imminent death forever foreclosed the possibility of seeking forgiveness for his betrayal—is obvious in very large part because we are the heirs of a culture that, in a sense, sprang from Peter's tears. To us, this rather small and ordinary narrative detail is unquestionably an ornament of the story, one that ennobles it, proves its gravity, widens its embrace of our common humanity. In this sense, all of us—even unbelievers—are "Christians" in our moral expectations of the world. To the literate classes of late antiquity, however, this tale of Peter weeping would more likely have seemed an aesthetic mistake; for Peter, as a rustic, could not possibly have been a worthy object of a well-bred man's sympathy, nor could his grief possibly have possessed the sort of tragic dignity necessary to make it worthy of anyone's notice. At most, the grief of a man of Peter's class might have had a place in comic literature: the querulous complaints of an indolent slave, the self-pitying expostulations of a witless peon, the anguished laments of a cuckolded taverner, and so on. Of course, in a tragic or epic setting a servant's tears might have been played as accompaniment to his master's sorrows, rather like the sympathetic whining of a devoted dog. But, when one compares this scene from the Gospels to the sort of emotional portraiture one finds in great Roman writers, comic or serious, one discovers—as the great literary critic Erich Auerbach noted half a century ago—that it is only in Peter that one sees "the image of man in the highest and deepest and most tragic sense."[1] Yet Peter remains, for all that, a Galilaean peasant. This is not merely a violation of good taste; it is an act of rebellion.

This is not, obviously, a claim regarding the explicit intent of any of the evangelists. But even Christianity's most implacable modern critics should be willing to acknowledge that, in these texts and others like them, we see something beginning to emerge from darkness into full visibility, arguably for the first time in our history: the human person as such, invested with an intrinsic and inviolable dignity, and possessed of an infinite value. It would not even be implausible to argue that our very ability to speak of "persons" as we do is a consequence of the revolution in moral sensibility that Christianity brought about. We, after all, employ this word with a splendidly indiscriminate generosity, applying it without hesitation to everyone, regardless of social station, race, or sex; but originally, at least in some of the most crucial contexts, it had a much more limited application. Specifically, in Roman legal usage, one's person was one's status before the law, which was certainly not something invariable from one individual to the next. The original and primary meaning of the Latin word *persona* was "mask," and as a legal term its use may well have harked back to the wax funerary effigies by which persons of social consequence were represented after their deaths, and which families of rank were allowed to display as icons of their ancestral pedigrees. Thus, by extension, to have a persona was to have a face before the law—which is to say, to be recognized as one possessing rights and privileges before a court, or as being able to give testimony upon the strength of one's own word, or simply as owning a respectable social identity, of which jurists must be conscious.

For those of the lowest stations, however—slaves, base-born non-citizens and criminals, the utterly destitute, colonized peoples—legal personality did not really exist, or existed in only the most tenuous of forms. Under the best of the pagan emperors, such as Augustus, certain legal protections were extended to slaves; but, of themselves, slaves had no real rights before the law, and no proper means of appeal against their masters. Moreover, their word was of no account. A slave was so entirely devoid of any "personal" dignity that, when called to testify before a duly appointed court, torture might be applied as a matter of course. For the slave was a man or woman *non habens personam:* literally, "not having a persona," or even "not having a face." Before the law, he or she was not a person in the fullest and most proper sense. Nor did he or she enjoy any greater visibility—any greater countenance, one might say—before society at large. In a sense, the only face proper to a slave, at least as far as the cultural imagination of the ancient world went, was the brutish and grotesquely leering "slave mask" worn by actors on the comic stage: an exquisitely exact manifestation of how anyone who was another's property was (naturally) seen.

We today have our bigotries, of course; we can hardly claim to have advanced so far as to know nothing of racism, for instance, or of its most violent expressions; it was not so long ago that blackface and the conventions of the minstrel show were as inoffensive to us as the slave mask was to ancient audiences; and certainly there is no such thing as a society without class hierarchies. All we can claim in our defense is that we have names for the social inequities we see or remember; we are, for the most part, aware—at least, those of us who are not incorrigibly stupid or cruel—that they violate the deepest moral principles we would be afraid not to profess; we are conscious also—the great majority of us, at any rate—that they are historical accidents, which do not reflect the inmost essence of reality or the immemorial decrees of the gods or of nature, and therefore can and should be corrected. But this is only because we live in the long twilight of a civilization formed by beliefs that, however obvious or trite they may seem to us, entered ancient society rather like a meteor from a clear sky. What for us is the quiet, persistent, perennial rebuke of conscience within us was, for ancient peoples, an outlandish decree issuing from a realm outside any world they could conceive. Conscience, after all, at least in regard to its particular contents, is to a great extent a cultural artifact, a historical contingency, and all of us today in the West, to some degree or another, have inherited a conscience formed by Christian moral ideals. For this reason, it is all but impossible for us to recover any real sense of the scandal that many pagans naturally felt at the bizarre prodigality with which the early Christians were willing to grant full humanity to persons of every class and condition, and of either sex.

A few modern men, it is true, have been able to induce a similar dismay in themselves, or have at least succeeded in mimicking it. Nietzsche, for instance, did his very best to share the noble pagan's revulsion at the sordid social sediments the early church continuously dredged up into its basilicas (though, middle-class pastor's boy that he was, he never became quite as effortlessly expert in patrician disdain as he imagined he had). But to hear that tone of alarm in its richest, purest, and most spontaneous registers one really has to repair to the pagans themselves: to Celsus, or Eunapius of Sardis, or the emperor Julian. What they saw, as they peered down upon the Christian movement from the high, narrow summit of their society, was not the understandable ebullition of long-suppressed human longings but the very order of the cosmos collapsing at its base, drawing everything down into the general ruin and obscene squalor of a common humanity. How else could they interpret the spectacle but as a kind of monstrous impiety and noisomely wicked degeneracy? In his treatise *Against the Galilaeans*, Julian complained that the Christians had from the earliest days swelled their ranks with the most vicious, disreputable, and contemptible of persons, while offering only baptism as a remedy for their vileness, as if mere water could cleanse the soul. Eunapius turned away with revulsion from the base gods that the earth was now breeding as a result of Christianity's subversion of good order: men and women of the most deplorable sort, justly tortured, condemned, and executed for their crimes, but glorified after death as martyrs of the faith, their abominable relics venerated in place of the old gods.

The scandal of the pagans, however, was the glory of the church. Vincent of Lérins, in the early fifth century, celebrated the severe moral tutelage of the monasteries in his native Gaul precisely because it was so corrosive of class consciousness: it taught the sons of the aristocracy humility, he said, and shattered in them the habits of pride, vanity, and luxuriance. It is arguable that, during the second century, the legal and social disadvantages of the lower classes under Rome had grown even more onerous than they had been in previous centuries, and that the prejudices of class had become even more pronounced than they had been in the Hellenistic or earlier Roman world. During this same period, however, Christians not only preached but even occasionally realized, something like a real community of souls, transcendent of all natural or social divisions. Not even the most morally admirable of the pagan philosophical schools, Stoicism, succeeded so strikingly in making a spiritual virtue of indifference to social station. The very law of the church was an inversion of "natural" rank: for Christ had promised that the first would be last and the last first. The *Didascalia*, for instance, prescribed that a bishop ought never to interrupt his service to greet a person of high degree who had just entered the church, lest he—the bishop—be seen to be a respecter of persons; but, on seeing a poor man or woman enter the assembly, that same bishop should do everything in his power to make room for the new arrival, even if he himself should have to sit upon the floor to do so. The same text also makes it clear that the early church might often have arranged its congregations into different groups, distinguished by age, sex, marital status, and so on, simply for propriety's sake, but that social degree was not the standard by which one's place was assigned among "the brethren."[2] Men of high attainment—literate, accomplished, propertied, and free—had to crowd in among slaves, laborers, and craftsmen, and count it no disgrace.

I do not wish to exaggerate the virtues of the early Christians on this count. Perfection is not to be found in any human institution, and the church has certainly always been that. Even in the early days of the church, certain social distinctions proved far too redoubtable to exterminate; a Christian slaveholder's Christian slaves were still slaves, even if they were also their master's brothers in Christ. And, after Constantine, as the church became that most lamentable of things—a pillar of respectable society—it learned all too easily to tolerate many of the injustices it supposedly condemned. The enfranchised church has never been more than half Christian even at the best of times; often enough, it has been much less than that. Neither, however, should we underestimate how extraordinary the religious ethos of the earliest Christians was in regard to social order, or fail to give them credit for the attempts they did make to efface the distinctions in social dignity which had traditionally separated persons of different rank from one another, but which had been (they believed) abolished in Christ. When all is said and done, the pagan critics of the early church were right to see the new faith as an essentially subversive movement. In fact, they may have been somewhat more perspicacious in this regard than the Christians themselves. Christianity may never have been a revolution in the political sense: it was not a convulsive, violent, or intentionally provocative faction that had some "other vision" of political power to recommend; but neither, for that reason, was the change it brought about something merely local, transient, and finite. The Christian vision of reality was nothing less than—to use the words of Nietzsche—a "transvaluation of all values," a complete revision of the moral and conceptual categories by which human beings were to understand themselves and one another and their places within the world. It was—again to use Nietzsche's words, but without his sneer—a "slave revolt in morality." But it was also, as far as the Christians were concerned, a slave revolt "from above," if such a thing could be imagined; for it had been accomplished by a savior who had, as Paul said in his Epistle to the Philippians, willingly exchanged the "form of God" for the "form of a slave," and had thereby overthrown the powers that reigned on high.

Perhaps even more striking than the episode of Peter's tears—at least, in regard to its cultural setting—is the story of Christ before Pilate, especially as related in the Gospel of John. Again, an immense historical distance intervenes between us and the age in which the text was produced; and, again, the moral meaning of the scene is one to which most of us today are prepared, at least emotionally, to assent; so we cannot quite *feel* its strangeness, or the novelty of its metaphysical implications. To its earliest readers, however, what could such a scene have meant? On one side of the tableau stands a man of noble birth, invested with the full authority of the Roman Empire, entrusted with the responsibility of imposing the *pax Romana,* in a barbarous country, upon an uncouth and intractable indigenous population too much given to religious fanaticism. On the other side stands a poor and possibly demented colonial of obscure origins and indiscernible ambitions who, when asked if he is King of the Jews, replies only with vague and enigmatic invocations of a kingdom not of this world and of some mysterious truth to which he is called to bear witness. In the great cosmic hierarchy of rational powers—descending from the Highest God down to the lowliest of slaves—Pilate's is a particularly exalted place, a little nearer to heaven than to earth, and imbued with something of the splendor of the gods. Christ, by contrast, has no natural claim whatsoever upon Pilate's clemency, nor any chartered rights upon which he might call; simply said, he has no person before the law. One figure in this picture, then, enjoys perfect sway over life and death, while the other no longer belongs even to himself. And the picture's asymmetry becomes even starker (and perhaps even more absurd) when Jesus is brought before Pilate for the second time, having been scourged, wrapped in a soldier's cloak, and crowned with thorns. To the ears of any ancient person, Pilate's question to his prisoner now—"Where do you come from?"—would almost certainly have sounded like a perfectly pertinent, if obviously sardonic, inquiry into Christ's pedigrees, and a pointed reminder that, in comparison to Pilate, Christ is no one at all. And Pilate's still more explicit admonition a moment later—"I have power to crucify you"—would have had something of the ring of a rhetorical coup de grâce. Christ's claim, on the other hand, that Pilate possesses no powers not given him from above would have sounded like only the comical impudence of a lunatic.

Could any ancient witness to this scene, recognizing how fate had apportioned to its principals their respective places in the order of things, have doubted on which side the full "truth" of things was to be found? For what measure of reality is there, in a world sustained by immutable hierarchies of social privilege, apart from the relative calculus of power: Who has the authority to judge others? Who possesses the right to kill? This much, in fact, Pilate had already communicated at his first interrogation of Christ, and with the tersest eloquence, when he asked, "What is truth?"—expecting and needing no reply. Nietzsche, who—better than almost any other modern critic or champion of Christianity—understood how vast a confrontation between worlds is concentrated in this scene, spoke for practically the whole of antique culture when he pronounced this question of Pilate's the only commendable sentence to be found anywhere in Christian scripture, a shining instance of noble irony that had, through the curious inattention of the evangelist, become anomalously fixed in the frozen morass of the New Testament, like a glittering dragonfly preserved in a particularly dark amber.

I have to assume, however, that most of us today simply *cannot* see Christ and Pilate in this way. We come too late in time to think like ancient men and women, and few of us, I hope, would be so childish as to want to. Try though we might, we shall never really be able to see Christ's broken, humiliated, and doomed humanity as something self-evidently contemptible and ridiculous; we are instead, in a very real sense, *destined* to see it as encompassing the very mystery of our own humanity: a sublime fragility, at once tragic and magnificent, pitiable and wonderful. Obviously, of course, many of us are quite capable of looking upon the sufferings of others with indifference or even contempt. But what I mean to say is that even the worst of us, raised in the shadow of Christendom, lacks the ability to ignore those sufferings without prior violence to his or her own conscience. We have lost the capacity for innocent callousness. Living as we do in the long aftermath of a revolution so profound that its effects persist in the deepest reaches of our natures, we cannot *simply* and guilelessly avert our eyes from the abasement of the victim in order to admire the grandeur of his persecutor; and for just this reason we lack any immediate consciousness of the radical inversion of perspective that has occurred in these pages. Seen from within the closed totality of a certain pre-Christian vision of reality, however, Pilate's verdict is essentially a just one: not because the penalty it imposes is somehow proportionate to the "crime" (what would that mean anyway?), but because it affirms the natural and divine order of reality, by consigning a worthless man to an appropriately undignified death, and by restoring order through the destruction of the agent of disorder. For, in the end, the gods love order above all else. The Gospel of John, however, approaches the confrontation between Christ and Pilate from a vantage unprecedented in human culture: the faith of Easter. And the result of this new angle of approach, soberly considered, is somewhat outrageous. God, it seems, far from approving the verdict of his alleged earthly representatives—Gentiles or Jews, priests or procurators, emperors, generals, or judges—entirely reverses their judgment, and in fact vindicates and restores to life the very man they have "justly" condemned in the interest of public tranquility. This is an astonishing realignment of every perspective, an epochal reversal of all values, a rebellion against reality. Once again, no one ever evinced a keener sense of the magnitude of this subversion than did Nietzsche, or deplored it more bitterly; but Nietzsche saw no motive behind this Christian audacity deeper than simple resentment, and here his insight certainly failed him. Resentment is, of its nature, crude and ponderous; by itself, it can destroy, but it cannot create; and whatever else this inverted or reversed perspective was, it was clearly a powerful act of creativity, a grand reimagining of the possibilities of human existence. It would not have been possible had it not been sustained by a genuine and generous happiness.

The new world we see being brought into being in the Gospels is one in which the whole grand cosmic architecture of prerogative, power, and eminence has been shaken and even superseded by a new, positively "anarchic" order: an order, that is, in which we see the glory of God revealed in a crucified slave, and in which (consequently) we are enjoined to see the forsaken of the earth as the very children of heaven. In this shockingly, ludicrously disordered order (so to speak), even the mockery visited on Christ—the burlesque crown and robe—acquires a kind of ironic opulence: in the light cast backward upon the scene by the empty tomb, it becomes all at once clear that it is not Christ's "ambitions" that are laughable, but those emblems of earthly authority whose travesties have been draped over his shoulders and pressed into his scalp. We can now see with perfect poignancy the vanity of empires and kingdoms, and the absurdity of men who wrap themselves in rags and adorn themselves with glittering gauds and promote themselves with preposterous titles and thereby claim license to rule over others. And yet the figure of Christ seems only to grow in dignity. It is tempting to describe this vision of reality as—for want of a better alternative—a total humanism: a vision, that is, of humanity in its widest and deepest scope, one that finds the full nobility and mystery and beauty of the human countenance—the human person—in each unique instance of the common nature. Seen thus, Christ's supposed descent from the "form of God" into the "form of a slave" is not so much a paradox as a perfect confirmation of the indwelling of the divine image in each soul. And, once the world has been seen in this way, it can never again be what it formerly was.

◆ ◆ ◆

This, of course, again raises rather obvious questions regarding the general
failure of the church after Constantine to translate this "total humanism"
into what, in long retrospect, looks to us like plain social justice. Not that
such questions should be allowed to degenerate into facile sanctimony. It
would be an almost perfect anachronism, for instance, to ask why post-
Constantinian society was satisfied with mere legal ameliorations of the
conditions of slaves (and those of a frequently inconsistent nature) rather
than with the complete abolition of slavery as an institution. Christians of
the fourth through the sixth centuries, many of whom would have been
only "lightly baptized" in any event, would have found it scarcely any easier
to imagine that they could replace the entire economic and social system
of their world with another, better system than to imagine that they could
persuade the mountains to exchange places with the clouds. But, still, one
has to admit that the Great Church of the imperial era was not exactly
heroic in its vision of the social implications of its creed. As a rule, only
certain extraordinary individuals—certain saints—were willing to press
the principles of the faith to their most unsettling conclusions.

Nevertheless, what should really astonish us by its improbability is
not that so few Christians behaved in a way perfectly consistent with
their beliefs but that such beliefs had ever come into existence in the
first place. Every true historical revolution is a conceptual revolution first,
and the magnitude of any large revision of the conditions or premises of
human life (to say nothing of the time required for it to bear historical
fruit) is determined by the magnitude of that prior "spiritual" achievement. Considered thus, the rise of Christianity was surely an upheaval of
unprecedented and still unequaled immensity. Naturally, when we look
back to the early centuries of the enfranchised church for signs of revolutionary vitality, we do so from the privileged position of late modern
men and women, and so tend to think we see only fugitive gleams amid
a general and otherwise unrelieved darkness. If we are somewhat more
attentive, we become aware of a number of gradual—but substantial—in-
cremental changes that took place within certain of the institutions and
traditions of antiquity. But still, if this is all we see, we have missed what
is most essential. Considering the hierarchy of values that began to find
expression in those centuries, what we should be able to discern on looking back is a massive tectonic shift in the spiritual culture common to

the minds and wills of ancient men and women. There is more than a formal difference, after all, between the soul that is merely unaware of its sins and the soul that is obstinately unrepentant; and the same is true of society as a whole. Once a person or a people comes to recognize an evil for what it is, even if that evil is then allowed to continue for a time, in whole or in part, the most radical change has already come to pass. Thereafter, everything—penitence, regeneration, forgiveness, rebellion, reconciliation—becomes possible. For what it is to be human has been, in some real way, irrevocably altered.

Take for example, once again, what to us constitutes the most obvious case of Christian dereliction in the early centuries of the Constantinian church: the persistence of slavery. Even if it is, as I have said, anachronistic to expect ancient persons to have viewed the institution as an accidental or dispensable feature of their society, and even if it is equally anachronistic to think of slavery in ancient Roman culture as a perfect corollary of the slave systems that flourished in the Americas in the early modern period, it is still entirely reasonable to wonder at the ability of so many ancient Christians to believe simultaneously that all men and women should be their brothers and sisters in Christ and also that certain men and women should be their legal property. The greater marvel, however, in purely historical terms, is that there were even a few who recognized the contradiction. And there were.

Admittedly, the attitudes of many of the fathers of the church toward slavery ranged from (at best) resigned acceptance to (at worst) a kind of prudential approval. All of them regarded slavery as a mark of sin, of course, and all could take some comfort in the knowledge that, at the restoration of creation in the Kingdom of God, it would vanish altogether. They even understood that this expectation necessarily involved certain moral implications for the present. But, for most of them, the best that could be hoped for within a fallen world (apart from certain legal reforms) was a spirit of charity, gentleness, and familial regard on the part of masters and a spirit of longsuffering on the part of servants. Basil of Caesarea found it necessary to defend the subjection of some men to others, on the grounds that not all are capable of governing themselves wisely and virtuously. John Chrysostom dreamed of a perfect (probably eschatological) society in which none would rule over another, celebrated the extension of legal rights and protections to slaves, and fulminated against Christian masters who would dare to humiliate or beat their slaves. Augustine, with his darker, colder, more brutal vision of the fallen world, disliked slavery but did not think it wise always to spare the rod, at least not when the welfare of the soul should take precedence over the welfare of the flesh. Each of them knew that slavery was essentially a damnable thing—which in itself was a considerable advance in moral intelligence over the ethos of pagan antiquity—but damnation, after all, is reserved for the end of time; none of them found it possible to convert that eschatological certainty into a program for the present. But this is hardly surprising. All three were creatures of their time, and we should not expect them to have seen very far beyond the boundaries of the world they knew. Given the inherently restive quality of the human moral imagination, it is only natural that certain of the moral values of the pagan past should have lingered on so long into the Christian era, just as any number of Christian moral values continue today to enjoy a tacit and largely unexamined authority in minds and cultures that no longer believe the Christian story.

And yet—confusingly enough for any conventional calculation of historical probability—there is Gregory of Nyssa, Basil's younger and more brilliant brother, who sounded a very different note, one that almost seems to have issued from some altogether different frame of reality. At least, one searches in vain through the literary remains of antiquity—pagan, Jewish, or Christian—for any other document remotely comparable in tone or content to Gregory's fourth sermon on the book of Ecclesiastes, which he preached during Lent in 379, and which comprises a long passage unequivocally and indignantly condemning slavery *as an institution*. That is to say, in this sermon Gregory does not simply treat slavery as an extravagance in which Christians ought not to indulge beyond the dictates of necessity, nor does he confine himself to denouncing the injustices and cruelties of which slaveholders are frequently guilty. These things one would naturally expect, since moral admonitions and exhortations to repentance are part of the standard Lenten repertoire of any competent homilist. Moreover, ever since 321, when Constantine had granted the churches the power of legally certifying manumissions (the power of *manumissio in ecclesia*), propertied Christians had often taken Easter as an occasion for emancipating slaves, and Gregory was no doubt hoping to encourage his parishioners to follow the custom. But if all he had wanted to do was recommend manumission as a spiritual hygiene or as a gesture of benevolence, he could have done so quite (and perhaps more) effectively by using a considerably more temperate tone than one actually finds in his sermon. For there he directs his anger not at the abuse of slavery but at its use; he reproaches his parishioners not for mistreating their slaves but for daring to imagine they have the right to own other human beings in the first place.

One cannot overemphasize this distinction. On occasion, scholars who have attempted to make this sermon conform to their expectations of fourth century rhetoric have tried to read it as belonging to some standard type of penitential oration, perhaps rather more hyperbolic in some of its language but ultimately intended to do no more than impress the consciences of its hearers with the need for humility. The problem with such an approach, of course, is that a "type" of which no other example exists is hardly a type in any meaningful sense. More to the point, Gregory's language in the sermon is simply too unambiguous to be read as anything other than what it is. He leaves no room for Christian slaveholders to console themselves with the thought that they, at any rate, are merciful masters, generous enough to liberate the occasional worthy servant but wise enough to know when they must continue to exercise stewardship over less responsible souls. He certainly could have done just this; he begins his diatribe (which is not too strong a word) with a brief exegetical excursus on a single, rather unexceptional verse, Ecclesiastes 2:7 ("I got me male and female slaves, and had my home-born slaves as well"): a text that would seem to invite only a few bracing imprecations against luxuriance and sloth, and nothing more. As he warms to his theme, however, Gregory goes well beyond this. For anyone at all, he says, to presume mastery over another person is the grossest imaginable arrogance, a challenge to and a robbery of God, to whom alone all persons belong. Moreover, he continues, for one person to deprive another of the freedom granted to all human beings by God is to violate and indeed to overturn the law of God, which explicitly gives us no such power over one another. At what price, Gregory goes on to ask his congregation, could one ever be said to have purchased the image of God—which is what each person is—as God alone possesses resources equal to such a treasure? In fact, says Gregory, directly linking his argument to the approaching Easter feast, since God's greatest gift to us is the perfect liberty vouchsafed us by Christ's saving action in time, and since God's gifts are entirely irrevocable, it lies not even in *God's* power to enslave men and women. Anyway, he reasons, it is known that, when a slave is bought, so are all of his or her worldly possessions; but God has given dominion over all of creation to each and every person, and there simply is no sum sufficient for the purchase of so vast an estate. So, he tells his congregation, you may imagine that the exchange of coin and receipt of deed really endows you with superiority over another, but you are deceived: all of us are equal, prey to the same frailties, capable of the same joys, beneficiaries of the same redemption, and subject to the same judgment. We are therefore equal in every respect, but—says Gregory—"you have divided our nature between slavery and mastery, and have made it at once slave to itself and master over itself."

Where does this language come from? We can try to identify certain of the immediate influences on Gregory's thought. His sister Macrina, for example, was a theologian and contemplative of considerable accomplishment who had persuaded her (and Gregory's and Basil's) mother to live a common life of service, prayer, and devotion with her servants; and Gregory revered Macrina. But even his sister's example cannot account for the sheer uncompromising vehemence of Gregory's sermon, or for the logic that informs it—which, taken at face value, seems to press inexorably toward abolition. And there are other mysteries in Gregory's language as well. What, for instance, does it mean to complain that slaveholders have divided our common nature as human beings by their deeds? To answer this question fully would require a long investigation of Gregory's metaphysics (and he was, as it happens, a philosopher of considerable originality), but that is not necessary here. Suffice it to say that Gregory obviously cannot understand human nature as, for instance, Aristotle did: as merely an invariable, abstract set of properties, of which any given man or woman constitutes either a more excellent or a more degenerate expression. For Aristotle, it is precisely knowledge of what human nature is that allows us to judge that some human beings are deficient specimens of the kind and therefore suited only to serve as the "living tools" of other men (which is how he defines slaves in both the *Nicomachean* and the *Eudemian Ethics*). Human nature, understood in this sense, is simply the ideal index of the species, one which allows us to arrange our understanding of human existence into exact and obvious divisions of authority: the superiority of reason over appetite, of course, but also of city over nature, man over woman, Greek over barbarian, and master over slave. For Gregory, by contrast, the entire idea of human nature has been thoroughly suffused with the light of Easter, "contaminated" by the Christian inversion of social order; our nature is, for him, first and foremost our community in the humanity of Christ, who by descending into the most abject of conditions, even dying the death of a criminal, only to be raised up as Lord of history, in the very glory of God, has become forever the face of the faceless, the persona by which each of us has been raised to the dignity of a "co-heir of the Kingdom."

This, perhaps, is all the explanation we need—or can hope to find— for Gregory's sermon. Modern persons of a secularist bent, who believe that the roots of their solicitude for human equality reach down no deeper in the soil of history than the so-called Age of Enlightenment, often tend to imagine that their values are nothing more than the rational impulses of any sane conscience unencumbered by prejudice. But this is nonsense. There is no such thing as "enlightened" morality, if by that one means an ethics written on the fabric of our nature, which anyone can discover simply by the light of disinterested reason. There are, rather, moral traditions, shaped by events, ideas, inspirations, and experiences; and no morality is devoid of the contingencies of particular cultural histories. Whatever it is we think we mean by human "equality," we are able to presume the moral weight of such a notion only because far deeper down in the historical strata of our shared Western consciousness we retain the memory of an unanticipated moment of spiritual awakening, a delighted and astonished intellectual response to a single historical event: the proclamation of Easter. It was because of his faith in the risen Christ that Gregory could declare in his commentary on the Beatitudes, without any irony or reserve, that if Christians truly practiced the mercy commanded of them by their Lord humanity would no longer admit of divisions within itself between slavery and mastery, poverty and wealth, shame and honor, infirmity and strength, for all things would be held in common and all persons would be equal one with another. In the sermon he preached for Easter 379, Gregory resumes many of the themes of his Lenten addresses on Ecclesiastes, including that of the moral odium of slavery; Easter, he makes it clear, is a time to celebrate every form of emancipation, and thus he seamlessly unites the theme of our liberation from the household of death to his renewed call for the manumission of slaves. There is nothing at all forced in this association of ideas, at least not for anyone who truly believes that Jesus of Nazareth, crucified by Pontius Pilate, is Lord.

Needless to say, it is somewhat disheartening that what, in Gregory's sermon, has something of the blinding brilliance of a lightning flash seems so quickly to have subsided into a pale and feeble flicker in the centuries that followed, all but lost in the darkness of the immense historical tragedy of institutional Christianity. On the other hand, however, much depends on how one chooses to tell the story of those centuries. Chattel slavery did, after all, gradually disappear in the West during the Middle Ages, and not solely for economic reasons (though such reasons cannot be discounted or ignored). If nothing else, in a society composed of baptized men and women Christian principles could not help but be, if not catastrophic, at least corrosive in their effects upon a slave economy, and indeed upon all forms of forced servitude. There is, in fact, some (fitful) evidence to this effect. For instance, in 1256 the city of Bologna decided to place all bonded servants within the city under ecclesiastical jurisdiction and then to grant them liberty; and the municipal government reached this decision explicitly on Christian grounds.[3] Local anecdotes are, of course, of only limited significance. It would be much more impressive, obviously, if medieval men and women had succeeded far more broadly, throughout all their cities and villages, in creating the sort of social justice the gospel would seem to demand. It would also have been considerate of them to have discovered a cure for cancer. But reality is a particularly inert and intransigent substance. What is remarkable about an incident such as this Bolognese mass emancipation is that it testifies to the spiritual ferment of a whole religious culture, and to the capacity of a Christian society—even one constrained by the severest material and conceptual limitations—to find itself moved, perplexed, troubled, and perhaps tormented by moral ideals that ancient society could never have imagined, and then to act upon those ideals, in defiance of its own economic interests. It allows us also to see more clearly the continuity of a certain, often hidden but ultimately inextinguishable, contrarian impulse within the Christian moral vision of reality (of the sort that surfaced again in, for instance, the great abolitionist movements of the eighteenth and nineteenth centuries).

In any event, this much is certain: Gregory broke with all known precedent in his sermon, and this can only be because one pure instant of piercing clarity—one great interruption of history and of the tediously repetitive stories men and women tell about themselves and about their prerogatives and privileges and eminence and glories—had allowed him to see the true measure of human worth, and of divine love, precisely where all worldly wisdom would say it cannot be found. All of humanity's self-serving myths, all of its romances of power, had been shattered at Easter, even if a great many Christians could not fully grasp this. Three years after the Ecclesiastes sermon, Gregory wrote a treatise against the teachings of the "semi-Arian" theologian Eunomius. At one point in his argument, Gregory notes that Eunomius claims that Christ could not really be God in the fullest sense, because Paul describes Christ as bearing the form of a slave. To this Gregory's indignant response is to say that slavery, no less than sin, disease, or death, is a consequence of our alienation from God, and that God in Christ assumes the greater slavery in which all human beings are bound in order to purge slavery (along with every other evil) from our nature. In this particular text, Gregory's reasoning does not necessarily extend beyond eschatological anticipation; but the moral import of treating slavery as an evil specifically defeated by Christ's saving acts clearly does. When Western peoples came to believe that the verdict of God had been passed upon all persons in Christ—on Christ's side of the tableau, so to speak, rather than Pilate's—a boundary had been crossed in time that, once crossed, continued constantly to recede from them, even if they were not always much disposed to move any farther than they already had. At certain critical moments in history, the past (even the fairly recent past) becomes all at once a foreign land, immeasurably remote. For peoples that had come to believe in Easter, even if only for a brief cultural moment, it was no longer possible to believe with perfect innocence that divine justice recognized the power of one person to own another; for, in coming to believe in the resurrection of Christ—much to their consternation, maybe, but also perhaps for their salvation—they found that the form of God and the form of the human person had been revealed to them all at once, completely, then and thenceforth always, in the form of a slave.

CHAPTER FOURTEEN

The Death and Birth of Worlds

VIOLENT, SUDDEN, AND calamitous revolutions are the ones that accomplish the least. While they may succeed at radically reordering societies, they usually cannot transform cultures. They may excel at destroying the past, but they are generally impotent to create a future. The revolutions that genuinely alter human reality at the deepest levels—the only real revolutions, that is to say—are those that first convert minds and wills, that reshape the imagination and reorient desire, that overthrow tyrannies within the soul. Christianity, in its first three centuries, was a revolution of the latter sort: gradual, subtle, exceedingly small and somewhat inchoate at first, slowly introducing its vision of divine, cosmic, and human reality into the culture around it, often by deeds rather than words, and simply enduring from one century to the next. It was probably a largely urban phenomenon, appealing to the moderately affluent and educated as well as to the poor, though as time passed it won patrons and sympathizers among the nobility. As I have noted already, it was somewhat conspicuous by its general indiscriminacy regarding the social stations of its converts and by its special attraction for women, and it may have entered many households through wives and daughters. It endured obloquy and false rumor, but over time won admiration from many for its charitable zeal, even toward unbelievers. Persecutions were sporadic, though sometimes fierce, but their ultimate effect was to refine and strengthen the faith. As the new faith mastered the instruments of philosophy and increasingly drew converts from among the philosophically trained, it acquired the ability to articulate its vision of things with ever greater clarity, richness, and persuasiveness. And only then, after many generations, and directly following one last, especially savage period of persecution, it was unexpectedly granted not only political security but political influence.

It is impossible to say with any real certainty what the number of Christians in the empire was at the dawn of the fourth century, or what portion of the population they constituted. Neither can we establish what the rate of conversion had been in the preceding centuries, nor can we measure the intensity of faith among the converted. The distribution of Christians, moreover, was irregular; the church in Rome was fairly large, but Christianity's most fertile field of growth was in the East. It seems likely that in some Eastern cities, such as Ephesus, Antioch, and Smyrna, Christians were in the majority. Even then, the countryside remained more generally pagan. Occasional notes of triumphalism on the part of ancient Christians or of alarm on the part of their pagan contemporaries might tempt us to imagine a great mass movement toward the church: Pliny writing in 112 from a town of the northern Pontus that buyers could not be found for meat from sacrificial animals, presumably on account of the number of Christians in the region; Tertullian boasting in 197 that adherents of a faith so young "already fill the world"; Diocletian fretting over the number of "the just" in the empire; the emperor Maximin in 312, in the course of revoking the persecution of the Eastern churches, sheepishly explaining that the policy of persecution had been adopted in the first place only because "almost everyone" had been abandoning worship of the gods. One should not, however, read too much into such pronouncements; a movement need not be large, but only sufficiently substantial to attract attention, to inspire confidence in its members or dismay in its enemies. There is just as much anecdotal evidence of paganism's durability. "Hellenes" could be found among the privileged classes two centuries and more after Constantine's accession, and, in both East and West, parts of the provinces long remained quite cheerfully heathen. Even among the baptized the old ways were not hastily abandoned: as late as 440, Pope Leo was dismayed to see Roman Christians on the steps of St. Peter's basilica reverently bowing their heads to the rising sun, as if to Sol Invictus himself; and, as late as 495, Pope Gelasius I could not dissuade the Romans from celebrating the Lupercalia, the ancient "wolf festival" of purification and fertility, during which young men ran naked through the streets. And surely it is of some significance that well into the sixth century Justinian still had to resort to such heavy-handed coercion to suppress the old beliefs.

So what can we say of the size of the empire's Christian population in the year 300? Among modern historians, estimates range from as low as 4 percent of the entire population of the empire to as high as 10. I incline toward the latter number, or one even slightly higher, only because I suspect that there is a certain critical demographic threshold below which the religion would still have been too marginal to seem a plausible option for a man of Constantine's enormous ambitions (unless we are really to believe that his conversion was entirely free of political calculation). The ferocity of the Great Persecution, the pathetic capitulation of Galerius on his bed of pain, Constantine's final adoption of the Christian God as his own—all of this suggests, at the very least, that Christianity had by this period become not only an ineradicable movement but a genuinely potent cultural and social force. But this is still only conjecture on my part. What is certain is that by 350 many Christians were convinced that their numbers had swelled to more than half the empire's population of roughly sixty million, and most historians have tended to interpret this as evidence of a sudden flood of new conversions in the wake of Constantine's. On the other hand, the sociologist Rodney Stark has made a rather convincing case that such a shift in demographic proportion would in fact have followed naturally from a rate of expansion more or less arithmetically constant with that of previous centuries, which would suggest that Constantine's conversion was not so much the chief cause of the Christianization of the empire as its most salient symptom.[1]

Without real statistical evidence, however (and none, alas, exists), any purely mathematical model of the rate of conversion remains at most an educated guess. A better approach to the matter would perhaps be a more purely historical attempt to ascertain from the events of the fourth century to what degree Christianity or Christian ideas had by then already come to pervade and shape imperial society. In this regard, perhaps no episode is more instructive than that of the short, startling career of Constantine's nephew, Julian the Apostate, and of the failure of his great plan to restore the worship of the old gods among the peoples of the empire. Of course, it is conceivable that, had he lived longer, Julian might have succeeded in halting or stalling Christianity's triumphant advance through history, or at least in rousing a more than tepid enthusiasm among his subjects for the great religious revival he envisaged; but I sincerely doubt that the ultimate defeat of his designs can be attributed solely to the brevity of his reign. In a very real sense, even if he had succeeded he would still have failed, for the simple reason that the "paganism" he preached was so thoroughly saturated with Christian ideals and hopes, and so colored with a Christian sensibility, that it could never have coalesced into a stable system of thought or belief in its own right. Julian's religion could have survived only by imitating the strengths of Christianity; but then it would have been a contradiction and a mystery to itself, to which the only solution would have been a return to faith in Christ.

Had Julian's repudiation of Christianity been merely a matter of executive prudence, it might have been an essentially sound policy. Constantine probably never quite grasped how volatile and unpredictable a force he had introduced into imperial politics in adopting Christianity, but his sons almost certainly did. Constantius II (317–361) in particular seems to have realized that the church—with its appetite for precise dogma and its pretensions to the kind of ultimacy that no temporal institution could claim—was anything but a perfectly acquiescent ally of the imperial court. Sharing little or nothing of his father's faith, such as it was, he was also better prepared to recognize the need securely to incorporate the offices of the church into the apparatus of the state. To this end he set about corrupting the clergy with patronage, property, usufructs, special immunities, and unwarranted privileges. He also convoked a series of synods through which to impose an ever more elaborate official theology upon the faithful; even the pagan Ammianus expressed a certain revulsion at the (as he saw it) effeminate intricacy of the doctrines with which the emperor had sought to cloud an essentially "lucid and uncomplicated faith." And, in imposing legal penalties on dissenters from the theology of his imperial church—which happened to be Arian rather than Nicene (that is, "Catholic")—Constantius won for himself the special distinction of having inaugurated institutional Christianity's history of internecine persecution. Ultimately, though, he discovered that the intransigence of truly devout Christians was invincible. The perverse obstinacy, for instance, of Athanasius of Alexandria (c. 293–373)—the great champion of Nicene orthodoxy who endured at least five exiles from his see rather than submit to Arian doctrine, and who even went so far as to denounce Constantius as a forerunner of the Antichrist—must have served as a sobering reminder to the imperial court of just how fractious and indomitable this religion of "true believers" really was. Would any sensible pagan have willingly suffered so much over matters of such rarified interest and of so little consequence? And would any pagan faction have exhibited the temerity of those Nicene Christians in Alexandria who signed their names to a public reprimand of the emperor for his deviations from the true faith? If Julian had decided to end the court's flirtation with this religion of voluble fanatics, simply for the sake of civic tranquility, no one could really have reproached him.

Julian, however, was himself a true believer, and his disenchantment with Christianity came early in life. His formation in the faith, moreover, was hardly superficial; the tutor and guardian of his earliest years was the Arian bishop Eusebius of Nicomedia, and, according to Eunapius, Julian's knowledge of scripture soon surpassed that of his teachers. But he had no reason to love the creed of his cousin Constantius, who on ascending to the purple had slaughtered Julian's family as potential rivals for his throne. And, according to Ammianus, Julian had seen too much of the savagery with which Christians could treat one another to entertain any exorbitant illusions regarding the personal sanctity certified or produced by baptism. The truth, however, is that Julian was not simply repelled by Christianity; had he been, he might merely have sunk into a cynicism even more callous than his cousin's. Rather, he was genuinely and reverently drawn to paganism, especially the mystical—and magical—Neoplatonism he learned from Maximus of Ephesus, and his conversion in 351, when he was at most twenty years old, was sincere and irrevocable. It was also motivated by a real and commendable love of Hellenistic civilization, as well as a touching inability to recognize that the religious forms of that civilization were largely exhausted. Of all the emperors in the Constantinian line, Julian alone stands free of any suspicion of bad faith. He was also without question the most estimable and attractive of the lot: a devout lover of the gods, an avid scholar, a military leader of unexpected brilliance and dashing bravery, and a fine—and on occasion exquisite—writer; when he was appointed Western Caesar in 355 he showed himself a conscientious ruler, genuinely concerned for the welfare of his subjects; and on becoming Augustus (emperor) in 360 he proved for the most part a mild and equable sovereign, modest, restrained, capable of self-mockery, possessed of a ready wit, and magnanimous to those who did not offend his taste in religion. He was spiteful in his treatment of the Christians, it is true, but that can be ascribed to a predictable emotional purblindness; and he certainly exhibited none of his cousin's murderous proclivities.

Julian was also, however, a spiritual enthusiast, and this is part of the peculiar contradiction of his religious psychology. He was, not to belabor the point, pagan in the way that the ideal Christian was expected to be Christian. I am not referring to the obviously rapturous quality of his personal piety and devotion to the gods; that was common enough in, for instance, many of the savior cults of late antiquity. As for his personal austerities—the rough garb, uncropped beard, somewhat unfastidious hygiene, and general abstemiousness—they were no more Christian than they were Platonist. But there was also a proselytizing, moralizing, and activist element in his approach to religion that one can describe only as evangelical zeal. At the center of his spiritual vision was an experience of *metanoia*, repentance, a humble return of the prodigal heart to the High God who calls his errant children home; and he seems truly to have believed that the emotional warmth with which he desired this reconciliation with the divine world could be communicated to his fellow pagans as an experience immediately convincing and profound. Moreover, it may not be too much to say that many aspects of the kind of Neoplatonism he embraced—with its amalgamation of theurgy and metaphysical system, faith and dialectic, worship and contemplation, supplication and self-abnegation, revelation and reason—was already influenced by Christianity's attractive synthesis of the communal and the private, the intellectual and the emotional, the philosophical and the devotional, the institutional and the ethical.

Unfortunately, and notoriously, Julian was also remarkably and even at times vulgarly credulous. Apparently Maximus was able to impress him with the theurgic rites of Hecate, including the "telestic" technique of bringing a statue of the goddess to life. This was accomplished, one assumes, with a mechanical automaton of the sort often in those days employed by religious charlatans. In fact, the numerous divine visions and auditions that Libanius ascribes to Julian may well have been induced, at least on many occasions, by nothing more supernatural than dark alcoves, guttering torches, hidden pulleys, and concealed speaking trumpets (though, then again, the gods might have put in a real appearance or two). His mind, moreover, was hospitable to every imaginable mystification and occult fascination. And his passion for the sacrificial slaughter of hecatombs of oxen, in which he often participated with his own hands, verged on the genocidal. Despite his native intellectual gifts, his philosophical writings are a syncretic midden of superstitions, myths, and metaphysical obscurantism. The mystery religions evidently exercised considerable appeal for him, and he may himself have submitted to more than one ritual rebirth and clutched to his bosom more than one corpus of secret revelations. He seems to have harbored a special affection for the Metroac cult of the Great Mother or Cybele, whose worship he quixotically hoped might eventually expunge the stain of Christian atheism from the empire, and whom he accorded a place in public devotion equal to that of Zeus or Apollo.[2]

It was, I think, more a result of his religious ardor than of political strategy that, after becoming emperor, Julian soon also became—in his own modest but increasingly impatient way—a persecutor. I have already mentioned his rescript depriving Christian professors of classical literature, rhetoric, and philosophy of their license to teach, as well as his firm policy of preference for pagans over "Galilaeans" in all government appointments. He also proscribed the willing of legacies to churches. Some of his anti-Christian legislation, however, was perhaps no more than simple justice: he revoked the special privileges and exemptions Constantius had granted the Christian clergy; he abrogated the church's state subsidies; he had several churches that had been erected on or near the sites of pagan shrines demolished; local Christian communities were obliged to indemnify the cost of restoring the temples they had despoiled or destroyed; and some churches—reversing an older history of unpunished theft—were forcibly converted into pagan fanes, including two Syrian basilicas in which idols of Dionysus were installed. When, however, these policies provoked protest, he was not entirely above using violence. For instance, he ordered the removal of the relics of the Christian martyr Babylas from the grove of Daphne in Antioch, where an ancient shrine of Apollo stood, in order to purge the site of the pollution produced by moldering bones (which had, it seems, silenced the god's oracles); when local Christians expressed their resentment by forming a funeral cortege to conduct the relics to their new resting place, and by singing hymns against idolatry as they walked, Julian was sufficiently incensed to have a number of Christians arrested and tortured for information regarding the identities of the chief agitators. (A few days later, the Apolline temple burned down, probably as a result of arson, but no culprits were ever found.) He was also notably swift and fierce in punishing violence against pagans, but leisurely and mild in punishing violence against Christians. A number of pagan riots, resulting in Christian deaths, were met by no more than a general profession of official displeasure. When the Arian bishop of Alexandria George was torn apart by a mob, Julian satisfied himself with a fairly gentle rebuke of the city's citizens for their understandable but excessive and unseemly zeal. At the end of the day, though, Julian's measures against the "Galilaeans" look almost kindhearted in comparison to the measures taken by Constantius against "heretics" and "Hellenes."

That Julian honestly believed he was engaged in restoring the ancient ways can hardly be doubted; but one has to wonder, nonetheless, whether he was ever aware of how curiously unlike the religions of antiquity his version of paganism frequently was. It has been often suggested (though also often denied) that he hoped to create a kind of pagan "church" on the Christian model, centrally organized, uniform in basic tenets, and rigorist in morals. He certainly could strike a somewhat pontifical tone when instructing pagan priests on matters of faith and morals. His infatuation with sumptuous sacrificial spectacle may indicate a craving for forms of worship that could rival the Eucharistic liturgy in ceremonial theatrics and affective power. And other aspects of his religious policy perhaps suggest a desire for an imperial cult as capable as Christianity of uniting every level of society in a common creed, and of appealing with equal force to persons of the highest and of the lowest intellectual attainments. But, whether any of this was his conscious purpose or not, it is certainly the case that his vision of a renewed paganism was almost absurdly "Galilaean" in coloration. In his "Letter to a Priest" he describes his ideal pagan cleric as pious, sober, and unostentatious, loving God and his neighbor above all else, and giving freely and cheerfully to all who come in need, even from small stores. After all, he reasons, it was neglect of the poor by the pagan priesthood in the past that had made Christian philanthropy so enticing a lure to the indigent and weak-minded. Anyway, he argues, surely all of us should wish to imitate the benevolence of the gods, who pour out the bounties of the earth to be shared by all in common; poverty is caused solely by the greed of the rich, who hoard these divine blessings to themselves rather than share them with their neighbors; we should give lavishly to the poor, naturally preferring the virtuous among them, perhaps, but realizing that it is a pious act to care even for the wicked: "For it is to their humanity, not to their character, that we give." For the same reason, we should be generous in caring for those shut up in prison. In his twenty-second epistle, written to the high priest of Galatia Arsacius, Julian's tone at times waxes positively envious: no Jew is so forsaken of his coreligionists as to have to go begging; the "Galilaeans"—to our disgrace—support not only their poor but ours also; yet we give not even to our own. It is, he argues, by their "pretense" of benevolence and holiness that the Christians win so many recruits to their cause. Still, we should imitate them. For instance, he suggests, pagan priests should establish hostels in every city to shelter those in duress, "not only our own, but also others lacking in funds." Generally speaking, we must, for the good of all, teach our fellow Hellenes how to serve others willingly and unstintingly.

What, one has to ask, did this achingly, poignantly deluded man think to accomplish by such exhortations? Did he really imagine that the sort of charity he wished to recommend could have any compelling rationale apart from the peculiar moral grammar of Christian faith? Where did he imagine the moral resources for such an ethics were to be found in pagan culture? Hospitality to strangers, food and alms for beggars: these were indeed, as he insisted, ancient traditions of the "Hellenes." But giving to all and sundry, freely, heedless of their characters, out of love for their humanity; visiting those in prison, provisioning the poor from temple treasuries, ceaselessly feeding the hungry, providing shelter to all who might have need of it; loving God and neighbor as the highest good, priestly poverty, universal civic philanthropy: all of this emanates from another quarter altogether. Did Julian truly believe that the fervency of his faith would take fire in others if pagan priests would only undertake the sort of superficial imitation of Christian behavior he enjoined? And did he really fail to understand that the Christians had been able to surpass the pagans in benevolence because active charity was organically part of—indeed, central to—their faith in a way that it was not for pagans? As Gibbon observed, "The genius and power of Julian were unequal to the enterprise of restoring a religion which was destitute of theological principles, of moral precepts, and of ecclesiastical discipline; which rapidly hastened to decay and dissolution, and was not susceptible of any solid or consistent reformation."[3]

In the end, Julian's schemes probably would not have succeeded even if he had reigned as long as Constantine: arrayed against him were not only the stubborn forces of Christian fanaticism but the unconquerable legions of pagan indifference. The Jews, he tells the high priest Theodorus, know the traditions of their fathers, keep the laws of their faith, and prefer death to even the violation of kosher prescriptions; but we Hellenes, he laments, are so uninterested in our own traditions that we have entirely forgotten what the laws laid down by our ancestors actually are. During his sojourn in Antioch, not long before his death, he was chilled not only by the animosity of the Christian majority but by the apathy of the local pagans, who viewed many of the special features of his religion—his mortifications, his moralism, the extravagance of his sacrificial liturgies, his apparently insatiable malice toward cows—as rather shrill and alarming. For his part, Julian especially resented the Antiochenes for the immense disappointment he had suffered on their account when, eagerly hastening to the ancient Apolline temple in the grove of Daphne to realize his boyhood dream of attending the local festival of Apollo—expecting paeans, cakes, libations, sweet incense, processions, sacrifices, and pious youths clad in pure white garments—he found instead only a solitary old priest who had no sacrifice to offer but a goose that he himself had brought from home. Nor was this the only such disappointment the young emperor suffered. When he made his pilgrimage to the Anatolian city of Pessinus, the "birthplace" of Cybele, he could induce the locals to participate in rites for the goddess only by paying them to do so. Episodes of this sort are painfully emblematic of the pervasive element of fantasy in Julian's project of religious restoration. A still vital and viable pagan religion would not have required the exaggerated, artificial, and traumatic resuscitation he attempted; nor would a few decades of Christian dominance have reduced a truly robust tradition to so feeble a condition. The cultural transition from paganism to Christianity had been occurring naturally—and inexorably—for centuries, and Julian (arriving so very late in the day) could do nothing to reverse it. What he desired was simply impossible. One cannot make a fire from ashes.

◆ ◆ ◆

With Julian's premature death, while on campaign against the Sassanid Empire, the inevitable course of imperial history resumed and began to move toward a religious settlement that Constantine surely could not have foreseen and that Constantius would certainly have deplored. Julian's successors did, it is true, reinstate much of the earlier imperial policy toward the church, but they were not necessarily eager to emulate Constantius's incubation of a state church, or his suffocating indulgence of a compliant clergy. The emperor Valentinian I (321–375), for instance, who reigned from 364 to his death, restored many of the clergy's privileges and exemptions but also took measures to prevent abuses of ecclesiastical power and to bring an end to corruption within the church. Whereas, for instance, Constantius had allowed men to retain their estates (and the profits therefrom) when they entered the priesthood, Valentinian insisted upon complete divestment and a binding rule of priestly poverty. He also revived the Edict of Milan's law of universal religious tolerance rather than Constantius's antipagan legislations. But, in the end, the relationship of church and state remained an uneasy contradiction. Tertullian had once proudly proclaimed that no one could serve both God and Caesar, since the armies of Christ and those of the devil can never be reconciled; Christians acknowledge, he said, no commonwealth smaller than the entire world, nor any allegiance but to Christ. Now, however, the impossible was a concrete reality. Two entities with no natural compatibility, each more likely to weaken or corrupt the other than to strengthen or invigorate it, were now so thoroughly interwoven that separation had become inconceivable. Given their intrinsic irreconcilability, each would now have to surrender something of its essence to survive, and each would have to strive for supremacy over the other. In the event—to their mutual advantage but individual disadvantage—both won.

The critical moment at which the future shape of this improbable liaison was effectively decided came during the reign of Theodosius I, from 379 to 395. Theodosius was, it is fair to say, a convinced Catholic Christian, who regarded the theology of Nicaea as authoritative for the church as a whole, and who believed that it was the obligation of a Christian monarch to bring the laws of his realm into as close a conformity with the moral precepts of his faith as was practically possible, and to assure the ascendency of orthodoxy among his subjects. This is not, of course, to imply that he was insensible to the political value of a unified imperial church. And his desire to introduce a spirit of Christian leniency into the laws of the empire, while producing many genuine and admirable improvements, did not prevent him from resorting to the most draconian methods where the financial or military needs of his beleaguered empire were at stake. And over against his more humanitarian legislations one must place in the balance the inequity of his treatment of pagans and "heretics." In the year 380 he proclaimed Catholic Christianity the official faith of the realm. In 381 he proscribed pagan rites for the purpose of divination, at any altar, public or private. In 382 he converted all remaining pagan temples into imperial museums and their possessions into mere objets d'art. He abolished all traditional auspication in 385. In 388 he adopted a policy of destroying temples and of dissolving pagan societies. In 389 he abolished the old calendar of pagan feasts. In 391 he definitively forbade the restoration of the altar of Victory in the Roman Senate, ended all remaining subsidies of pagan festivals, and reiterated the ban on blood sacrifice. In 392 he prohibited all offerings of any kind to the gods, made haruspication equivalent to treason, and threatened fines and confiscations for those who used public altars for sacrifice or adored graven images. In 393 he ended the Olympic Games. As for aberrant Christians, in 383 and 388 he imposed heavy fines on "heretics" and forbade their assemblies and ordinations. And harsher measures would be taken by his sons after his death.

All of this was a great boon for the institutional church, perhaps, but was obviously an almost irreparable catastrophe for Christianity. Not that it was a moment of perfect victory for the state either. It is tempting to read this history as nothing more than the depressing chronicle of how the great initial surge of Christianity's revolutionary interruption of human history was at last subdued and absorbed by a society that, as the price of its victory, was willing to submit to nominal baptism; and of how the church was reduced to an instrument of temporal power and worldly order; and of how the gospel was taken captive and subverted by the mechanisms of the state. All of this is quite true, of course, as far as it goes, but there is more to the story too. The most remarkable aspect of Theodosius's edict of 380 was that it did not merely establish an imperial preference in matters of religion, or even merely identify the Christian Church in a general sense as the cult of the empire. It identified a specific body of doctrine, established and preserved by the authority of a specific hierarchy of bishops, as the index of true Christianity, to which even the power of the empire was now in some sense logically subservient. Constantius had simply used theology as a means of creating a servile clergy and laity; he certainly never meant to concede any kind of institutional autonomy to the church. Theodosius, by contrast, professed his loyalty to a set of dogmas and to the institution that alone had authority to interpret and amplify upon them. What this meant in practical terms cannot be reduced to a simple formula, but it definitely implied a certain relativity in the moral and legal authority of the state. As much as Theodosius made submission to Catholic teaching a sign of true allegiance to the state, he also made the legitimacy of the state in some sense contingent upon its fidelity to the church.

Some of the implications of so radical a compromise can perhaps be glimpsed in the famous tale of Theodosius's humiliation in the winter of 390 at the hands of the formidable bishop of Milan Ambrose (a man whose entire career in the church was marked by an almost perfect implacability, both for good and for ill, wherever matters of faith or ecclesial "principle" were at stake). That year, Theodosius happened to be sojourning in Milan when word reached him from Thessalonica of a riot in which certain citizens, as reprisal for the just imprisonment of a popular racer of horses, had brutally murdered the imperial governor and his assistants. Theodosius ordered a stern military retaliation, and approximately seven thousand inhabitants of Thessalonica were massacred by his soldiers in the city's hippodrome. Theodosius had certainly not envisaged such carnage, and he quickly regretted what he had done, but Ambrose refused to be satisfied by private professions of shame. Before the bishop would again allow the emperor to be present at the Eucharistic celebration in the cathedral of Milan, Theodosius would have to do public penance for his crime. In fact, Ambrose would not allow the emperor even to enter the cathedral unless he came as a penitent. Astonishingly, after several weeks, Theodosius submitted to Ambrose's authority, approached the church in plain attire, openly confessed his guilt, and implored God for absolution. This was unprecedented. The old cults had certainly never wielded any power like this or arrogated to themselves a sacred office higher than that of the emperor himself. Here, though, for perhaps the first time in the history of the West, the supreme power of the state surrendered to the still higher power of the church, and a spectacular demonstration was given of the transcendence of divine over human law. It was now clear that the one true sacred community was the church, of which even the temporal sovereign was only one member, and of which even the empire was only one "local" region. This same drama, or one very like it, would be played out again and again throughout the history of Christendom, and often—though not always—the temporal power would emerge victorious over the spiritual. Still, a principle had been established on the day of Theodosius's penance: the state could never again enjoy the unquestioned divine authority or legitimacy it had possessed before the rise of Christianity. If Theodosius's imposition of Catholic orthodoxy on the empire was in some sense the Christian revolution's greatest defeat (and it was), it was also an irremediable blow to the ultimacy of the state; and this much, at least, the church bequeathed to the future. In some sense the ferment, fecundity, and turmoil of later Western history—political, social, ideological, and so on—was born in this moment when the unhappy marriage of church and state also, quite unexpectedly, began to desacralize the state. Of course, from that point on it was inevitable that these two allied but essentially irreconcilable orders would continue to struggle for advantage, one over the other. And only in the early modern period would that struggle be decided, with the reduction of the church to a state cult, as part of the West's transition to late modernity's cult of the state.

Julian was in many respects wise, I think it fair to say, to mourn the passing of the pagan order, and to detest the rising barbarism of his age, and to recognize that the bizarre Asiatic mystery cult upon which Constantine had bestowed his favor was in some sense destined to destroy the world he loved. And perhaps it was a tragedy for Christianity that Julian did not succeed in extinguishing the emerging state church before it could assume its final dimensions (just as it might have been better, all things considered, if Ambrose had lost to Theodosius). But, speaking in purely practical terms, the old civilization had long been dying, and in an age of dissolution—waning faith, demographic attrition, cultural exhaustion, economic decline, constant military duress, and so forth—the new religion brought with it the possibility of a new civilization, continuous with but more vital than its predecessor. Christianity produced a unique synthesis of Hellenic and Jewish genius; it gathered the energies of imperial culture together under the canopy of a religious logic capable of reaching every level of society and of nourishing almost every spiritual aspiration; it made temporal adversity more tolerable by illumining this world with the light of an eternal Kingdom immune to the vicissitudes of earthly societies; it promised every soul that sought God's Kingdom an eternal welcome; it gave the course of human history a meaning and a design; its great epic narrative of fall and redemption, sin and sanctification, divine incarnation and human glorification provided the human imagination with a new universe in which to wander, expand, and flourish; and it infused the culture it inherited with a far profounder, far richer, far more terrible moral consciousness than had ever existed under the rule of the old gods. The established church, moreover, provided the Western half of the old Roman world with an institution that could endure through the long night of the barbarian kingdoms and that—in its monasteries—would shelter the remnants of a vanished civilization. The East, on the other hand, it provided with the binding force for a new empire, a new Roman Christian civilization, able to preserve much of the Hellenistic past but possessed also of an artistic, intellectual, religious, and moral genius wholly its own. And to both West and East, by virtue of its transcendence of any particular national or imperial order, it provided a means for forging alliances and absorbing enemies.

In the end, though, one can be too easily distracted by the grand and momentous events of the history of hierarchies and governments, bishops and princes. The Christian revolution with which this book is concerned has very little to do with the triumph of the institutional Catholic order, except insofar as the latter might be understood as an unforeseen and, in retrospect, ambiguous consequence of the former. I am not much interested in either the church of the empire or the empire of the church. The true revolution was something that happened at far deeper—though often far humbler—levels; its true victories were so subtle as to be often all but invisible; it advanced not only by the conversion of individuals but also by the slow, tacit transformation of the values around it; and it became an object of genuine imperial concern only after it had achieved its principal victory among and through those whom no one would have imagined capable of threatening the foundations of the ancient order. Compared to this fundamental, essential, and really quite incredible revision of the prevailing understanding of God, humanity, nature, history, and the moral good, the delinquent response of the powerful of the earth was of only minor import. The truest sign of the revolution's triumph was, as I have said, the reign of Julian. Not because of his personal defeat: the old and rather nasty Christian legend of his last moments—filling his hand with the blood pouring from his wounded side, flinging it at the sun, and crying "Thou hast conquered, Galilaean!"—is nothing more than a spiteful lie. In fact, his final hours were adorned by a moving profession of faith on his part, full of gratitude to the divine, and free of any trace of resentment or self-pity. The real proof of what the gospel wrought in its first three centuries lay in Julian himself, as he was in the full splendor of his pagan prime. From Constantine to Theodosius, the emperor most genuinely Christian in sensibility—in moral feeling, spiritual yearning, and personal temper—was Julian the Apostate. At least, none merits greater admiration from a Christian of good will. It is simply one of the great ironies of history that everything Julian wanted from his chosen faith—personal liberation and purification, a united spiritual culture, a revived civilization, moral regeneration for himself and his people—was possible only through the agency in time of the religion he so frantically despised. And nothing, I think, gives better evidence of how great and how total a victory the true Christian revolution had by his time achieved.

CHAPTER FIFTEEN

Divine Humanity

WE BELIEVE IN nature and in history: in the former's rational regularity and in the latter's genuine openness to novelty. The physical order, we know, is governed by uniform laws written into the very fabric of space and time; and the course of the ages, we believe, moves in a single direction, from one epoch to another, constantly developing, assuming cultural and material configurations that no one can foretell, and proceeding relentlessly toward an ineluctable, though unknowable, conclusion. Neither conviction is in itself extraordinary, perhaps, even if the peoples of most ages have subscribed to neither. What is remarkable is that we hold them both simultaneously; and this peculiar confluence of two really rather incongruent certitudes is one of the more striking ways in which we differ from ancient men and women.

At the common level of society and religion, pagan culture was largely devoid of any distinct concept of either nature or history, at least as we understand them today. The average person had every reason to assume that all the familiar institutions and traditions of his or her world were more or less immutable, and imbued with a quality of divine or cosmic necessity. There was really, therefore, no such thing as history, though there might be annals, oral or written, recounting certain predictable fluctuations in earthly fortune: the rise and fall of generations, territorial expansion or contraction, dynastic succession, wars and conquests, omens and lamentations. Behind all of that, of course, lay a vast mythic prehistory: theogonies, cosmogonies, the founding of cities, and so on. There was of course a sense of time and of time past, but no concept of the future as a realm of as yet unrealized possibilities; there was only the prospect of the present, or of something only inconsequentially different, more or less interminably repeated. As for nature, any rustic knew of the perennial cycle of its recurrences, the unvarying sequence of the seasons and sidereal rotations, the waxing and waning of the moon, fallow time, seed time, and harvest, birth and death, and all the rest. But this is not the same thing as believing the world to possess a perfectly rational basis or frame. The natural order was also the habitation of numinous powers, sometimes capricious elemental spirits, genii, daemons, gods and goddesses (under their various local aspects), and occult agencies, all of whom expected to be honored, invoked, supplicated, and appeased. Sea and land, streams and forests, mountains and valleys, the whole of animal and vegetal creation constituted as much a spiritual as a physical ecology, suffused with beauty, mystery, and menace. And the worship of the gods was an adoration of death no less than of life. Some, such as Dionysus or Cybele, even on occasion demanded madness, inebriation, or violent ecstasies as their tribute.

At the more elevated levels of pagan intellectual culture, of course, there were both historians and natural philosophers, and among those inclined to a truly "rational worship" of God there was a firmly settled habit of viewing the natural order as an internally coherent system of ordered causes (though not strictly, as a rule, material causes). But by "belief in history" I do not mean simply the ability to construct narratives of past human affairs, or even to extract edifying epitomes of more or less static human truths. I mean a consciousness of the "arrow of time," a sense that humanity as a whole traverses a temporal terra incognita, by a series of often unrepeatable steps, toward a future that may well be unlike the past and yet may also bring the essence of the past to a new and unforeseen synthesis—or fail to do so. To believe in history is to assume that human time obeys a certain narrative logic, one that accommodates both disjunction and resolution and that moves toward an end quite different from its beginning. This we do not find among the pagans. The only philosophy of history known to antiquity was one that simply assimilated history to nature: its cycles and repetitions, a vast regularity punctuated by chance upheavals. Which is to say that, from a philosophical perspective, history and nature alike shared in the same ultimate meaninglessness. For the late Platonist, for example, everything subject to change—here below in the "region of dissimilitude"—was at best a dim and distant reflection of an order of eternal splendors, which was the true homeland of the spirit, and to which the mind could rise only to the degree that it divested itself of mutability and contingency; one's inmost identity was pure intellection, to which one's personal psychology and body were secondary and even somewhat accidental accretions that had to be set aside before one could enter into perfect union with the One. For the Stoic, the entire cosmos, with all its joys and pains, grandeurs and abysses, was an eternally repeated cycle of creation and dissolution, without beginning or end, and the highest philosophical virtue was the cultivation of perfect detachment, in a soul immune to the effects of time and nature alike.

As, however, the pagan mythos was displaced by the Christian, and Christianity's immense epic of creation and salvation became for ancient men and women the one true story of the world, the conceptual shape of reality necessarily changed for them as well. For common believers, Christ's victory—his triumph over the powers of the air, the elemental spirits, the devils, death itself—had purged the natural world of its more terrifying mysteries and tamed its more impulsive spiritual agencies. The old divinities, from the most awesomely cosmic to the most daintily local, found themselves demoted to the status of either demons or, if they were more fortunate, legends (though in later centuries a more relaxed and generous Christian civilization would invite some of them back, suitably chastened and contrite, as allegorical figures, personifications of nature or art, poetic metaphors, ornamental motifs, and bits of fabulous bric-a-brac). For the more educated and philosophically inclined, the doctrine of creation ex nihilo, by God's free action, raised the principle of divine transcendence to an altogether vertiginous height. It produced a vision of this world as the gratuitous gift of divine love, good in itself: not merely the defective reflection of a higher, truer world, not a necessary emanation of the divine nature or a sacrificial economy upon which the divine in some sense feeds, but an internally coherent reality that by its very autonomy gives eloquent witness to the beauty and power of the God who made it. And history now acquired not only meaning but an absolute significance, as it was within time that the entire drama of fall, incarnation, and salvation had been and was being worked out. The absolute partition between temporal and eternal truth had been not only breached but annihilated.

All of this is probably quite obvious; similar observations have been made often enough, in one form or another, frequently as a prelude to some more ambitious assertions regarding the unique energy or power of innovation infused into Western culture by Christian principles. This latter topic bores me, I have to confess. It is too often discussed in tones of unwarranted confidence, as though it were the simplest of matters to discern precisely which immaterial ideas shape which material events, and how, or to discriminate between necessary and fortuitous historical developments. In a general sense, any philosophically sophisticated monotheism has the advantage over any unreflective polytheism in fostering a culture of scientific investigation. But, historically speaking, pagan and Christian culture alike nurtured both forms of religion, the former being characteristic of the educated classes and the latter of the uneducated, and in either pagan or Christian culture—not surprisingly—science was a pursuit of the very educated, and was susceptible of periods both of creativity and of stagnation. In an equally general sense, a people who believes in the purposiveness of history and the possibility of new and redemptive historical developments is somewhat more likely to conceive and realize great social, political, and economic projects than is a people without such beliefs. But new forms of political association were generated in pre-Christian cultures as well; Rome, for instance, passed quite nimbly from monarchy to republic to empire without the mighty impetus of Christian salvation history at its back. And unless Christian apologists are eager to accept credit for much that is not creditable, and to argue that their faith made straight the way for all the large political movements of Western history, including the very horrid ones, they should venture claims regarding the inevitable political and economic consequences of Christian beliefs only tentatively and, as it were, sotto voce.

What interests me—and what I take to be genuinely demonstrable and important—is the particular ensemble of moral and imaginative values engendered in numberless consciences by Christian beliefs. That such values had political and social consequences I certainly do not deny; I feel fairly safe in saying, for instance, that abolitionism—as a purely moral cause—could not easily have arisen in any non-Christian culture of which I am aware. That is quite different, however, from claiming that

Christianity ineluctably or uniquely must give rise to, say, democracy or capitalism or empirical science. It is to say, rather, that the Christian account of reality introduced into our world an understanding of the divine, the cosmic, and the human that had no exact or even proximate equivalent elsewhere and that made possible a moral vision of the human person that has haunted us ever since, century upon century.

It may be that the truly distinctive nature of Christianity's understanding of reality first began to assume concrete conceptual form only in the course of the great doctrinal disputes of the fourth and fifth (and, by extension, sixth and seventh) centuries, when theologians were forced by the exigencies of debate to formulate their beliefs as lucidly and as thoroughly as possible. The dogmatic controversies of those years constitute at once one of the peculiar embarrassments and one of the peculiar glories of Christian tradition. The embarrassment follows not (as critics such as Gibbon would have it) from the supposedly too abstract or needlessly precise nature of the arguments regarding the Trinity or the person of Christ but from the rancor and occasional violence that surrounded them. And the glory lies in the remarkable conceptual visions and revisions those debates involved, and the way in which they gave form to a uniquely Christian philosophy.

One cannot really understand the Trinitarian debates of the fourth century, in particular, without some knowledge of the metaphysical picture of reality that many of the major intellectual traditions of the time—pagan, Jewish, and Christian—to some degree shared. Especially in the great intellectual center of the Eastern empire, Alexandria, a fairly uniform understanding (at least, in terms of general morphology) of the relation between God and lower reality had held sway for centuries. According to this vision of things, all of reality was arranged in a hierarchy of beings, the "shape" of which might be described as a pyramid, with purely material nature at its base, and God Most High or the eternal One at its summit. Between the lowest and the highest places, moreover, were a plurality of intermediate agencies, powers, and substances, but for which there would have been no relation between high and low, and thus no universe at all, spiritual or material. God was understood as that supreme reality from which all lesser realities came, but also as in a sense contained within the hierarchy, as the most exalted of its entities. Such was his magnificence

and purity, moreover, high up atop the pyramid of essences, that he literally could not come into direct contact with the imperfect and changeable
order here below. He was in a sense a God limited by his own transcendence, fixed up "there" in his proper place within the economy of being.
In order to create or reveal anything of himself, therefore, he was obliged
to generate a kind of secondary or lesser god through whom he could
act, an economically "reduced" version of himself who could serve as his
instrument and surrogate in creating, sustaining, and governing the universe of finite things. For the first century Alexandrian Jewish philosopher
Philo (20 B.C.–A.D. 50), this secondary divine principle could be called
God's "Son" or "Wisdom" or "Logos." The term "Logos" came to enjoy a
special favor among Christians, as it had been adopted by the author of
the prologue of John's Gospel to identify the pre-incarnate Christ. The
Neoplatonist Plotinus, for reasons peculiar to his metaphysics, preferred
the term "Nous" ("intellect" or "spirit"). And different schools used different names. As a general rule, the "articular" form *ho Theos*—literally, "the
God"—was a title reserved for God Most High or God the Father, while
only the "inarticular" form *theos* was used to designate this secondary
divinity. This distinction, in fact, was preserved in the prologue to John,
whose first verse could justly be translated as: "In the beginning was the
Logos, and the Logos was with God, and the Logos was a god."

It was entirely natural, therefore, for many Christians—especially
those within Alexandria or the Alexandrian orbit—to think of Christ as
the incarnation of this derivative divine being who, though he functions
in all respects as God for us, is still a lesser being than the Father. This
understanding of the divine realm—that the Father is forever beyond the
reach of created beings, while the Son is a necessarily diminished expression of deity able to "touch" this world, and the Spirit is at most a further
diminished emanation or angel of the Son—is called "subordinationism"
by historians of dogma. But to many generations of early Christians it
would have seemed merely the plain import of scripture and the most
philosophically respectable form of their faith.

The crisis that led to the first "ecumenical council," the council of
Nicaea, was occasioned by the Alexandrian priest Arius (c. 250–336),
who—though later generations of Christians would remember him as
the prototype of all heretics—was in many respects quite a conservative
Alexandrian theologian, to whom a great many of his contemporaries

readily rallied as a champion of what they regarded as orthodoxy. Arius's great indiscretion, so to speak, was to follow the logic of traditional Alexandrian subordinationism to one of its possible ends and then openly to declare his conclusions. Generally those who habitually thought in Alexandrian terms allowed a certain generous vagueness to enshroud the question of the precise metaphysical status of the divine Son's relation to the Father. Some spoke of the Logos as having been "emanated" or "generated" directly from the Father, and as therefore somehow continuous with or participating in the Father. Others, however, often out of a concern to preserve a proper sense of God's utter transcendence of inferior reality, thought of him as a creature: the most exalted of all creatures, to be sure, the "first-born of creation," so resplendently glorious and powerful as to be, for all intents and purposes, God for us; but still, nevertheless, not God as such but an "Angel of Mighty Counsel" or great "Heavenly High Priest," leading all of creation in its worship of the unseen Father, who is forever hidden in unapproachable darkness. Arius and the so-called Arians subscribed to this latter view, apparently in its most austere construal; they even, it seems, denied that the divine Son had always existed.

There is certainly no need here for a historical reconstruction of the debates and councils of those years. It is enough to note that the ultimate defeat of Arius's position was fairly inevitable. This was not because he stood on scriptural grounds weaker than those of his opponents. The Arians could adduce any number of passages from the Bible to support their case, including in fact the first verse of John. And what we might term the "Nicene party" could respond by citing passages seeming to corroborate their views, such as John 20:28, where the apostle Thomas appears to address the risen Christ as "my *God*" in the articular form: *ho Theos*. And each side could produce fairly cogent arguments for why the other's interpretations of the verses in question were flawed. Here neither side enjoyed the advantage. Ultimately, though, the Arian position was untenable simply because it reduced to incoherence the Christian story of redemption as it had been understood, proclaimed, prayed, and lived for generations. This was understood with particular clarity by all the great Nicene fathers who, in the decades following the council, continued to struggle against Arianism and its theological derivatives, often despite the opposition of the imperial court. For Athanasius, Basil of Caesarea, Gregory of Nazianzus, Gregory of Nyssa, and many others, it was first and foremost the question of salvation that must determine how the identity of Christ is to be conceived. And they understood salvation, it must be appreciated, not in the rather impoverished way of many modern Christians, as a kind of extrinsic legal transaction between the divine and human by which a debt is canceled and the redeemed soul issued a certificate of entry into the afterlife; rather they saw salvation as nothing less than a real and living union between God and his creatures. To be saved was to be joined to God himself in Christ, to be in fact "divinized"—which is to say, in the words of 2 Peter 1:4, to become "partakers of the divine nature." In a lapidary phrase favored, in one form or another, by a number of the church fathers, "God became man that man might become god." In Christ, the Nicene party believed, the human and divine had been joined together in a perfect and indissoluble unity, by participation in which human beings might be admitted to a share in his divinity.

This being so, salvation is possible only if, in Christ, God himself had descended into our midst. For if we have been created for nothing less than real and intimate communion with the eternal God—if ours is indeed a destiny so great—then the end for which we are intended is one to which no mere creature, however exalted, could ever raise us. Only God can join us to God. And so, if it is Christ who joins us to the Father, then Christ must himself be no less than God, and must be equal to the Father in divinity. By this same logic, of course, as the doctrinal debates of the latter half of the century would make clear, the Spirit too must be God of God, coequal with the Father and the Son. For it is only by the action of the Spirit—in the sacraments, in the church, in our own lives of inward sanctification—that we are joined to the Son: and only God can join us to God. This is, if nothing else, a strange, daring, and luminous idea, one that did not easily recommend itself to the minds of ancient persons: not only that God is in our midst but also that we—saved by being incorporated into the Trinitarian life of Father, Son, and Spirit—are in the midst of God.

Quite apart from their spiritual significance, moreover, the doctrinal determinations of the fourth century are notable for a number of rather remarkable metaphysical implications. What emerged from these debates was the grammar of an entirely new understanding not only of God but of the nature of created reality. Whereas, on the old and now obsolete Alexandrian model, God was understood principally as an impenetrable mystery, at an impossible remove from created beings, for whom the Logos functioned as a kind of outward emblem and ambassador, and of which the Spirit was an even more remote and subordinate emissary; now God was understood as a living fullness of internal and dynamic relation, an infinite movement of knowledge and love, in whom the Logos is the Father's own infinite self-manifestation to himself, and the Spirit the infinitely accomplished joy of that life of perfect love. And thus, in the revelation of God in Christ, through the Spirit, the Father himself had made himself known to his creatures. More to the point here, with the adoption of this language of God as Trinity, an entire metaphysical tradition had been implicitly abandoned. No longer could God in the "proper" sense be conceived of as an inaccessible Supreme Being dwelling at the top of the scale of essences, who acts upon creation only from afar, by a series of ever more remote deputations, and who is himself contained within the economy of the high and the low. If all of God's actions in the Son and Spirit are nothing less than immediate actions of God himself, in the fullness of his divine identity, then creation and redemption alike are immediate works of God.

At this point, a new, more developed understanding of both divine transcendence and created goodness has taken shape. On the one hand, the somewhat absurd and mythological picture of transcendence as sublime absence, as the sheer supremacy of some discrete superbeing up "there" at the summit of reality, had been replaced by a more cogent understanding of transcendence as God's perfect freedom from limitation, his ability to be at once infinitely beyond and infinitely within finite reality; for a God who is truly transcendent could never be confined merely to the top of the hierarchy of beings. And, on the other hand, a certain "pathos of distance" had been banished from the philosophical understanding of creation, for it was no longer the case—as once it had been—that finite reality had to be understood as, of its nature, something defective and tragically severed from the wellspring of being and truth: this world is not merely the realm of unlikeness, forever alien to God, from which the soul must flee to be saved; and God does not lie forever beyond the reach of finite natures. The world is in itself good and beautiful and true; it is in fact the very theater of divine action. And all of this, moreover—and this is not a contradiction—followed precisely from the affirmation of the real difference between divine and created being. On the older model, the actual distinction between the Father's generation of the Son and God's creation of the world was somewhat indiscernible; the Logos was, in some sense, merely the first movement in a kind of cascading pullulation of lesser beings, each level of existence ever more remote and estranged from its highest source. Now, however, with God's full transcendence and creation's inherent integrity both established, as it were, it was no longer necessary to think of this world as a distortion or dilution of divine reality, which must be negated or forsaken if the divine is to be known in its own nature.

It is difficult to exaggerate, I think, how great a difference this vision of things made at a purely personal and psychological level. In a very significant sense, it freed spiritual longing from that residue of melancholy that I spoke of above: that tragic if glorious sadness that followed from believing that the journey of the soul to God requires an almost infinitely resigned leave-taking, a departure from all the particularities of one's finite identity and all that attaches thereto, including the whole of creation and all those whom one loves. In the older metaphysical scheme, the reverse of the metaphysical descent of God's power along the scale of beings, from the purity of divine existence down into the darkness of mutable nature, was the mind's ascent to God along that same pathway, which necessarily involved the methodical stripping away of everything truly "personal" within the self. For the devout Neoplatonist, for instance, the longing for spiritual liberation was also a desire for emancipation from one's "lower" identity, as well as from time and all lesser associations. The pure inner core of the self—the nous—needed to be extracted from the pollutions and limitations of the vital soul and the animal flesh. For Christians, by contrast, even the most ascetically inclined or temperamentally Platonist among them, personality could not be viewed simply as a condition of distraction from eternity. It is the image of God within us and truly reflects that interior life of knowledge and love that God is. It is, moreover, the place where God meets us, not only in the drama of sin and redemption, free will and grace, but in the incarnation of the eternal Logos, the divine person who takes on our humanity in order that we, as human persons reborn in him, might take on his divinity.

For Christian thought the full import of this last point emerged fully into the light only with the controversies regarding the person and nature of the incarnate Son that began in the late fourth century, achieved their first shattering "resolution" midway through the fifth, and did not reach their final culmination until the seventh. In many ways, these Christological debates constitute an even greater embarrassment for Christian memory than those that preceded them: not only were incidents of popular violence more numerous and episodes of imperial persecution more savage, the result of the fourth ecumenical council convoked at Chalcedon in 451 was a fragmented church—divided for the most part by terminology rather than by faith. At the same time, the evolution of Christological dogma must also be remembered as one of the most extraordinary intellectual achievements of Christian tradition. Again the principal engine of dogmatic definition was the theology of salvation, and again the chief concern was how the church might coherently affirm that, in Christ, the divine and the human had been perfectly reconciled and immediately joined. That Christ was wholly God had been proclaimed by the Council of Nicaea; but, in order for his incarnation to have created a truly divinized humanity, he must also have been wholly man. Gregory of Nazianzus stated the matter in a rather elegant aphorism in his "Epistle to Cledonius": "That which [Christ] has not assumed he has not healed, but whatever is united with his divinity has been saved." That is to say, if any natural aspect of our shared human-ity—body, mind, will, desire—was absent from the incarnate God, then to that degree our nature has never entered into communion with his and has not been refashioned in him. So it was that, pursuing this logic to its most radical consequences, the theologians who participated in the Christological debates were led into an ever-deepening consideration of how it was that Christ was human; and, in the process, they necessarily found themselves drawn into an ever-deepening consideration of what it is for any of us to be human, and into an ever more precise investigation of all those hidden realms within where God (they believed) had united us to himself.

It is no exaggeration to say that what followed, over the course of centuries, was the most searching metaphysics of the self undertaken to that point in Western thought. At every step, the process was guided by the conviction that Christ had entered history not as some sort of furtive phantom, merely arraying himself in the outward appearance of a man in order to teach each of us how to free his or her spiritual quintessence from the shell of the lower soul or the degrading prison of the body, but as a human being in the fullest possible sense, bringing us salvation within the very complexity of our earthly existence. As a consequence, many aspects of human experience that many ancient philosophies might have dismissed as accidental to our natures, scarcely worthy of attention, Christian thought came to regard as essential to who and what we are. At the most basic level, the belief that God himself had really assumed human flesh at once dispelled a certain antique reserve with regard to the body, a certain pious conviction that the material and carnal are a kind of corruption within which God cannot possibly dwell. Not only was it the case that, for the Christian, the body was much more than merely one of the pilgrim soul's transient associations or degrading entanglements; it was the real vehicle of divinization in Christ, as essential to our humanity as the rational will, to be chastened only that it might be redeemed and made glorious. But even more remarkable was the continuous Christological "clarification" of the inward and outward workings of the self. It was, as one might imagine, necessary first to establish that Christ had possessed a genuinely human mind. But then, as one theological attempt after another was made to end the controversies of those centuries by producing a position agreeable to all parties, excluding from the incarnate Christ some small defectible element of human personality—say, a naturally human "energy" (operation) or a naturally human will—it became necessary to define how that element was in fact integral to the full complexity of our humanity, and so indispensable to his. And within every distinction still finer distinctions could be discerned. This process reached its greatest sophistication in the seventh century, in the thought of Maximus the Confessor, whose reflections on, for instance, the ways in which the various "energies" of our persons realize our natures, or on the difference within us between our natural and deliberative acts of will, achieve an almost inexhaustible subtlety, and often startling insightfulness.

There is, though, a still more astonishing implication to the Christian understanding of salvation in Christ. The final formula of Christology adopted at Chalcedon was that in the one person of the incarnate Logos two natures—human and divine—both subsisted complete and undiminished, in perfect harmony and yet unconfused. In purely historical terms, one cannot call this formula the definitive expression of the Christian certainty of the fullness of both the humanity and the divinity of Christ, because of those terminological differences I mentioned above: the church of Alexandria (the Coptic Church), for instance, due largely to a very particular understanding of the word "nature" in the traditions of the city's philosophical schools, rejected the language of the council. That said, the actual theology of the council differed from that of Alexandria not at all. However one phrases it, the essential intuition of the great churches remains the same: that Christ is one divine person, who perfectly possesses everything proper to God and everything proper to humanity without robbing either of its integrity, and who therefore makes it possible for every human person to become a partaker of the divine nature without thereby ceasing to be human. The rather extraordinary inference to be drawn from this doctrine is that personality is somehow transcendent of nature. A person is not merely a fragment of some larger cosmic or spiritual category, a more perfect or more defective expression of some abstract set of attributes, in light of which his or her value, significance, legitimacy, or proper place is to be judged. This man or that woman is not merely a specimen of the general set of the human; rather, his or her human nature is only one manifestation and one part of what he or she is or might be. And personality is an irreducible mystery, somehow prior to and more spacious than everything that would limit or define it, capable of exceeding even its own nature in order to embrace another, ever more glorious nature. This immense dignity—this infinite capacity—inheres in every person, no matter what circumstances might for now seem to limit him or her to one destiny or another. No previous Western vision of the human being remotely resembles this one, and no other so fruitfully succeeded in embracing at once the entire range of finite human nature, in all the intricacy of its inner and outer dimensions, while simultaneously affirming the transcendent possibility and strange grandeur present within each person.

It is not my intention, I should pause to note, to suggest that the dogmatic decisions of the imperial church or the theological arguments made by the Nicene and Chalcedonian theologians in some way caused the rise of what is sometimes called Christian "personalism" or "humanism." Christian culture did not form itself around the Nicene formula, or set itself the task of developing Maximus's concept of the deliberative will into a special program for philosophy, law, or the arts. When we encounter, say, Gregory of Nyssa's intense reflections on the inherent mutability and

dynamic finitude of human spiritual nature, or Evagrius Ponticus's deli-
cately precise delineation of the different promptings and hidden causes
within the intellect and will, or Augustine's discovery of the interrelated
multiplicities of mental and emotional life, we are not encountering the
consequences of conciliar decisions or dogmatic commitments. Rather,
as Christianity permeated and then absorbed the ancient civilization in
which it was born, a new moral, spiritual, and intellectual atmosphere
came into being, within which all of these things naturally took shape,
and of which particular dogmatic determinations were simply especially
concentrated crystallizations. And that atmosphere was generated first
and foremost by the story of God and creation that Christians told: this
strange, fascinating epic of the God-man, of a divine source of all being
that is also infinite self-outpouring love, of a physical universe restored
and glorified in an eternal Kingdom of love and knowledge, and of a God
who dwells among us so that we might dwell in him.

Needless to say (at least, it ought to be needless to say), it was only
within the expansive embrace of this story that all those great revisions of
human thought took place that would define the special ideals, ethos, and
accomplishments of a Christian civilization. And these revisions occurred
at every level of society, however gradually, irregularly, or imperceptibly. It
was this story—and only secondarily the remarkably sophisticated metaphysics that developed from it—that first severed the bond of necessity
that almost every antique philosophical school presumed between this
world and its highest or divine principle, and that first broke open the
closed system or "fated" economy within which reality was comprised.
Christian thought taught that the world was entirely God's creature, called
from nothingness, not out of any need on his part, but by grace; and that
the God who is Trinity required nothing to add to his fellowship, bounty,
or joy, but created out of love alone. In a sense, God and world were both
set free: God was now understood as fully transcendent of—and therefore
immanent within—the created order, and the world was now understood
entirely as gift. And this necessarily altered the relation between humanity
and nature. This world, it was now believed, was neither mere base illusion and "dissimilitude," nor a quasi-divine dynamo of occult energies,
nor a god, nor a prison. As a gratuitous work of transcendent love it was
to be received with gratitude, delighted in as an act of divine pleasure,
mourned as a victim of human sin, admired as a radiant manifestation of

divine glory, recognized as a fellow creature; it might justly be cherished, cultivated, investigated, enjoyed, but not feared, not rejected as evil or deficient, and certainly not worshipped. In this and other ways the Christian revolution gave Western culture the world simply *as* world, demystified and so (only seemingly paradoxically) full of innumerable wonders to be explored. What is perhaps far more important is that it also gave that culture a coherent concept of the human as such, endowed with infinite dignity in all its individual "moments," full of powers and mysteries to be fathomed and esteemed. It provided an unimaginably exalted picture of the human person—made in the divine image and destined to partake of the divine nature—without thereby diminishing or denigrating the concrete reality of human nature, spiritual, intellectual, or carnal. It even produced the idea (which no society has ever more than partially embodied) of a political order wholly subordinate to divine charity, to verities higher than any state, and to a justice transcending every government or earthly power. In short, the rise of Christianity produced consequences so immense that it can almost be said to have begun the world anew: to have "invented" the human, to have bequeathed us our most basic concept of nature, to have determined our vision of the cosmos and our place in it, and to have shaped all of us (to one degree or another) in the deepest reaches of consciousness.

All of the glories and failures of the civilizations that were born of this revolution, however, everything for which Christendom as a historical, material reality might be praised or blamed, fades in significance before the still more singular moral triumph of Christian tradition. The ultimate power and meaning of the Christian movement within the ancient world cannot be measured simply by the richness of later Christian culture's art or architecture, the relative humanity or inhumanity of its societies and laws, the creativity of its economic or scientific institutions, or the perdurability of its religious institutions through the ages. "Christendom" was only the outward, sometimes majestic, but always defective form of the interaction between the gospel and the intractable stuff of human habit. The more vital and essential victory of Christianity lay in the strange, impractical, altogether unworldly tenderness of the moral intuitions it succeeded in sowing in human consciences. If we find ourselves occasionally shocked by how casually ancient men and women destroyed or ignored lives we would think ineffably precious, we would do well to reflect that theirs was—in purely pragmatic terms—a more "natural" disposition toward reality. It required an extraordinary moment of awakening in a few privileged souls, and then centuries of the relentless and total immersion of culture in the Christian story, to make even the best of us conscious of (or at least able to believe in) the moral claim of all other persons upon us, the splendor and irreducible dignity of the divine humanity within them, that depth within each of them that potentially touches upon the eternal. In the light of Christianity's absolute law of charity, we came to see what formerly we could not: the autistic or Down syndrome or otherwise disabled child, for instance, for whom the world can remain a perpetual perplexity, which can too often cause pain but perhaps only vaguely and fleetingly charm or delight; the derelict or wretched or broken man or woman who has wasted his or her life away; the homeless, the utterly impoverished, the diseased, the mentally ill, the physically disabled; exiles, refugees, fugitives; even criminals and reprobates. To reject, turn away from, or kill any or all of them would be, in a very real sense, the most purely practical of impulses. To be able, however, to see in them not only something of worth but indeed something potentially godlike, to be cherished and adored, is the rarest and most ennoblingly unrealistic capacity ever bred within human souls. To look on the child whom our ancient ancestors would have seen as somehow unwholesome or as a worthless burden, and would have abandoned to fate, and to see in him or her instead a person worthy of all affection—resplendent with divine glory, ominous with an absolute demand upon our consciences, evoking our love and our reverence—is to be set free from mere elemental existence, and from those natural limitations that pre-Christian persons took to be the very definition of reality. And only someone profoundly ignorant of history and of native human inclinations could doubt that it is only as a consequence of the revolutionary force of Christianity within our history, within the very heart of our shared nature, that any of us can experience this freedom. We deceive ourselves also, however, if we doubt how very fragile this vision of things truly is: how elusive this truth that only charity can know, how easily forgotten this mystery that only charity can penetrate.

All of which, as I take leave of this phase of my argument, raises certain questions for me. A civilization, it seems obvious, is only as great or as wonderful as the spiritual ideals that animate it; and Christian ideals have shown themselves to be almost boundless in cultural fertility and dynamism. And yet, as the history of modernity shows, the creativity of these ideals can, in certain times and places, be exhausted, or at least subdued, if social and material circumstances cease to be propitious for them. I cannot help but wonder, then, what remains behind when Christianity's power over culture recedes? How long can our gentler ethical prejudices—many of which seem to me to be melting away with fair rapidity—persist once the faith that gave them their rationale and meaning has withered away? Love endures all things perhaps, as the apostle says, and is eternal; but, as a cultural reality, even love requires a reason for its preeminence among the virtues, and the mere habit of solicitude for others will not necessarily long survive when that reason is no longer found. If, as I have argued in these pages, the "human" as we now understand it is the positive invention of Christianity, might it not be the case that a culture that has become truly post-Christian will also, ultimately, become posthuman?

PART FOUR REACTION AND RETREAT:
MODERNITY AND THE ECLIPSE
OF THE HUMAN

CHAPTER SIXTEEN

Secularism and Its Victims

THE RATHER PETULANT subtitle that Christopher Hitchens has given his (rather petulantly titled) *God Is Not Great* is *How Religion Poisons Everything*. Naturally one would not expect him to have squandered any greater labor of thought on the dust jacket of his book than on the disturbingly bewildered text that careens so drunkenly across its pages—reeling up against a missed logical connection here, steadying itself against a historical error there, stumbling everywhere over all those damned conceptual confusions littering the carpet—but one does still have to wonder how he expects any reflective reader to interpret such a phrase. Does he really mean precisely *everything*? Would that apply, then—confining ourselves just to things Christian—to ancient and medieval hospitals, leper asylums, orphanages, almshouses, and hostels? To the golden rule, "Love thine enemies," "Judge not lest ye be judged," prophetic admonitions against oppressing the poor, and commands to feed and clothe and comfort those in need? To the music of Palestrina and Bach, Michelangelo's Pietà, "ah! bright wings," San Marco's mosaics, the Bible of Amiens, and all that gorgeous blue stained glass at Chartres? To the abolitionist movement, the civil rights movement, and contemporary efforts to liberate Sudanese slaves? And so on and so on? Surely it cannot be the case that, if only purged of the toxin of faith, these things would be even better than they are; were it not for faith, it seems fairly obvious, most of them would have no existence at all. And since none of these things would seem to fall outside the general category of "everything," it must be that Hitchens means (assuming he means anything at all) that they fall outside the more specific category of "religion." This would, at any rate, be in keeping with one of the rhetorical strategies especially favored in New Atheist circles: one labels anything one dislikes—even if it is found in a purely secular setting—"religion" (thus, for example, all the twentieth-century totalitarianisms are "political religions" for which secularists need take no responsibility), while simultaneously claiming that everything good, in the arts, morality, or any other sphere—even if it emerges within an entirely religious setting—has only an accidental association with religious belief and is really, in fact, common human property (so, for example, the impulse toward charity will doubtless spring up wherever an "enlightened" society takes root). By the same token, every injustice that seems to follow from a secularist principle is obviously an abuse of that principle, while any evil that comes wrapped in a cassock is unquestionably an undiluted expression of religion's very essence.

As I have already complained, the tribe of the New Atheists is something of a disappointment. It probably says more than it is comfortable to know about the relative vapidity of our culture that we have lost the capacity to produce profound unbelief. The best we can now hope for are arguments pursued at only the most vulgar of intellectual levels, couched in an infantile and carpingly pompous tone, and lacking all but the meagerest traces of historical erudition or syllogistic rigor: Richard Dawkins triumphantly adducing "philosophical" arguments that a college freshman midway through his first logic course could dismantle in a trice, Daniel Dennett insulting the intelligence of his readers with proposals for the invention of a silly pseudo-science of "religion," Sam Harris shrieking and holding his breath and flinging his toys about in the expectation that the adults in the room will be cowed, Christopher Hitchens bellowing at the drapes and potted plants while hoping no one notices the failure of any of his assertions to coalesce with any other into anything like a coherent argument. One cannot begrudge these men the popularity of their screeds, obviously; sensationalism sells better than sense. One still has to wonder, however, at their thoughtless complacency: the doctrinaire materialism—which is, after all, a metaphysical theory of reality that is almost certainly logically impossible—and the equally doctrinaire secularism

—which is, as even the least attentive among us might have noticed, a historical tradition so steeped in human blood that it can hardly be said to have proved its ethical superiority. And, even if one is disposed to pardon the New Atheists for the odd insensibility that seems to insulate them against any decent anxiety regarding their positions, or even any impulses toward simple intellectual modesty, one still might complain that they rarely pause to consider where so many of the moral principles they tirelessly and confidently invoke as their own really come from, or show any sign of that grave curiosity and foreboding that characterized the thought of the great unbelievers of earlier generations as they forced themselves to consider what possibilities the future after Christianity's decline might hold.

Even in purely practical terms, to despise religion in the abstract is meaningless conceit. As a historical force, religion has been neither simply good nor simply evil but has merely reflected human nature in all its dimensions. For our remote ancestors it was the force that shaped society, law, and culture, by pointing to one or another "higher truth" that could fuse individual wills into common aspirations and efforts. In its more developed forms it has functioned as a source of prohibition and injunction, burning moral commands into obstinate minds with visions of hell and heaven, endless reincarnation or final repose in God, or what have you, fashioning conscience by breaking and binding inflexible wills, applying now the cautery of fear, now the balm of hope (we may not much like this, but—to paraphrase Freud—inhibition is the price of civilization). In its even more developed forms, it has encouraged love or compassion or peacefulness in numberless souls, even if it has also inspired or abetted sanctimony and intolerance in others. And the more imaginatively stirring the spiritual longings it has awakened in various peoples, the more extraordinary the cultural accomplishments it has elicited from them. Both the most primordial artistic impulses in a people and the most refined expressions of those impulses have always been indissolubly united to visions of eternal order. In the end, to regret "religion" as such is to regret that humanity ever became more as a species than a collection of especially cunning brutes. But, as I have said, I am not much concerned with the issue of religion.

By the same token, and also in purely practical terms, it borders upon willful imbecility to lament the rise of Christendom, or to doubt the singular achievements of the culture that the Christian synthesis of Judaism and Hellenism produced, or to refuse to grant that whatever it is Hitchens means by "religion" gave life to both the soul and the body of that culture. This should scarcely require saying. The special glories of Christian civilization—in its arts and sciences, in its institutions and traditions, in its philosophies and ideals—speak for themselves, and it would be undignified to cosset intellectual perversity by pleading the obvious. That Christendom may also justly be indicted of any number of sins and failings, incidentally, also should not need to be said. But I am not much concerned with the issue of Christendom either. In fact, I am content to leave "purely practical terms" out of my argument altogether, inasmuch as it is the sheer "impracticality" of Christianity itself that interests me: its extraordinary claims, its peculiar understandings of love and service, which down the centuries have not so much dominated Western civilization as haunted it, at times like a particularly engrossing dream, at others like an especially forlorn specter. And, again, the question with which I find myself left at the far side of my narrative is what must become of our culture once that benignant or terrible spirit has finally departed.

Can one really believe—as the New Atheists seem to do—that secular reason, if finally allowed to move forward, free of the constraining hand of archaic faith, will naturally make society more just, more humane, and more rational than it has been in the past? What evidence supports such an expectation? It is rather difficult, placing everything in the scales, to vest a great deal of hope in modernity, however radiantly enchanting its promises, when one considers how many innocent lives have already been swallowed up in the flames of modern "progress." At the end of the twentieth century—the century when secularization became an explicit political and cultural project throughout the world—the forces of progressive ideology could boast an unprecedentedly vast collection of corpses, but not much in the way of new moral concepts. At least, not any we should be especially proud of. The best ideals to which we moderns continue to cling long antedate modernity; for the most part, all we can claim as truly, distinctively our own are our atrocities. One could, I suppose, argue that the secular project had somehow been diverted from its proper course at the dawn of the twentieth century, just as the new ideologies were assuming concrete political forms, or had been stalled or subverted by certain intransigent forces of unreason. This would be a more credible claim, however, if the twentieth century's horrors were demonstrably aberrations within the larger story of the modern world. But, in fact, the process of secularization was marked, from the first, by the magnificent limitlessness of its violence. One does not have to harbor any nostalgia for the old political order of Christendom, or for the church's degrading association with the state, to be conscious of secularity's cost. As I noted in my remarks upon the early modern period's "wars of religion," when one looks back upon the historical sequels of the settlement of Westphalia, it is hard not to conclude that the chief inner dynamism of secularization has always been the modern state's great struggle to free itself from those institutional, moral, and sacramental allegiances that still held it even partially in check, so that it could now get on with all those mighty tasks—nationalist wars, colonial empires, universal conscription, mass extermination of civilians, and so on—that would constitute its special contribution to the human experience. In purely arithmetic terms, one cannot dispute the results. The old order could generally reckon its victims only in the thousands. But in the new age, the secular state, with all its hitherto unimagined capacities, could pursue its purely earthly ideals and ambitions only if it enjoyed the liberty to kill by the millions. How else could it spread its wings?

One does occasionally hear it argued, I should note, that the great utopian projects of the twentieth century were not, in fact, genuinely secular movements but, rather, displaced messianisms, and as such should be seen as only the delayed aftereffects of the old arrangement. On this telling, Christianity—with its promise of a future Kingdom of God—planted a kind of persistent hope in Western culture that, once robbed of its supernatural trappings, naturally mutated into a demonic rage to establish heaven on earth, through a great process of election and dereliction, culminating in historical fires of judgment. I suppose something can be said for this view. Perhaps if Christianity had not introduced its peculiar variant of apocalyptic yearning into Western culture, we would never have become susceptible to eschatological visions of an impossible future or to the beguilements of false messiahs. But, really, one should not take these sorts of speculation too seriously. Long before the rise of Christianity, the great empires of antiquity—Egyptian, Persian, Chinese, Roman, and so forth—all claimed a sacred mission and a divine warrant for their conquests, plunders, enslavements, and murders. Temporal power will kill when it chooses to do so, according to its interests and desires, and will employ whatever mythic or ideological instruments lie ready to hand to advance its aims. That Jewish and Christian apocalyptic motifs can be vaguely discerned in the grotesque tapestries of twentieth-century ideology is hardly any indication of causal order. After all, the only language of election and dereliction and judgment explicitly invoked by the ideological precursors of the Third Reich was that of natural selection and survival of the fittest; but it would be rather crude to assert that Darwinism "caused" the death camps. Since the one explicit and inviolable rule that has always governed Christian eschatology is that God's Kingdom is not of this world and comes only at God's bidding (ignoring the occasional blasphemous hyperbole of this or that sycophantic court orator), and since, for just this reason, Christian culture never produced any movement of salvation through political action, it is only to the degree that eschatological rhetoric is entirely alienated from any traditional Christian context that it can be exploited for a political project of human redemption. But this is only to reiterate that, in the end, it is the process of secularization itself—and not those elements of the "religious" grammars of the past that the secular order might have misappropriated for its purposes—that is the chief cause of the modern state's curious talent for mass murder.

The tale of the modern nation-state's struggle for liberation, however, should really be situated within the still larger narrative of (for want of another name) the "triumph of the will." As I said above, modern thinking differs from premodern nowhere more starkly than on the matter of freedom. And, as I also said above—again, without intending any denigration—the modern notion of freedom is essentially "nihilistic": that is, the tendency of modern thought is to see the locus of liberty as situated primarily in an individual subject's spontaneous power of choice, rather than in the ends that subject might actually choose. Freedom, thus understood, consists solely in the power of choosing as such. Neither God, then, nor nature, nor reason provides the measure of an act's true liberty, for an act is *free* only because it might be done in defiance of all three. I am not, by the way, railing against the "godless" depravity of this idea. As it happens, in fact, it is an idea with something of a theological genealogy. Traditionally, throughout most of Christian history, theologians followed classical precedent in conceiving of creaturely freedom principally as the freedom of any being's *nature* from any alien constraint or external limitation or misuse that might prevent that nature from reaching its full fruition in the end appropriate to it. And much the same was true, though in infinite magnitude, of divine freedom: God, it was assumed, is free because his nature, being infinite, cannot be hindered, thwarted, or corrupted by any other force. Hence he can do no evil precisely because he is infinitely free, and so nothing can prevent him from being fully what he is: infinite goodness itself. The "ability" to choose evil would have been thought a defect in God, a limitation of the divine substance, a distortion of the divine nature, all of which is quite impossible. In late scholastic thought, however, principally in the fourteenth and fifteenth centuries, there arose a new theological tendency, traditionally referred to as "voluntarism," which placed an altogether unprecedented metaphysical emphasis—among the divine attributes—upon the sheer sovereignty of the divine will, and upon the inscrutable liberty of that sovereignty. Certain theologians began to worry that to grant any of God's other attributes—his goodness, mercy, rationality, and so on—priority over his will could not help but dilute a proper sense of the majesty of divine freedom. A few particularly extreme formulations of the voluntarist position even seemed to describe a God whose will is somehow supreme over his own nature, and seemed to suggest that this God's acts toward created reality should be understood solely as demonstrations of his power, and nothing else. By this logic, the laws of nature and of morality could no longer be said to reflect who or what God is, or to communicate any knowledge of his nature or character, but should be seen simply as inexplicable decisions emanating from the unfathomable abyss of his will. Here explicitly, for the first time in Western thought, freedom was defined not as the unobstructed realization of a nature but as the absolute power of the will to determine even what that nature might be. One might even say that, in this view of things, God's essence simply *is* will. And if this is what freedom is for God, then this must be what freedom is for us as well.

Whatever the fate of voluntarism as a theological position (which was mixed), the routes of its migration out of the theological realm and into modern philosophy, law, psychology, politics, and social theory are easily traced. René Descartes spoke at once as an heir to the late scholastic tradition and as the father of modern Western philosophy when he declared in his *Meditations* that the true image of God within human beings consists in the godlike liberty and incomprehensibility of the will. One can, though, accord too much importance to abstract ideas. Theological voluntarism as such was not the *cause* of the ascendancy of a "libertarian" model of freedom in later Western culture. It was, rather, a theology that conformed well to any number of the concrete material and social changes of its time: the continuous rise of the middle class, the genesis of early capitalism, the increasing wealth and influence of educated commoners, the solidifying alliance between the governing and commercial classes, the expansion of freely contracted labor, the slow disintegration of older forms of social subsidiarity, the growth of urban economies, the consequent evolution of new forms of "individualism," and so on. Not to sound more like a Marxist than I absolutely must, the social, political, and economic *habit* of voluntarism, however inchoate, surely preceded the theological *concept*, as a result of several social and economic developments, some of which may have had quite happy consequences for culture at large, and all of which were quite inexorable in any event.

A laborious cultural history, however, is neither necessary nor possible here. For the purposes of my argument, it is enough simply to ask where the ascendancy of our modern notion of freedom as pure spontaneity of the will leads the culture it pervades. At a rather ordinary level of public discourse, it obviously leads to a degradation of the very notion of freedom, its reduction in the cultural imagination to a fairly banal kind of liberty, no more—though no less—significant than a consumer's freedom to choose among different kinds of bread, shoes, televisions, political parties, or religions. At the level of conventional social behaviors, it leads perhaps toward a decay of a shared sense of obligation or common cause, or toward an increasingly insipid and self-absorbed private culture, or toward a pronounced tendency in society at large less to judge the laudability of particular choices by reference to the worthiness of their objects than to judge objects worthy solely because they have been chosen. As prognostication goes, however, none of this is very daring; all of it is at once obviously true and obviously vague. Our modern concept of freedom can, however, lead to other, more terrible things as well: for what the will may will, when it is subordinate to nothing but its own native exuberance, is practically without limit. As a matter purely of logic, absolute spontaneity is an illusion; all acts of the will are acts toward some real or imagined end, which prompts volition into motion. But something dangerously novel entered our culture when we began to believe that the proper end of the will might simply be willing as such. Nor does the truly liberated will have to confine its energies to the adventure of the self's discovery and invention of itself; collective will is ever so much more exhilaratingly potent than individual will, at least if it can be disciplined and marshaled for some "greater" purpose, and the material upon which it can exercise its plastic powers is ever so much more immense than the paltry canvas of a private psychology. Moreover, if there really is no transcendent source of the good to which the will is naturally drawn, but only the power of the will to decide what ends it desires—by which to create and determine itself for itself—then no human project can be said to be inherently irrational, or (for that matter) inherently abominable. If freedom of the will is our supreme value, after all, then it is for all intents and purposes our god. And certain kinds of god (as our pagan forebears understood) expect to be fed.

I do not think I can really be accused of alarmism when I talk this way, inasmuch as my remarks emerge not from premonition but simply from retrospection. The whole record of the modern attempt to erect a new and more rational human reality upon the ruins of the "age of faith" is thronged, from beginning to end, with lists of sacrificial victims—or, I suppose I should say, not lists but statistical registers, since so many of those victims must remain forever nameless. From the days of the Jacobin Club and the massacres in the Vendée to the great revolutionary socialisms, nationalist and internationalist, of the twentieth century, with their one hundred million or so murders, the will to lead modern humanity onward into a postreligious promised land of liberty, justice, and equality has always been accompanied by a willingness to kill without measure, for the sake of that distant dawn. And something of the special ethos generated by this modern idea of the supremacy of will over nature declared itself with particular vividness at the end of the nineteenth century and beginning of the twentieth, when the rise of "scientific" racial theories and the new "progressive" politics of eugenics encouraged a large number of educated and idealistic men and women to begin conceiving of humanity as merely another kind of technology, an object to be manipulated, revised, and perfected by the shaping hand of scientific pragmatism. There was scarcely a forward-thinking soul of the time who did not dabble in such ideas at one point or another. Marx and Engels eagerly anticipated the day when inferior or reactionary races such as the Slavs would be exterminated to make way for a better, more forwardly mobile stock. That most "progressive" of men, Francis Galton—Darwin's half-cousin—first popularized the view that traditional social sentimentalities, inspired and maintained by religious myths, had conspired to retard the natural process of evolution by preserving idiots, criminals, weaklings, and the feckless from nature's just—if pitiless—verdicts, and that a project of selective breeding was now needed to correct the problem. Darwin himself, alas, concurred; at least, in *The Descent of Man* he speaks quite bloodlessly of the injury done the human race in developed lands by the unnatural preservation of, and procreative license granted to, defective persons; and he foretells—with, to his credit, no sign of relish—the ultimate annihilation of the "savage" races by the civilized. H. G. Wells predicted the same thing, albeit somewhat more buoyantly, and pronounced the extermination of lesser races a rational imperative. And any number of other earnest souls shared these ideas, arguing the need for an ethical approach to society and race that was no longer bound to the obsolete Christian superstition that every life is of equal—which is to say, of equally infinite—value.

It would be comforting to believe, needless to say, that such thinking belonged to a particular and unfortunate cultural moment, and has been banished forever to the past by the "sobering" lessons of the last century. The reality is that this is not quite the case. We can certainly hope that such ideas will one day be relegated exclusively to the malarial margins of global culture, of course. I should observe, though, that—given the special premises upon which the moral metaphysics of modernity rests—there is no obvious reason why they should be.

CHAPTER SEVENTEEN

Sorcerers and Saints

NIETZSCHE CANNOT BE SAID to have shed many tears over the thought of European Christianity's demise; but even he was not entirely sanguine regarding what would follow from the gradual collapse of faith in the Continent. In part, this was because he believed that the pathogens of Christian pity and resentment had so weakened the wills of Western men that a meaningful recovery might be impossible. Now that the sacred canopy had been rolled back and the empty heavens exposed, a moment of potentially shattering crisis had arrived; and it was not obvious to him that post-Christian humanity had the energy to respond to it with anything more than an ever-deeper descent into triviality and narcissism. The "death of God" has certainly come, he believed—which is to say that belief in the transcendent has ceased to be even a possibility, except for the self-deluding —but who can know what sort of thing this unprecedented animal, "godless man," will ultimately become?

It may well be that, when Christianity passes away from a culture, nihilism is the inevitable consequence, precisely because of what Christianity itself is. Once, ages ago, the revolution that the gospel brought into the ancient world discredited the entire sacred order of the old religion. Christianity took the gods away, subdued them so utterly that, try though we might, we can never really believe in them again. The world was in one sense demystified, even as it was imbued with another kind of sacramental splendor. And so powerful was the new religion's embrace of reality, and so comprehensive and pervasive its effects, that even the highest achievements of antique pagan wisdom were easily assumed into its own new intellectual, aesthetic, and ethical synthesis. When, therefore, Christianity departs, what is left behind? It may be that Christianity is the midwife of nihilism precisely because, in rejecting it, a people necessarily rejects everything except the bare horizon of the undetermined will. No other god can now be found. The story of the crucified God took everything to itself, and so—in departing—takes everything with it: habits of reverence and restraint, awe, the command of the Good within us. Only the will persists, set before the abyss of limitless possibility, seeking its way—or forging its way—in the dark. What, though, arises from such a condition?

One answer, again, is that what arises may very well be mere banality. There is something to be said, surely, for Nietzsche's prophecies regarding the "Last Men." At least, when one considers our culture's devotion to acquisition, celebrity, distraction, and therapy, it is hard not to think that perhaps our vision as a people has narrowed to the smaller preoccupations and desires of individual selves, and that our whole political, social, and economic existence is oriented toward that reality. On the other hand, perhaps that is simply what happens when human beings are liberated from want and worry, and we should therefore gratefully embrace the triviality of a world that revolves around television, shopping, and the Internet as a kind of blessedness that our ancestors, oppressed by miseries we can scarcely now imagine, never even hoped to enjoy in this world. Even so, it is hard not to lament the loss of cultural creativity that seems an inevitable concomitant of this secular beatitude. When one looks, for instance, at the crepuscular wasteland of modern Europe—with its aging millions milling among the glorious remnants of an artistic and architectural legacy that no modern people could hope to rival, acting out the hideously prolonged satyr play at the end of the tragic cycle of European history—it is hard to suppress a feeling of morbid despair. This was Nietzsche's greatest fear: the loss of any transcendent aspiration that could coax mighty works of cultural imagination out of a people. When the aspiring ape ceases to think himself a fallen angel, perhaps he will inevitably resign himself to being an ape, and then become contented with his lot, and ultimately even rejoice that the universe demands little more from him than an ape's contentment. If nothing else, it seems certain that post-Christian civilization will always lack the spiritual resources, or the organizing myth, necessary to produce anything like the cultural wonders that sprang up under the sheltering canopy of the religion of the God-man.

Would that banality were the only thing to be feared, however. Another possible direction in which our new freedom from obsolete constraints, natural or moral, evidently can lead (as I also remarked above) is toward monstrosity. We should never cease to be somewhat apprehensive regarding our own capacity, as a people, to destroy or corrupt things that, as individuals, we might be disposed to treat with reverence or respect. The twentieth-century philosopher who pondered the origins and nature of nihilism with, to my mind, the profoundest insight was Martin Heidegger. For him (to simplify his arguments to an altogether criminal degree), the essential impulse of nihilism arises first from a long history of human forgetfulness of and indifference toward the mystery of being, abetted by the "metaphysical" desire to master reality by the exercise of human power. Over many cultural and philosophical epochs, he believed, this drive to reduce being's mystery to a passive object of the intellect and will has brought us at last to the "age of technology," in which we have come to view all of reality as just so many quanta of force and come to see the world about us as nothing more than a neutral reserve of material resources waiting to be exploited by us. Technological mastery, he believed, has become for us not merely our guiding ideal but our only convincing model of truth, one that has already shaped our whole understanding of nature, society, and the human being.

One of the more distressingly distinctive features of modern thought, it often seems, is its almost invincible tendency toward fundamentalism. Even religious fundamentalism in the West is primarily a modern phenomenon (as anyone who knows the history of biblical exegesis is aware), an absurd and reactive mimicry of modern scientific positivism. And nowhere, at present, is the fundamentalist tendency more prevalent and indurated than in certain quarters of the scientific community, or among those who look exclusively to the sciences for guidance in this world. It is astonishing, really (and evidence that a good scientific education can still leave a person's speculative aptitudes entirely undeveloped), how many very intelligent scientists cling to an illogical, inflexible, and fideistic certainty that empirical science should be regarded not only as a source of factual knowledge and theoretical hypotheses but as an arbiter of values or of moral and metaphysical truths. At times, this delusion can take a form no more threatening than Richard Dawkins's philosophically illiterate inability to distinguish between, say, theoretical claims about material causality and logical claims about the mystery of existence, or simply between the sort of matters that the sciences are competent to address and those they are not. At other times, however, it can take the form of a chilling conviction that the advance of the sciences, under any circumstances, is its own justification, and that all moral values are therefore in some sense corrigible and elective. As I have already argued, no good historian of science believes that the rise of modern science is a special achievement of secular rationality; but the occasional pitilessness that follows from making an ideology out of science most definitely is. At least, ancient Christian pieties regarding the integrity of human nature and the absolute value of each person had to be put aside before the eugenics movement could arise and prosper and bear fruit. A culture could remain quite contentedly Christian in all its convictions and still achieve space travel. The mass manufacture of nerve toxins and nuclear weaponry, court-mandated sterilizations, lobotomies, the miscegenation of human and porcine genetic materials, experimentation on prison populations, clinical studies of untreated syphilis in poor black men, and so on: all of this required the scientific mind to move outside or "beyond" Christian superstitions regarding the soul and the image of God within it.

The world of late antiquity, during the first few centuries of the rise of Christianity, knew many cults that promised salvation through the possession of knowledge and power, some even promising the assistance of various kinds of higher magic. And in some circles the figure of the savior was all but indistinguishable from the darkly glamorous figure of the hermetic sorcerer, understood as a master of inexplicable powers and a possessor of secret wisdom. And vulgar belief in witchcraft and in the occult potencies residing in the cosmic elements was, of course, ubiquitous. For the most part, ancient culture regarded magic not as a supernatural power called down from above (though there were certain forms of "theurgy" or higher "magia" that were conceived of in this way) but as a kind of terrestrial technology concerned with impersonal cosmic forces, a technology neutral in itself but susceptible of uses both "white" (in which case it was called simply "magia") and "black" (in which case it was called "goetia"). In the Christian period, however, belief in magic was discouraged and treated as a superstition; the world, according to Christian teaching, is an internally rational creature, governed by God's providence, and so contains no hidden extraphysical mechanisms that can be manipulated by word or gesture. Even the late medieval and early modern panics over witches did not generally involve actual belief in magic; the fear, rather, was of diabolism, murder, and demonic illusion. It seems perfectly obvious to me, though, that in the post-Christian era something more like real magical thinking has come back into vogue, albeit with a modern inflection. I am not speaking of popular interest in astrology, Wicca, runes, mystical crystals, or any other New Age twaddle of that sort; these things are always with us, in one form or another. I am speaking rather of the way in which, in modern society, technology and science (both practical and theoretical) are often treated as exercises of special knowledge and special power that should be isolated from too confining an association with any of the old habitual pieties regarding human nature or moral truth (these being, after all, mere matters of personal preference). That is, we often approach modern science as if it were magic, with the sort of moral credulity that takes it as given that power is evidence of permissibility. Of course, our magic—unlike that of our ancestors—actually works. But it is no less superstitious of us than it was of them to think that the power to do something is equivalent to the knowledge of what it is one is doing, or of whether one should do it, or of whether there are other, more comprehensive truths to which power ought to be willing to yield primacy. We seem on occasion, at least a good number of us, to have embraced (often with a shocking dogmatism) the sterile superstition that mastery over the hidden causes of things is the whole of truth, while at the same time pursuing that mastery by purely material means. Knowledge as power—unmoored from the rule of love or simply a discipline of prudent moral tentativeness—may be the final truth toward which a post-Christian culture necessarily gravitates. After all, if the modern story of freedom is what I have said it is, then in a sense each of us is already a sorcerer, attempting to conjure a self out of the infinite vacuum of indeterminate possibility. And today's magicians truly possess the powers they claim: the occult energies of matter have really been unlocked, the secrets of the cosmos truly fathomed, and the realms of physics, biology, chemistry, and so on—the chief glories of the modern age—are also now places where real monsters can be bred, and real terrors summoned out of the depths of nature.

Once again, I believe I can be exonerated of alarmism, though in this instance my remarks emerge from neither retrospection nor premonition but simply from attention to the present. I do not, I should say, fear that the honorable and industrious race of research scientists will all, any day now, suddenly cast off the fetters of reason and morality and devote themselves to projects to exterminate the race or breed supermen or invent new kinds of biological and radioactive weapons and then use them, just out of curiosity or just for the amusement the exercise might provide. My unease, rather, has to do with the kind of moral imagination that becomes possible in the aftermath of Christianity and in an age of such wonders, and how over time it might continue slowly and persistently to alter the culture's view of human nature, or even the experience of being human. One would think it would be more scandalous than it is, for instance, that a number of respected philosophers, scientists, medical lecturers, and other "bioethicists" in the academic world not only continue to argue the case for eugenics, but do so in such robustly merciless terms. The late Joseph Fletcher, for example, who was hardly an obscure or insignificant public philosopher, openly complained that modern medicine continues to contaminate our gene pool by preserving inferior genetic types, and advocated using legal coercion—including forced abortions—to improve the quality of the race. It was necessary, he maintained, to do everything possible to spare society the burden of "idiots" and "diseased" specimens, and to discourage or prevent the genetically substandard from reproducing. Indeed, he asserted, reproduction is not a right, and the law should set a minimum standard of health that any child should be required to meet before he or she might be granted entry into the world. He also favored Linus Pauling's proposed policy of segregating genetic inferiors into an immediately recognizable caste by affixing indelible marks to their brows, and suggested society might benefit from genetically engineering a subhuman caste of slave workers to perform dangerous or degrading jobs. Nor was Fletcher some lone, eccentric voice in the desert. Peter Singer argues for the right to infanticide for parents of defective babies, and he and James Rachels have been tireless advocates for more expansive and flexible euthanasia policies, applicable at every stage of life, unencumbered by archaic Christian mystifications about the sanctity of every life.

"Transhumanists" like Lee Silver look forward to the day when humanity will take responsibility for its own evolution, by throwing off antique moral constraints and allowing ourselves to use genetic engineering in order to transform future generations of our offspring into gods (possessed even, perhaps, of immortality). Some of the giddier transhumanists even envisage the possibility of a kind of posthuman polygenesis, a process by which the partitions between species might be breached and whole new hybrid strains might be bred—men with canine hearing and elephants' tusks, perhaps, women with wings and cuttlefish tentacles, androgynies able to see in the dark, breathe underwater, change colors, and lick clean the scales on their own backs. The possibilities are without number.[1]

The transhumanists, of course, should be ignored, principally on grounds of good taste, but also because genomic science does not as yet even remotely foreshadow the sort of organic technologies they like to fantasize about. Those, however, who advocate more modest projects of genetic engineering and more vigorously active policies of prudential euthanasia do have to be taken seriously, in part because the science exists, and in part because a growing number of persons in the academic and medical worlds are sympathetic to their positions. In general, I have to say (and this is probably evidence of the antique moral prejudices that continue to enslave my thinking), I am not sure what the pressing need to "improve" the race is. The science of special evolution seems to me to imply no ethical imperatives at all—that is one of the ways in which it is recognizable as a science, after all—and I am not at all certain what needs correcting or why. Severe Down syndrome, for instance, can be a very grave disability. But most of us who have known persons with Down syndrome also know that a great many of them seem more capable of cheer than the average run of mortal, and seem to have a spontaneous gift for gentleness, patience, and hope that is positively enviable. Their lives seem no more obviously impoverished or meaningless than those of academic bioethicists, nor any more burdensome than enriching for others. I cannot quite see what crisis so threatens our race that it dictates that these persons, for the greater good, really should have been done away with in the womb or in the basinet. And yet, for a certain number of bien pensants who have some voice in discussions of social policy in many countries of the developed world, this sort of incomprehension would seem like stupidity compounded by the profoundest irresponsibility.

Admittedly, I am still talking about only a small number of particular individuals here, and those manifestly moral idiots. Living in the academic world, moreover, I am acquainted with their kind to a perhaps unhealthy degree. Some of them are, however, influential, and it is not entirely insignificant that their ideas—which at one time would have been rightly regarded by almost anyone as the degenerate ravings of sociopaths—are strangely palatable and even morally compelling to many of their fellows. Their voices may, then, be acute manifestations of a more chronic condition. If nothing else, their ideas demonstrate how easy it is even for educated persons today to believe—for no reason other than unreflective intellectual prejudice—that knowing how genes work is the same thing as being authorized to say what a person is or should be. This is one of the many reasons that I suspect that our contemporary "age of reason" is in many ways an age of almost perfect unreason, one always precariously poised upon the edge of—and occasionally slipping over into—the purest barbarism. I suspect that, to a far greater degree than we typically might imagine, we have forsaken reason for magic: whether the magic of occult fantasy or the magic of an amoral idolatry of our own power over material reality. Reason, in the classical and Christian sense, is a whole way of life, not the simple and narrow mastery of certain techniques of material manipulation, and certainly not the childish certitude that such mastery proves that only material realities exist. A rational life is one that integrates knowledge into a larger choreography of virtue, imagination, patience, prudence, humility, and restraint. Reason is not only knowledge, but knowledge perfected in wisdom. In Christian tradition, reason was praised as a high and precious thing, principally because it belonged intrinsically to the dignity of beings created in the divine image; and, this being so, it was assumed that reason is also always morality, and that charity is required for any mind to be fully rational. Even if one does not believe any of this, however, a rational life involves at least the ability to grasp what it is one does not know, and to recognize that what one does know may not be the only kind of genuine knowledge there is.

It may very well be the case that the "total humanism" I have described above—this fabulous, impractical, unverifiable Christian insistence upon the infinite dignity of every soul and the infinite value of every life—describes merely one moral epoch in the history of culture, impermanent, imposing for a time, but destined to pass away. As a social ideal, in fact, its successes have always been notably limited. There is no reason why a more "realistic" (which as often as not means more nihilistic) vision of the good should not come again to prevail among us or our distant descendants. The idea that humanity relentlessly progresses toward ever more "rational" and "ethical" forms of life is a modern myth, which we use to flatter ourselves for being what we are and to justify every alteration we make in our moral preferences. Over the course of many centuries, Christianity displaced the reigning values of a civilization with its own values, and for a time its rather extraordinary idea of the human, illumined by the unearthly radiance of charity, became the shining sun around which all other values were made to revolve, and in the light of which the good or evil of any act had to be judged. That may all have been a dream, though, from which we have all begun to awaken. There is no reason to assume that this Christian humanism will not now, in its turn, be replaced by another central value, perhaps similar to certain older ideas of the good, perhaps entirely new. Whatever the case may be, though, it seems quite likely that the future that beckons us will be one that will make considerable room, in its deliberations regarding the value of human life, for a fairly unsentimental calculus of utility.

I would, therefore, advise all of those whom Daniel Dennett likes to refer to as "brights"—that is, all those decent, conscientious, and altogether effulgently clever men and women who know better than to take religious ideas seriously—not to be too terribly dismayed if their politely humanitarian ethos proves ultimately less durable than they might have imagined. To use Richard Dawkins's justly famous metaphor (which, unfortunately, he does not quite grasp is a metaphor), "memes" like "human rights" and "human dignity" may not indefinitely continue replicating themselves once the Christian "infinite value of every life" meme has died out. It is true that it is an example of the so-called genetic fallacy to assume that an idea's value or meaning is always limited to the context in which it arose; just because certain moral premises have their ground in the Christian past does not mean that they must cease to carry authority for those who no longer believe. But it is also true that ideas are related to one another not only genetically but structurally. If the beliefs or stories or logical principles that give an idea life are no longer present, then that idea loses its organic environment and will, unless some other ideological organism can successfully absorb it, perish. If there is a God of infinite love and goodness, of whom every person is an image, then certain moral conclusions must be drawn; if there is not, those conclusions have no meaning. Many cultures, after all, have thrived quite well without ever adopting our "humanistic" prejudices; there is no reason we should not come more to resemble them than they us. As I suggested above, Nietzsche was a prophetic figure precisely because he, almost alone among Christianity's enemies, understood the implications of Christianity's withdrawal from the culture it had haunted for so many centuries. He understood that the effort to cast off Christian faith while retaining the best and most beloved elements of Christian morality was doomed to defeat, and that even our cherished "Enlightenment" virtues may in the end prove to have been only parasitic upon inherited, but fading, cultural predilections, and so prove also to be destined for oblivion.

Or perhaps not. There really is little point in extravagant and doom-fraught prognostication. The shape of the future may be legible in certain lineaments of the present, but the movement of culture's evolution invariably escapes the reach of our foresight when we attempt to follow it very far beyond the present. It is enough for me, as I draw my argument to a close, to declare my skepticism, not only in regard to our modern habits of magical thinking, but also in regard to a great many of modernity's larger claims for its moral, political, and rational character. The highest ideals animating the secular project are borrowed ideals, even if they have occasionally been profoundly altered by their new uses; taken by itself, the modern post-Christian order has too long proved a bizarre amalgamation of the banal and the murderous to be granted very much credence. And I am apprehensive, I confess, regarding a certain reactive, even counter-revolutionary, movement in late modern thinking, back toward the severer spiritual economies of pagan society and away from the high (and admittedly "unrealistic") personalism or humanism with which the ancient Christian revolution colored—though did not succeed in wholly forming—our cultural conscience. Peter Singer's meltingly "reasonable" advocacy of prudential infanticide, for instance, naturally reminds one of the ancient world's practice of exposing supernumerary infants (though lacking in the ancient piety that left the ultimate fate of the abandoned child to the gods). It seems to me quite reasonable to imagine that, increasingly, the religion of the God-man, who summons human beings to become created gods through charity, will be replaced once again by the more ancient religion of the man-god, who wrests his divinity from the intractable material of his humanity, and solely through the exertions of his will. Such a religion will not in all likelihood express itself through a new Caesar, of course, or a new emperor or Führer; its operations will be more "democratically" diffused through society as a whole. But such a religion will always kill and then call it justice, or compassion, or a sad necessity.

I should note here—not in order to strike a mournful note on departing, but only in order to clarify my intentions—that I have not written this book as some sort of frantic exhortation to an improbable general religious renewal. Such a renewal may in fact take place, I imagine, as the Spirit moves, and as a result of social and political forces I cannot hope to foresee. But I have operated throughout from the presupposition that, in the modern West, the situation of Christianity in culture at large is at least somewhat analogous to the condition of paganism in the days of Julian, though Christianity may not necessarily be quite as moribund. I do not, at any rate, anticipate a recovery under current circumstances, and I cannot at the moment envisage how those circumstances might change. Even in America, I assume, despite its special hospitality to transcendental ecstasies and enduring pieties, the intellectual and moral habits of materialism will ultimately prevail to an even greater degree than they have in Europe. And neither a person nor a people can will belief simply out of dread of the consequences of its absence. In one sense, Christianity permeates everything we are, but in another it is disappearing, and we are changing as a result; and something new is in the centuries-long process of being born. I suppose some sort of invocation of Yeats's "The Second Coming" would be appropriate here, but the uncanny and disturbing power of its lines has long since been irreparably weakened by overuse. It might be better, therefore, simply to note that what it is for us to be human—what, that is, our aesthetic and moral imaginations are capable of—is determined by the encompassing narrative of reality we inhabit. First, for any people, comes its story, and then whatever is possible for that people becomes conceivable within that story. For centuries the Christian story shaped and suffused our civilization; now, however, slowly but relentlessly, another story is replacing it, and any attempt to reverse that process is probably futile. We are not pagans; we are not moved by their desires or disquieted by their uncertainties. We live after the age of Christendom, and cultures do not easily turn back to beliefs of which they have tired or with which they have become disenchanted.

Perhaps here, however, the history of Christian antiquity offers a lesson from which Christians might derive some comfort. It was precisely as Christianity was on the verge of assuming political and social power, during the days of the final, ineffectual persecutions of the church, that the movement of Christian monasticism began to flower in the Egyptian desert; and, after the conversion of Constantine, the movement grew at a remarkable rate. Indeed, it became such a fashion that it soon began to swell its ranks with "monks" of distinctly questionable moral character (for there were, at first, no monasteries or abbots to control the flood). Hence those notorious gangs of black-clad rabble who, at the end of the fourth century, liked to raid pagan temples or, in the fifth, acted as shock troops for various theological factions. These tales are so outlandish, though, that they tend to distract us from the meaning and nature of the larger (and quite peaceful) monastic movement, and from the somewhat less eventful, if more luminous, careers of those first "desert fathers" (and then desert mothers) who went apart, into the wastes, to devote themselves to prayer and fasting, and to the cultivation of "perfect charity." It was from them that another current opened up within Christian culture: a renunciation of power even as power was at last granted to the church, an embrace of poverty as a rebellion against plenty, a defiant refusal to forget that the Kingdom of God is not of this world. The sayings of the desert fathers have been copiously preserved, and they are fascinating testaments to the birth of a new spiritual polity in the very midst of the Christianized empire, a community whose sole concern was to discover what it really meant to live for the love of God and one's neighbor, to banish envy, hate, and resentment from the soul, and to seek the beauty of Christ in others. These sayings reflect, among other things, what one might best call the heroism of forgiveness, and frequently a piercingly wise simplicity, and just as frequently a penetratingly subtle psychology. And the guiding logic of the life they lived was that of spiritual warfare: that is to say, now that the empire had "fallen" to Christ and could no longer be regarded as simply belonging to the kingdom of Satan, the desert fathers carried the Christian revolution against the ancient powers with them into the wild, to renew the struggle on the battleground of the heart. And this, I think, might be viewed as the final revolutionary moment within ancient Christianity: its rebellion against its own success, its preservation of its most precious and unadulterated spiritual aspirations against its own temporal power (perhaps in preparation for the day when that power would be no more), and its repudiation of any value born from the fallen world that might displace love from the center of the Christian faith.

It may be that ultimately this will again become the proper model of Christianity in the late modern West. I am not speaking, of course, of some great new monastic movement. I mean only that, in the lands where the old Christendom has mostly faded away, the life of those ancient men and women who devoted themselves to the science of charity, in willing exile from the world of social prestige and power, may perhaps again become the model that Christians will find themselves compelled to emulate. Christian conscience once sought out the desert as a shelter from the empire, where those who believed could strive to cultivate the pure eye (that could see all things as gifts of God) and the pure heart (that could receive all persons with a generous love); now a very great deal of Western culture threatens to become something of a desert for believers. In other parts of the world, perhaps, a new Christendom may be in the process being born—in Africa and Asia, and in another way in Latin America—but what will come of that is impossible to say. We live in an age of such cultural, demographic, ideological, and economic fluidity that what seems like a great movement now may surprise us in only a very few years by its transience. Innumerable forces are vying for the future, and Christianity may prove considerably weaker than its rivals. This should certainly be no cause of despair for Christians, however, since they must believe their faith to be not only a cultural logic but a cosmic truth, which can never finally be defeated. Even so, it may be the case that Christians who live amid the ruins of the old Christendom—perhaps dwelling on the far-flung frontiers of a Christian civilization taking shape in other lands—will have to learn to continue the mission of their ancient revolution in the desert, to which faith has often found it necessary, at various times, to retreat.

NOTES

CHAPTER 1. THE GOSPEL OF UNBELIEF

1. Daniel C. Dennett, *Breaking the Spell: Religion as a Natural Phenomenon* (New York: Viking, 2006); Richard Dawkins, *The God Delusion* (New York: Houghton Mifflin, 2006); Christopher Hitchens, *God Is Not Great: How Religion Poisons Everything* (New York: Twelve, 2007); Sam Harris, *The End of Faith: Religion, Terror, and the Future of Reason* (New York: W. W. Norton, 2004).
2. *New York Times*, December 11, 2005.
3. Libanius, *Oration XXX.32.*
4. David B. Hart, "Daniel Dennett Hunts the Snark," *First Things*, January 2007.

CHAPTER 3. FAITH AND REASON

1. Jacques Le Goff, *Medieval Civilization 400–1500*, trans. Julia Barrow (Oxford: Basil Blackwell, 1988), p. 316.
2. See Guenter B. Risse, *Mending Bodies, Saving Souls: A History of Hospitals* (Oxford: Oxford University Press, 1999).
3. See, for instance, John Bossy, *Christianity in the West: 1400–1700* (Oxford: Oxford University Press, 1985).
4. One need not search too diligently to discover this sentiment in Gibbon, of course, but the actual phrase is found in the 1776 preface to the first volume of *The History of the Decline and Fall of the Roman Empire*, which many modern editions omit.
5. William Manchester, *A World Lit Only by Fire: Portrait of an Age* (Boston: Little, Brown, 1992).

CHAPTER 4. THE NIGHT OF REASON

1. Jonathan Kirsch, *God against the Gods: The History of the War between Mono-theism and Polytheism* (New York: Viking Compass, 2004), p. 278.

2. We know of the presence of the Septuagint in the library from the *Letter of Aristeas,* whose author appears to have been a Jewish scholar writing in the second century before Christ. The *Letter* also speaks of a store of two hundred thousand scrolls, still growing, an almost unimaginably large number by the standards of the time and given the space required for such a collection. In the first century A.D., Seneca, in *De tranquillitate animi* IX, 5, speaks of the loss of forty thousand books when the library was destroyed, as does Paul Orosius in the early fifth century, though certain (less trustworthy) codices of both works say four hundred thousand. In the second century A.D., Aulus Gellius's *Noctes Atticae* VII, 17, speaks either of seventy thousand or of seven hundred thousand, though the latter number had become fixed in lore by the late fourth century when Ammianus Marcellinus wrote his history. Still, in the fourth century A.D. Epiphanius, in his *De mensuris et ponderibus,* speaks of fifty-four thousand eight hundred; and Isidore of Seville, as late as the early seventh century, in his *Etymologies,* contracts the number to forty thousand, while John Tzetzes, in the twelfth, expands it again to four hundred thousand. Whether "Caesar's fire" ever actually burned, or ever consumed the library, is impossible to say. The story appears to have been recounted by Livy, to judge from Florus's second-century *Epitome* of his history (the relevant books of Livy's history now being lost), and late in the first century Plutarch treated Caesar's destruction of the library as an established fact, as did Ammianus Marcellinus three centuries later. Dio Cassius, in the early third century, recounted the story of the granary fire. Strabo (c. 64 B.C.–c. A.D. 23), in his *Geography,* already speaks of the library as something in the distant past: *Geography* II, 1, 5.

3. Aphthonius, in the late fourth century, in his *Progymnasmata* 12, speaks of rooms among the colonnades of the great Alexandrian temple, some of which hold stores of books for the use of those studious of philosophy; as this entire passage is presented as a specimen of good descriptive prose, it is uncertain that Aphthonius is describing a temple that he himself had seen.

4. On Orosius, see Gibbon, *The History of the Decline and Fall of the Roman Empire,* ch. 28; on Ammianus and the Serapeum, see ch. 51, and especially n. 124. See also Ammianus, *Res gestae* XXII, 16: "In quo Bybliothecae *fuerunt* inaestimabiles."

5. The great pagan rhetorician Libanius (c. 314–c. 394)—friend and encomiast of Julian, teacher to many of the great Christian theologians of his time, and advocate for the pagan peasantry—describes these desecrations and spoliations quite movingly in his thirtieth oration, "To Theodosius on Behalf of the Temples"; see especially sections 8–13.

6. Sozomen, *Ecclesiastical History,* V, 10.

7. Socrates, *Ecclesiastical History,* VII, 15.

8. Julian, Epistle 22.

9. The most convincing modern reconstruction of the events leading to Hypatia's death, as well as the best modern portrait of Hypatia herself, can be found in Maria Dzielska, *Hypatia of Alexandria*, trans. F. Lyra (Cambridge, Mass.: Harvard University Press, 1995). For a brief list of certain of this period's women scholars, see pp. 117–119.

10. Ramsay MacMullen, *Christianity and Paganism in the Fourth to Eighth Centuries* (New Haven: Yale University Press, 1997), p. 6.

11. Gibbon, *Decline and Fall*, ch. 28.

12. Theodoret, *Ecclesiastical History*, V, 22.

CHAPTER 5. THE DESTRUCTION OF THE PAST

1. Jonathan Kirsch, *God against the Gods: The History of the War between Monotheism and Polytheism* (New York: Viking Compass, 2004), p. 280.

2. See David C. Lindberg, "The Transmission of Greek and Arabic Learning to the West," in David C. Lindberg, ed., *Science in the Middle Ages* (Chicago: University of Chicago Press, 1978), pp. 52–90.

3. See John Henry Newman, *Essays and Sketches*, ed. C. F. Harrold, vol. 3 (New York: Longman, Green, 1948), pp. 315–21.

4. Kirsch, *God against the Gods*, p. 278.

5. Ramsay MacMullen, *Christianity and Paganism in the Fourth to Eighth Centuries* (New Haven: Yale University Press, 1997), p. 4. The footnote MacMullen provides to corroborate his remark is a veritable tangle of elliptical references to another of his own books, to which few readers can be expected to repair, and which in fact provides no relevant evidence.

6. Ramsay MacMullen, *Christianizing the Roman Empire* A.D. 100–400 (New Haven: Yale University Press, 1984), p. 124 n. 15, p. 164 n. 49.

7. See Werner Jaeger, *Early Christianity and Greek Paideia* (Cambridge, Mass.: Harvard University Press, 1961), pp. 68–85.

CHAPTER 6. THE DEATH AND REBIRTH OF SCIENCE

1. Charles Freeman, *The Closing of the Western Mind: The Rise and the Fall of Reason* (New York: Knopf, 2003), pp. xix, 322. Examples of Freeman's sketchy understanding of early Christian teachings and doctrinal disputes, to say nothing of classical philosophy, are plentiful; take, for instance, his remarks on p. 150 regarding Platonism, Aristotelianism, and the Christian doctrine of the divine image in man, which betray an almost perfect ignorance of all three topics.

2. David C. Lindberg, *The Beginnings of Western Science: The European Scientific Tradition in Philosophical, Religious, and Institutional Context, 600* B.C. *to* A.D. *1450* (Chicago: University of Chicago Press, 1992), pp. 98–105, 294–301.

3. To this day, one still encounters educated persons who believe that Galileo was tortured by the Roman Inquisition or imprisoned in its dungeons. Witness, for example, A. N. Wilson, *God's Funeral* (New York: W. W. Norton,

1999), p. x. It is true that, at the final forensic interrogation of Galileo, the court—following the judicial process of the time—mentioned the penalty of torture for perjury, but this was a legal formula (called the *territio verbalis*) and did not amount to an actual threat. That, of course, does not make the jurisprudential procedures of the time any less unsavory.

4. Arthur Koestler, *The Sleepwalkers* (New York: Macmillan, 1959), p. 426. On the arguments regarding comets, see pp. 466–71.

5. See the essays collected in *The Church and Galileo,* ed. Ernan McMullin (Notre Dame: University of Notre Dame Press, 2003).

6. See Koestler, *The Sleepwalkers,* pp. 432–39; 464–95; and see also pp. 522–23: "The Galileo affair was an isolated, and in fact quite untypical, episode in the history of the relations between science and theology, almost as untypical as the Dayton monkey-trial was. But its dramatic circumstances, magnified out of all proportion, created a popular belief that science stood for freedom, the Church for oppression of thought."

7. David C. Lindberg, "Science and the Early Church," in *God and Nature: Historical Essays on the Encounter between Christianity and Science,* ed. David C. Lindberg and Ronald L. Numbers (Berkeley: University of California Press, 1986), pp. 30, 33.

8. Jacques Le Goff, *Medieval Civilization 400–1500,* trans. Julia Barrow (Oxford: Basil Blackwell, 1988), p. 3.

9. The best treatment of Byzantine hospitals available in English is Timothy S. Miller, *The Birth of the Hospital in the Byzantine Empire,* 2nd edition (Baltimore: Johns Hopkins University Press, 1997). See also Demetrios Constantelos, *Byzantine Philanthropy and Social Welfare,* 2nd edition (New Rochelle, N.Y.: Caratzas, 1991).

10. See Lynn White Jr., *Medieval Technology and Social Change* (Oxford: Oxford University Press, 1962); Jean Gimpel, *The Medieval Machine: The Industrial Revolution of the Middle Ages* (New York: Holt, Rinehart and Winston, 1976).

CHAPTER 7. INTOLERANCE AND PERSECUTION

1. For good accounts of the great witch hunts, see Brian P. Levack, *The Witch-Hunt in Early Modern Europe,* 2nd edition (London: Longman, 1995); Gustav Henningsen, *The Witches' Advocate: Basque Witchcraft and the Spanish Inquisition (1609–1614)* (Reno: University of Nevada Press, 1980); H. C. Erik Midelfort, *Witch-Hunting in Southwestern Germany* (Stanford: Stanford University Press, 1972); Rodney Stark, *For the Glory of God: How Monotheism Led to Reformations, Science, Witch-Hunts, and the End of Slavery* (Princeton: Princeton University Press, 2003), pp. 201–88.

2. Stark, *For the Glory of God,* p. 221.

3. See Dan Burton and David Grandy, *Magic, Mystery, and Science: The Occult in Western Civilization* (Bloomington: Indiana University Press, 2004), pp. 180–81.

4. One might mention the works of Samuel de Casini, Bernard di Como,

Johannes Trithemius, Martin d'Arles, Silvestro Mazolini, Bartolommeo di Spina, Jean Bodin, René Benoist, Alfonso de Castro, Peter Binsfeld, Franz Agricola, and Nicholas Remi, among others. For a fuller list, see Emile Brouette, "The Sixteenth Century and Satanism," in *Satan* (London: Sheed and Ward, 1951), pp. 315–17.

5. See Henry Kamen, *The Spanish Inquisition: A Historical Revision* (New Haven: Yale University Press, 1998), pp. 28–54, 73.

CHAPTER 8. INTOLERANCE AND WAR

1. This point is powerfully argued by William T. Cavanaugh: Cavanaugh, *Theopolitical Imagination: Discovering the Liturgy as a Political Act in an Age of Global Consumerism* (Edinburgh: T. and T. Clark, 2002), pp. 20–31.

2. See Stephen Toulmin, *Cosmopolis: The Hidden Agenda of Modernity* (Chicago: University of Chicago Press, 1990), p. 49.

3. John Bossy, *Christianity in the West: 1400–1700* (Oxford: Oxford University Press, 1985), pp. 154–55.

4. Henri Daniel-Rops, *The Church in the Seventeenth Century*, trans. J. J. Buckingham (Garden City, N.Y.: Doubleday, 1965), vol. 1, pp. 200–201. Quoted in Louis Dupré, *Passage to Modernity: An Essay in the Hermeneutics of Nature and Culture* (New Haven: Yale University Press, 1993), p. 12.

CHAPTER 9. AN AGE OF DARKNESS

1. Richard Dawkins, *The Blind Watchmaker* (New York: Norton, 1986), p. 318. This sentence appears in the final paragraph of Dawkins's book and repeats an assertion made in the book's very first sentence.

CHAPTER 10. THE GREAT REBELLION

1. For a rich and detailed treatment of the Byzantine rite, see Alexander Schmemann, *Of Water and the Spirit: A Liturgical Study of Baptism* (Crestwood, N.Y.: St. Vladimir's Seminary Press, 1974).

2. See Peter Brown, *The Rise of Western Christendom*, 2nd edition (Oxford: Blackwell, 2003), p. 118.

3. See Robert L. Wilken, *The Christians as the Romans Saw Them* (New Haven: Yale University Press, 1984), pp. 94–125.

4. Gibbon, *The History of the Decline and Fall of the Roman Empire*, ch. 2.

5. Tacitus, *Annals*, XIV, 42–45.

6. Symmachus, Epistles 2 and 6.

7. Theodoret, *Ecclesiastical History*, V, 20.

CHAPTER 11. A GLORIOUS SADNESS

1. See especially Plotinus, *Enneads* II, 9. See also II, 6.

2. One finds this same formula in the Gnostic Gospel of Philip, verse 57.

3. The best general introductions to Gnosticism are Giovanni Filoramo, *A History of Gnosticism*, trans. Anthony Alcock (Oxford: Blackwell, 1990), and

Kurt Rudolph, *Gnosis: The Nature and History of Gnosticism*, trans. P. W. Coxon and K. H. Kuhn. (San Francisco: Harper San Francisco, 1987).

4. For a splendid survey of the mystery cults, as well as of the rise of hermeticism in the empire, see Robert Turcan, *The Cults of the Roman Empire*, trans. Antonia Nevill (Oxford: Blackwell, 1996).

5. Robin Lane Fox, *Pagans and Christians* (San Francisco: Harper and Row, 1986), p. 331.

CHAPTER 12. A LIBERATING MESSAGE

1. Ramsay MacMullen, *Christianity and Paganism in the Fourth to Eighth Centuries* (New Haven: Yale University Press, 1997), p. 27.

2. The verb is a late Greek construction, from the Latin *furca*, meaning in this instance a fork-shaped gibbet or gallows. The word has nothing to do with crucifixion.

3. John Malalas, *Chronographia*, 18, 119.

4. Ibid., 18, 42.

5. MacMullen, *Christianity and Paganism*, p. 8.

6. Ibid., p. 165 n. 19.

7. Ramsay MacMullen, *Christianizing the Roman Empire* A.D. *100–400* (New Haven: Yale University Press, 1984), pp. 106–10.

8. Julian, Epistle 22, written to Arsacius, the pagan high priest of Galatia.

9. Lane Fox, *Pagans and Christians*, pp. 329–30.

10. MacMullen, *Christianity and Paganism*, pp. 77–78, 99–100.

11. Ibid., pp. 7–8.

12. MacMullen, *Christianizing the Roman Empire*, pp. 54–55. Libanius's brief remarks on the beneficence of the pagan temples are found in Oration II.30–32.

13. Lane Fox is particularly illuminating on these matters; see especially *Pagans and Christians*, p. 325.

14. See Gregory's *Life of Macrina* and his treatise *On the Soul and Resurrection;* see also Basil's Letter 204.

15. Tertullian, *Apologeticus* XXXIX.

16. See Peter Brown, *The Rise of Western Christendom,* 2nd edition (Oxford: Blackwell, 2003), pp. 69–70.

17. Ammianus, *Res gestae* XXII.11; see also XXII.5.

CHAPTER 13. THE FACE OF THE FACELESS

1. Erich Auerbach, *Mimesis: The Representation of Reality in Western Literature,* trans. Willard R. Trask (Princeton: Princeton University Press, 1953), p. 41.

2. *Didascalia apostolorum* XII.ii.58.

3. See John T. Noonan Jr., *A Church That Can and Cannot Change* (South Bend, Ind.: University of Notre Dame Press, 2005), pp. 50–52.

CHAPTER 14. THE DEATH AND BIRTH OF WORLDS

1. Rodney Stark, *The Rise of Christianity* (San Francisco: HarperCollins, 1996), pp. 3–27.

2. The finest treatment of Julian's religion is Rowland Smith, *Julian's Gods: Religion and Philosophy in the Thought and Action of Julian the Apostate* (London: Routledge, 1995).

3. Gibbon, *The History of the Decline and Fall of the Roman Empire*, ch. 22.

CHAPTER 17. SORCERERS AND SAINTS

1. See Wesley J. Smith, *Consumer's Guide to a Brave New World* (San Francisco: Encounter Books, 2004).

INDEX